BUSINESS ENGLISH

March 6
March . 7

English

morning 11:15
11:00

84.
84.
7
98

The Bobbs-Merrill Business Education Series:

A Modern Approach to Business English / *Annie DeCaprio*

A Modern Approach to Business Spelling / *Annie DeCaprio*

Basic Accounting, Second Edition / *Calvin Engler*

Business Correspondence / *Waldo C. Wright*

Business English: A Worktext with Programed
      Reinforcement / *Donald A. Sheff*

Business Spelling and Word Power / *A. H. Lass*

Career Builder Business Management Case Studies

Career Builder Secretarial Case Studies

Principles of Landmark abc Shorthand, Series I

Principles of Landmark abc Shorthand Workbook, Series I

ABC Shorthand Dictation and Transcription, Landmark Edition,
     Series I / *Jordan Hale*

Theory Tapes for Landmark abc Shorthand, Series I

Principles of ABC Shorthand, Landmark Edition, Series II

ABC Shorthand Workbook, Landmark Edition, Series II

ABC Shorthand Dictation and Transcription, Landmark Edition,
     Series II

ABC Shorthand Dictionary, Landmark Edition

Theory Tapes for Principles of ABC Shorthand, Landmark Edition,
     Series II

Typing: College Edition / *Verleigh Ernest*

Typing Power—Spelling Power, Volume One / *Norman Elliott,
Rose Palmer, Steve Rosen*

BUSINESS ENGLISH

A WORKTEXT WITH
PROGRAMED REINFORCEMENT

by DONALD A. SHEFF

The Bobbs-Merrill Company, Inc.
Indianapolis

The Bobbs-Merrill Company, Inc.
4300 West 62nd Street
Indianapolis, Indiana 46268

First Edition
Seventh Printing—1975

ISBN 0-672-96927-0 (pbk.)

CONTENTS

INTRODUCTION

Some time ago *Harper's* Magazine featured an article entitled "Why Nobody Can't Write Good" in which the author bemoaned the very low level of grammatical know-how exhibited by the average college student. The author asked: "Why is grammar so difficult for so many students who do excellent work in other subjects?"

Time has not changed matters: Today's average student still has difficulty with grammar. But why?

We think that one reason is that English grammar is often taught as though it were a foreign language. The student is bombarded with a barrage of tongue-twisting terminology until he is lost amidst a fog of jargon that's strictly Greek to him. He is not shown the inner logic of grammar which is very much a matter of common sense and much less a matter of terminology. Can one blame the average student for often being confused?

Business English is different. Wherever possible we have blown away the fog of terminology and tried to focus light upon *proper usage* since usage is your major objective in studying grammar. Shortcuts and learning hints are offered wherever appropriate.

In addition, an entirely new theory of learning is yours in this book. After reading the step-by-step explanation of a concept in the text, you turn to what we call a *Programed Reinforcement* unit on that concept. As its name implies, this unit is designed to reinforce your learning of what you have just read. It *forces* you to think. It enables you to check yourself as you go along by asking you questions on every point, then immediately providing you with the answer. Step by step it develops your thinking from the simplest concepts to the most abstract.

Here then you have what was the "missing link" in previous English textbooks—books that expected you to jump the chasm from the reading of the text about a concept to the immediate application of that concept in exercises and tests. The *Programed Reinforcement* units in this book enable you to bridge that chasm easily and naturally. By the time you complete a *Reinforcement* unit, you will *thoroughly* understand the concepts it covered; and you will be able to move on to the *Practice Exercises* without fear or hesitation.

Your perfect command of English grammer will be a key to success in the business world. *Business English* will help provide you with that key.

THE SENTENCE

1. what is a sentence

2. sentence fragments

3. run-on sentences

4. agreement of subject and predicate

Zoologists tell us that almost all animals communicate — the jungles offer a symphony of meaningful grunts, whistles, howls, and clicks. Even the seas are filled with the soggy sounds of fish communicating with one another. Why, then, is man considered unique in his ability to communicate? Because the communication of all these other animals is limited to disconnected instinctive signals — a shriek of alarm...a mating call...a triumphal cry of "Food!" Man's uniqueness lies in his ability to go beyond these isolated instinctive signals and to weld them in the crucible of his mind into complex *abstract ideas*. Man's genius lies in his ability to communicate these complex ideas through the medium of *language*.

Language is simply the audible expression of thought. It is not an artificial creation, but rather a natural expression that follows the natural flow of ideas in the mind. The man who thinks clearly, writes clearly. The man who thinks fuzzily and lazily, writes the same way. In other words, your language reflects your mind.

The rules of language that we call *grammar* are not the creation of some bearded philosophers. Rather they are a *description* of the natural pattern of language that civilized man has evolved over hundreds of centuries. A rule of grammar does not say, "This is so because we say it's so." It says, in effect, "This is so because this is the way the mind thinks. Anything else is less clear, less meaningful, less logical."

The objective of language is to communicate thoughts completely and clearly. To achieve this objective, the *sentence* is the basic unit since it is the "lowest form" that expresses a *complete thought*. A word or phrase by itself is merely a fragment of thought — the cry of an animal in the jungle. A sentence is the full expression of thought.

So let's start with the *sentence* in our study of Business English — our study of grammar as it relates to the business world — for it is with the sentence that the art of language begins.

I. subject or predicate or verb.
3. complete thought.

1. what is a SENTENCE?

Since the sentence is the basic unit of language that expresses a complete thought, every sentence must contain two essential parts:

1. _A subject,_ which tells us whom or what we are talking about.
2. _A predicate,_ which tells us what the subject does.

John speaks. This is a sentence. It expresses a complete thought by telling us:

a. Who? _John._ (The subject)
b. Does what? _Speaks._ (The predicate)

Tall, handsome John speaks. This, too, is a complete sentence. We have merely added some words that _describe_ our subject. _They do not change the subject._ The subject is still _John_ and the predicate is still _speaks._

Tall, handsome John speaks with fluency and persuasion. Again, this is a complete sentence. _Tall, handsome_ describes _John. With fluency and persuasion_ describes _speaks._ The subject remains _John._ The predicate remains _speaks._

Use this approach whenever you want to find the subject and the predicate of a sentence. Just ask yourself two simple questions:

a. Who or what is the doer of the action? (The subject)
b. What does the subject do? (The predicate)

For the moment, disregard all other words that merely describe the subject or the predicate.

1. The manager works with diligence and initiative.

a. Who? _Manager._ (The subject)
b. Does what? _Works._ (The predicate)
c. Disregard _with diligence and initiative._

2. On Wednesday evening after the banquet, the executives will meet.

a. Who? _Executives._ (The subject)
b. Do what? _Will meet._ (The predicate)
c. Disregard _on Wednesday evening, after the banquet...._

In this sentence the predicate consists of more than one word, _will meet._ The word _will_ is what we call an _auxiliary verb._ You'll learn more about these in a later lesson. For now, be alert to recognize an auxiliary verb whenever it is part of the predicate. You'll see it in a number of the following examples.

3. The secretary, after taking dictation, transcribed her notes.

a. Who? _Secretary_ (The subject)
b. Did what? _Transcribed._ (The predicate)
c. Disregard _after taking dictation ... her notes._

4. No one in all this confusion can decide upon a course of action.

a. Who? _(No) one._ (The subject)
b. Does what? _Can decide._ (The predicate)
c. Disregard all other words.

5. Eye-catching and appealing are our new package designs.

a. What? _Designs._ (In this sentence the subject comes _after_ the predicate.)
b. Do what? _Are._ (The predicate)
c. Disregard all other words.

Would you have located the subject and predicate more easily if the sentence had been written in the more usual subject-before-predicate order, as follows: _Our new package designs are eye-catching and appealing._

Don't let the predicate-before-subject order fool you. Simply rearrange the sentence mentally into the usual subject-before-predicate order.

6. Can you mail me the invoice by Friday?
By rearranging this question into an affirmative statement, you can quickly locate the subject and predicate: *You can mail me the invoice by Friday.*
   a. Who? *You.* (The subject)
   b. Do what? *Can mail.* (The predicate)
   c. Disregard all other words.

7. There are two men to see you. Here again a little rearrangement will make it much easier for you to locate the subject and the predicate: *Two men are there to see you.*
   a. Who? *Men.* (The subject)
   b. Do what? *Are.* (The predicate)
   c. Disregard all other words.

8. Uranium and plutonium are fissionable materials.
   a. What? *Uranium (and) plutonium.* (The subject in this case consists of more than one item.)
   b. Do what? *Are.* (The predicate)
   c. Disregard all other words.
When, as in this example, the subject is composed of two or more items, it is called a *compound subject.* You may remember that in chemistry a compound is a substance that is composed of two or more elements. So too in grammar, where the word *compound* is used in a number of different instances to indicate that something is made up of *more than one* part. In this example, you see a compound *subject.* Why is it compound?

9. Sales last year rose in May and fell in June.
   a. What? *Sales.* (The subject)
   b. Did what? *Rose ... fell.* (The predicate in this case consists of more than one action.)
   c. Disregard all other words.
As you probably guessed, the predicate in

this example is called a *compound predicate.* Why?

10. Stand still!
   a. Who? *You.* (Understood)
   b. Do what? *Stand.*
   c. Disregard *still.*
What do we mean by *understood?* This is a particular type of sentence—a command. Most commands are given quickly and curtly. The subject of the command is understood to mean *you.* Remember, though, in all other types of sentences the subject must be specifically stated. *Only* in commands can the subject be left to the imagination.

Turn to Programed Reinforcement S1 through S23

2. sentence FRAGMENTS

Is this a sentence: *John.* Obviously not. It names a subject, *John,* but does not tell us what the subject *does.* In other words, it is not a sentence because it contains no predicate and does not express a complete thought. It is only a piece or *fragment* of a sentence.

Is this a sentence: *Tall, handsome John.* Again, the answer is *No.* Our subject is described to us, but we are still not told what he does. We still have no predicate and no complete thought. Remember, a sentence must contain both a subject and a predicate and also must express a complete thought. A frequent mistake that some careless people make is to write only part of a sentence as though it were a complete sentence. For example: *Wrong: John Smith, president of our firm. Was invited to the banquet.*

3

Is either of these parts a complete sentence?

1. **John Smith, president of our firm.**

2. **Was invited to the banquet.**

No. Neither part is a complete sentence. Part 1 contains a subject, but no predicate. Part 2 contains a predicate, but no subject. Alone, each part is merely a *fragment* of a sentence. *Guard against sentence fragments!* To correct sentence fragments like 1 and 2, above, is simple. **Right: John Smith, president of our firm, was invited to the banquet.** We now have one sentence that includes a subject and predicate and expresses a complete thought.

EXAMPLES

1. **Right:** **Our book, the latest, most authoritative word on the subject, has just been put on the market.**

Wrong: Our book, the latest most authoritative word on the subject. Has just been put on the market.

2. **Right:** **The course that we are offering you is the finest you can get anywhere.**

Wrong: The course that we are offering you. Is the finest you can get anywhere.

3. **Right:** **The committee of which you are a member met in secret session.**

Wrong: The committee of which you are a member. Met in secret session.

There is another type of sentence fragment of which you should be wary on the job. This is the fragment that *apparently* contains both a subject and a predicate, but does not express a complete thought. For example, is this a sentence: *John, running at full speed.* Let's test it:

a. Who? *John.* (The subject)

b. Doing what? *Running.* (The apparent predicate)

c. Complete thought? NO! It leaves us with the question: *John running at full speed,* did what? This sentence fragment may be completed as follows: *John, running at full speed, fell.* Remember, a sentence must express a complete thought! If it does not express a complete thought, it is not a sentence; it is merely a fragment of a sentence. Beware of sentence fragments.

Now let's turn to the final type of sentence fragment. Is this a complete sentence: *Since the order arrived.* Answer: NO! The word *since* limits our thought in such a manner that it does not express a complete thought although it contains a subject, *order,* and a predicate, *arrived.* The expression *since the order arrived* leaves you up in the air. You want to know: *Since the order arrived,* what happened? You must add something to complete the thought. For example, you might say: *Since the order arrived, we have made headway.*

In the sentence *Since the order arrived, we have made headway* there are clearly two distinct parts, each of which contains a subject and a predicate. *Since the order arrived* contains the subject *order* and the predicate *arrived.* *We have made headway* contains the subject *we* and the predicate *have made.* When a sentence contains two or more parts, each of which contains a subject and a predicate, we call each such part a *clause* of the sentence. In the above example, *Since the order arrived* is a clause; *we have made headway* is a clause.

A quick inspection of these two clauses shows you that there is an obvious difference between them. Do you see it? That's right. The clause *We have made headway*

4

expresses a complete thought; it could stand as a sentence by itself: *We have made headway.* For this reason it is called an *independent clause.* An independent clause is simply a clause that expresses a complete thought and, therefore, could stand by itself as a sentence.

What about the clause *Since the order arrived.* Can it stand by itself as a sentence? Obviously not. The word *since* makes it *dependent* upon the rest of the sentence. For this reason it is called a *dependent* clause. What does it depend upon to complete it? That's right. It depends upon the *independent* clause, *we have made headway.*

There are many words like *since* that limit a thought, render it incomplete by itself, and make it *dependent* upon a main thought. Here are some other examples:

1. Though we received your order, we could not fill it. The word *though* makes *Though we received your order* incomplete by itself. It makes it *dependent* upon the main thought, *we could not fill it. Though we received your order* is the dependent clause; *we could not fill it* is the independent clause.

2. As soon as we heard the news, we ran to congratulate you. *As soon as* makes *As soon as we heard the news* dependent upon *we ran to congratulate you. As soon as we heard the news* is the dependent clause. What is the independent clause? Why is it independent?

3. We left the theater because we failed to get the part. Here, the dependent part comes last. *Because* makes *because we failed to get the part* dependent upon *we left the theater.* What is the dependent clause? The independent clause?

4. We kept trying until it was too late. *Until* makes *until it was too late* dependent upon *We kept trying.*

When you have a sentence like any of the above examples that is composed of a dependent clause linked to an independent clause, that sentence is called a *complex sentence.* What is a *complex* sentence? That's right. It's a sentence composed of an independent clause and a dependent clause. For the moment the important thing to remember is that you must never write one of these dependent clauses by itself as though it were a complete sentence.

Wrong: *Since the order arrived.* This is not a complete sentence. It is merely a fragment of a sentence. Guard against sentence fragments! Be sure to connect a dependent clause with an independent clause to form a complex sentence.

EXAMPLES

1. Right: Though the weather was cloudy, we went sailing.
Wrong: Though the weather was cloudy. We went sailing.

2. Right: Although we received your last shipment, we feel it is of such inferior quality that we should not pay.
Wrong: Although we received your last shipment. We feel it is of such inferior quality that we should not pay.

3. Right: He won because he was the fastest.
Wrong: He won. Because he was the fastest.

4. Right: Because he was fastest, he won.
Wrong: Because he was fastest. He won.

Turn to Programed Reinforcement S24 through S45

5

3. RUN-ON sentences

too much for one sentence

Look at these two sentences:
1. **We hope to attend the banquet.**
2. **We may be detained by business.**

You could combine these two sentences into one thought, as follows:

3. **We hope to attend the banquet, but we may be detained by business.**

Don't you agree that Sentence 3 better expresses the relationship between the ideas of Sentences 1 and 2?

Very often you will have two sentences that are so closely related that you may want to combine them into one. Don't think, however, that you can throw them together in a haphazard fashion. A sentence is like a building block. To connect two building blocks, you would use a good strong glue. To attach one sentence to another, you also need a strong *glue* to hold them together. This *glue* is supplied in Sentence 3 by the comma and the word *but:* **We hope to attend the banquet, but we may be detained by business.**

As you will learn in Lesson 9, the word *but* is called a *conjunction*. Two other conjunctions that can be used as *glue* to hold sentences together are *and* and *or*. For example: **Mr. Jackson took the 5:15 train, and he should be here any minute. You must accept our offer, or you will suffer the consequences.**

One great mistake that you should always avoid is trying to attach two sentences without using a *strong enough* glue. Here are two examples of the use of *glue* that is too weak to do the job:

1. **Wrong:** We hope to attend the banquet we may be detained by business. Here no glue is used at all. There is nothing to hold the two sentences together. They fall apart.

2. **Wrong:** We hope to attend the banquet, we may be detained by business. Here a comma is used to hold the two sentences together, but a comma by itself is not a strong enough glue to do the job. The two sentences again fall apart.

These two sentences are examples of an error that we call the *run-on sentence*. When two sentences are thrown together without a strong enough glue to hold them, the result is a run-on sentence. To correct such run-on sentences, either separate the two parts into individual sentences or use a strong glue like *but, and,* or *or* preceded by a comma.

Right: **We hope to attend the banquet, but we may be detained by business.**

One other type of glue that is strong enough to hold two sentences together is the *semicolon* (;). This mark of punctuation should be used only when the two thoughts are very closely related.

Right: **Thank you for your note; it was most timely.**

Right: **We cannot send the dies; they are not yet in stock.**

You have probably guessed that the run-on sentence is the opposite of the sentence fragment. The run-on sentence contains too much while the sentence fragment does not contain enough. Both are equally undesirable.

Remember these points, then:
1. To connect two sentences, you must use a *strong* glue such as a semicolon, or one

of the conjunctions *and, but, or* preceded by a comma.

2. You cannot hold two sentences together by using no glue at all; by using only a comma by itself as *glue;* or by using the conjunction *(and, but, or)* by itself without a comma (except in very short sentences, as will be explained later).

EXAMPLES

1. Right: Here is your order. We look forward to your reply.

 Right: Here is your order, and we look forward to reply.

 Right: Here is your order; we look forward to your reply.

 Wrong: Here is your order we look forward to your reply.

 Wrong: Here is your order, we look forward to your reply.

2. Right: We are new in this field. Our clocks are unmatched in quality.

 Right: We are new in this field, but our clocks are unmatched in quality.

 Wrong: We are new in this field our clocks are unmatched in quality.

 Wrong: We are new in this field, our clocks are unmatched in quality.

3. Right: We must change our advertising appeal. We may lose a large part of our market.

 Right: We must change our advertising appeal, or we may lose a large part of our market.

Turn to Programed Reinforcement S46 through S51

4. AGREEMENT of SUBJECT and PREDICATE

When you answer your employer's phone, you would never say, *"Mr. Smith are here."* You wince just to think of it. When sentences are more complicated, however, you may fall into just such an error; and this is where knowing the subject and predicate can help you on the job.

For your sentence to be grammatically correct, *its predicate must agree with its subject in number.* This means that if the subject is singular you use a singular predicate. If the subject is plural, you use a plural predicate. For example, what would you do with a sentence like this: **One man in the firm of hundreds (is, are) to be honored.**

To solve this problem merely ask yourself: What is the subject of this sentence? Who is to be honored? *One man* is to be honored, not *this firm of hundreds.* Since the predicate must agree with the subject in number, use the singular predicate *is.* The sentence now reads: **One man in this firm of hundreds is to be honored.**

Below is a series of hints to help you determine whether to use a singular or a plural predicate.

HINTS on AGREEMENT of SUBJECT and PREDICATE

HINT 1.

Jack and Jill (is, are) going up a hill. This problem-sentence is easy. It contains two subjects (Jack, Jill) connected by *and.* The sentence means that both of them are going up a hill so it calls for the plural predicate *are.* **Jack and Jill are going up a hill.**

This illustrates the general rule: Whenever a sentence contains two or more subjects connected by *and*, use a plural predicate. Usually this is obvious and natural. **The Acme Company and the Omega Company are merging. Good bookkeepers and good stenographers are hard to find.**

There is one exception to this rule. When both subjects really refer to one person or one thing, use a singular predicate. For example: **The treasurer and secretary is here.** One man holds both positions. *He* is here. If the positions are held by two different men, however, then the general rule applies: **The president and the secretary are here.**

BUT: **Bread and butter is my favorite snack.** *Bread* and *Butter* are so closely identified in this sentence as to be considered one unit; therefore, use the singular predicate **is.**

BUT: **Bread and butter are on my shopping list.**

HINT 2.

1. Jack or Jill (is, are) going up the hill. In this problem, notice first that there are two subjects connected by *or* — *Jack or Jill.* Here's a little trick that will help you with sentences like this. Whenever two or more subjects are connected by *or* or *nor*, make the predicate agree with the subject *closest* to it.

Jack or Jill (is, are) going up the hill. *Jill* is closer to the predicate. *Jill* is singular. Therefore, use the singular predicate *is going.* **Jack or Jill is going up the hill.**

2. Either Mr. Jones or Mr. Smith is going to the meeting. *Mr. Smith* is closer to the predicate. *Mr. Smith* is singular. Therefore, use the singular predicate *is going.*

3. Neither the chair nor the table has arrived. Remember, the same rule applies to two or more subjects connected by *nor. Table* is closer to the predicate. *Table* is singular. Therefore, use *has.*

4. The boys or the girls are going to win. *Girls* is closer to the predicate. *Girls* is plural. Therefore, use the plural predicate *are.*

5. Neither the chairs nor the tables have arrived. *Tables* is closer to the predicate. *Tables* is plural. Therefore, use *have.*

6. Either the secretaries or their bosses are to blame. *Bosses* is closer to the predicate. *Bosses* is plural. Therefore, use *are.*

7. Mr. Sawyer or his sons (has, have) studied your problem. This sentence is a little more complicated. One of the subjects is singular, *Mr. Sawyer.* The other subject is plural, *sons.* By applying our general rule, we can easily determine the proper predicate. *Sons* is closer to the predicate. *Sons* is plural. Therefore, we use the plural word *have:* **Mr. Sawyer or his sons have studied your problem.**

8. The boys or Mr. Sawyer has studied your problem. Here *Mr. Sawyer* is closer to the predicate. Therefore, use *has.* It should be noted, however, that as a general rule of business usage, it is better to place the plural subject closer to the predicate. Thus Sentence No. 7 is a better sentence than Sentence No. 8. Read these sentences aloud. Don't you agree that Sentence No. 7 sounds better?

make verb agree with nearest subject

9. Neither the table nor the chairs have arrived. *Chairs* is plural. Therefore, use *have*.

10. Mr. Smith, Mr. Jones, or their aides have completed the report. In this sentence there are three subjects connected by *or*. This is no problem for our general rule. *Aides* is closest to the predicate. Therefore, we use the plural word *have*.

Turn to Programed Reinforcement S52 through S59

HINT 3.

Words such as *each, anybody,* and *nobody* are tricky. You can save yourself a great deal of grief on the job if you remember that when any one of the following words is the subject of a sentence, you use a *singular* predicate.

1. Each. Each of the officers in the firm is a future chairman. The subject is *each*, not *officers*. *Each* means *each one*. Therefore, use the singular predicate *is*.

2. Anyone. Anyone is qualified for the job. *Anyone* means *any one*, and is therefore singular.

3. Anybody. Anybody is capable of filling this position. *Anybody* is the same as *any one*, and is therefore singular.

4. Someone. Someone is going to suffer for this. *Someone* means *some one*.

5. Somebody. Somebody has missed the point. *Somebody* is the same as *some one*.

6. Everyone. Everyone in town was sad when the Mets lost. *Every one was sad.*

7. Everybody. Everybody here wants to go to the meeting.

(always singular verb singular)

HINT 4.

When determining the subject, disregard expressions beginning with words such as *of, in, at*. These small words are called *prepositions*. In Lesson 6 we will discuss prepositions at length. For now, just remember that you disregard an expression that begins with a word such as *of, in,* or *at* when looking for the subject of a sentence. Look at these examples:

1. Each of the soldiers is a potential leader. Disregard *of the soldiers. Each . . . is a potential leader.*

2. Nobody in the whole army is capable of doing a better job. Disregard *in the whole army. Nobody . . . is capable of doing a better job.*

3. Everyone at headquarters has his job outlined. Disregard *at headquarters. Everyone . . . has his job outlined.*

HINT 5.

Always disregard expressions beginning with *as well as, together with, in addition to, accompanied by,* etc. These expressions give supplementary, incidental information which could be omitted. They do not change the subject.

1. The book, as well as the papers, has been received. The subject is *book*. Disregard *as well as the papers.*

2. My employer, in addition to his associates, was pleased. The subject is *employer*. Disregard *in addition to his associates.*

3. Mr. Smith, together with his secretary, is scheduled to arrive at noon. The subject is *Mr. Smith.* Disregard *together with his secretary.*

(temporarily forget)

9

4. The salesman, accompanied by his family, takes the plane tonight. The subject is *salesman*. Disregard *accompanied by his family*.

HINT 6.

In determining whether a subject is singular or plural, always look to the *meaning* of the word rather than to its form. For example, take the word *news*. Though *news* ends in *s*, it is singular in meaning. Therefore, it calls for a singular predicate. **No news is good news. The news is encouraging.**

Similarly, though the word *series* ends in *s*, it too is singular. **The series of revisions is completed. A series of changes has been made.**

Finally, the names of some school subjects and some diseases end in **s**, but are singular in meaning. For example: *economics, politics, civics, physics, mathematics, measles, and mumps.* **Economics is a required subject, as is civics. Measles is a mild disease. Physics is a basic tool of modern industry. Mumps is a dangerous illness if not treated properly.**

HINT 7.

When a quantity is measured in *one lump sum*, it should be treated as though it were one item. For example:

1. Five tons is a lot of coal. We are really referring to one large amount of coal.

2. Eighty miles per hour is too fast. Eighty miles per hour is one speed.

3. Two hundred dollars is a fair amount. We are referring to one sum of money.

On the other hand, when a quantity is measured in *piece-by-piece* units, use a plural predicate.

There are five men waiting.
In this box are 80 shirts.
Two hundred units have been produced.

You may have trouble when the word *number* is the subject of a sentence. Remember this rule-of-thumb: When *number* is preceded by *the*, use a singular predicate. When any other word, including *a*, precedes *number*, use a plural predicate.

The number of failures is low.
A number of people have failed.

HINT 8.

Beware of titles of books and articles that sound plural. For example:

1. Right: **"Business Letters" is a fine book.** You are referring to one book, though its title sounds plural.

2. Right: **"Notes on Fashions" is in this issue of Jones Magazine.** This is one article; therefore, use the singular predicate.

HINT 9.

Certain words refer to a number of people or things that comprise one group — words such as *committee, jury, class, faculty, crowd,* and *mob*. These words may be either singular or plural depending upon their *meaning* in a sentence. When the entire group to which they refer acts as a *single unit*, use a *singular* predicate.

The committee is scheduled to meet at one o'clock.
The class was led in the procession by the principal.
The jury has rendered its verdict.

When, however, you refer to the *individuals* that make the groups, use a plural predicate.

The committee are violently debating the merits of the proposed system.
The class were arguing with one another.

10

The jury have been embroiled in major disagreement for three hours.

Although the latter three sentences are grammatically correct, there is no denying that they sound extremely awkward. They just don't *sound* right! For this reason, you would be well-advised to rewrite these sentences as follows:

The members of the committee are violently debating the merits of the proposed system.

The students in the class were arguing with one another.

The men and women of the jury have been embroiled in major disagreement for three hours.

These sentences sound better, don't they?

HINT 10.

The name of a firm frequently includes the names of more than one person, and it often includes the word *company*. Again, you must decide whether the company name is being used in a particular sentence in a singular or in a plural sense.

Merrill Lynch, Pierce, Fenner and Smith is America's largest brokerage house.

The American Steel Company has its main offices in Pittsburgh.

In both of the preceding sentences, we have treated the firm as a *single* unit and have therefore used a *singular* predicate. In actual business practice, however, it has become common for the representative of a firm to refer to his company as *we* rather than *it*. Compare these two sentences.

American Steel is pleased to announce that it has developed a new type of alloy especially designed to solve your problem.

American Steel is pleased to announce that we have developed a new type of alloy espe-cially designed to solve your problem.

The use of *it* in the first sentence is cold and impersonal. The use of *we* in the second sentence adds a slight dash of warmth to the statement; it conjures up an image of the many hard-working men and women who have toiled to create this new alloy. This *human* company image may be just the subtle touch that creates a sale for one firm rather than for another. For this reason, the use of a firm name in the plural sense has become an extremely common and accepted practice in American business today.

HINT 11.

You have already been introduced to the type of sentence in which the predicate appears *before* the subject. You learned that you can easily recognize the parts of this type of sentence if you mentally rearrange the sentence into the usual subject-before-predicate order. For example, try this sentence: **Listed among those men suggested for promotion (was, were) George Shultz.** By reversing the order for the sentence, you easily find the solution: **Reverse: George Shultz was listed among those men suggested for promotion.**

Many predicate-before-subject sentences begin with the word *there:* **There (is, are) three new designs that have been selected.** This problem can be solved the same way — by mentally reversing the elements. **Reverse: Three new designs that have been selected are there.**

See how this procedure works with the following sentence: **There (is, are) a large area of disagreement between the factions. Reverse: A large area of disagreement between** the factions is there.

How about this sentence?

There (is, are) a man and his child to see you, Doctor. Just reverse the order of the sentence, and the answer becomes obvious. **Reverse: A man and his child are there to see you, Doctor.**

HINT 12.

The word *none* can be either singular or plural depending upon its reference in a sentence. Most often it is considered plural and requires a plural predicate.

None of the orders have been processed yet, is preferred. **None of the orders has been processed yet,** is also correct since *none* can mean *not one;* therefore: **Not one... has been processed yet.**

HINT 13.

The word *some* may be singular or plural depending upon its meaning in a particular sentence. Here's an easy way to tell the difference in most sentences containing this word. Generally, *some* is followed by a phrase beginning with *of*. If the noun or pronoun in such a phrase is plural, treat *some* as plural. **Some of the men have returned the work.**

If the noun or pronoun in the phrase is singular, treat *some* as singular. **Some of the work is considered satisfactory. Some of the firm's capital is being ear-marked for expansion.**

HINT 14.

Frequently a fraction or percentage is used as the subject of a sentence. **Three-fifths of the men have arrived. Sixty percent of our quota has been met.**

The same rule-of-thumb that we used with *some* applies to these fractions and percentages:

Half of the farms in this area are for sale.
Fifty percent of this farm is lying fallow.
One quarter of the order has been shipped.
Twenty-five percent of the orders have been shipped.

Turn to Programed Reinforcement S60 through S84

Clauses

Independent - can stand alson
Dependent - relies on some other clause to make a complete sentence.

Jack talks very loudly - Independent Clause.

If Jack talks very loudly. - dependent

(Indepent + dependen)
Complex Sentence

(Indepent + Indepent)
compound sentence

12

PROGRAMED REINFORCEMENT

You are about to embark upon an exciting and unusual approach to further mastery of business English in this section which we call *Programed Reinforcement*. Before starting, be sure that you have read the required material in the text section of this book. Only then are you ready to *reinforce* the learning of what you have read by working through this carefully *programed* sequence of questions and answers.

Programed Reinforcement is based upon the very latest concept of educational psychologists. This concept — called *programed learning* — involves the breaking down of a complex idea into many tiny bits of information that you can easily learn one at a time. As applied in this section, you are asked a question about one simple bit of information and you write your answers in the space provided. *Immediately* you check your answer against the correct answer that is printed in the book. If your answer is correct, you proceed to the next question. If it is wrong, you go over it again to see why. Thus you never proceed unless you are certain that you have mastered each step. In this manner you proceed with certainty step by step to complete mastery of the complete concept. It's easy . . . it's satisfying . . . it's fun.

— WHAT TO DO IN THIS SECTION —

Generally you are instructed to do one of two things in each frame:

1. Where you find blanks, write the missing word or words.
   For example — A sentence is a group of words that expresses a complete t*hought*.

2. Where you find two more words in parentheses, circle the correct word.
   For example — The efficient typist. What is needed in this fragment to make it a sentence? (A predicate, A subject)

Questions are numbered in sequence S1 . . . S2 . . . S3 . . . and so on. The correct response to S1 is numbered R1 . . . the correct response to S2 is R2 . . . and so on. (S stands for *stimulus* — the term psychologists apply to the *question*. R stands for *Response* — the term psychologists apply to the answer.)

Begin with S1 which appears in the top right-hand frame. Cover the corresponding answer (R1) that appears in the left-hand box of the second frame. Simply follow the frames down the page and onto the next page until you have completed your assignment. Then turn to the *Practice Exercises* that are assigned.

Obviously, there is nothing to be gained by peeking at the correct response before you write in your answer. You will not be graded on your work in Programed Reinforcement, so you will only be cheating yourself out of valuable and irreplaceable practice.

By applying yourself diligently to this programed material, you will be able to move on to the *Practice Exercises* with ease and confidence.

Now . . . on to frame S1.

S1

A sentence is a group of words that expresses a complete t_h_o_u_g_h_t.

R1 thought

S2

To express a complete thought, every sentence must include a) someone or something to talk about, and b) something to say about that person or thing. True ☑ False ☐

R2 True

S3

The s_u_b_j_e_c_t of a sentence tells us whom or what we are talking about.

R3 subject

S4

The subject of a sentence is the d_o_e_r of the action.

R4 doer

S5

The p_r_e_d_i_c_a_t_e of a sentence tells us what the subject does.

R5 predicate

S6

Since every sentence must contain a subject and a predicate, how many essential parts must every sentence have? _2_

R6 two

S7

In the sentence **Mary types,** the subject **Mary** answers the question w____, while the predicate **types** answers the question d_____ w_____.

R7 who; does what

S8

Able, efficient Mary types with ease and correctness. Circle the words that describe (modify) the subject **Mary.**

R8 able; efficient

S9

Able, efficient Mary types with speed and accuracy. Circle the words that describe (modify) the predicate **types.**

R9 with speed and accuracy

S10

Able, efficient Mary types with speed and accuracy.
The subject is _____; the predicate is _____.

R10 Mary; types

S11

In the sentence **The foreman spoke with authority and directness,** the subject _____ answers the question w____; the predicate _____ answers the question d____ w____.

R11 foreman, who; spoke; does what

S12

In the same sentence, **The foreman spoke with authority and directness,** circle the words that should be disregarded in determining the subject and the predicate.

R12 with authority and directness

S13

On Tuesday morning after the coffee break the department heads met. The subject is _____; the predicate is _____.

R13 subject — **heads**; predicate — **met**

14

S14
Mr. Jones, after giving dictation, dismissed his secretary.
Circle the subject and underline the predicate.

R14
Mr. Jones;
dismissed

S15
No one, in my opinion, can deliver a better sales talk than Mrs. Reynolds. The subject consists of two words, n ___ o ___ ___, and the predicate here also has two words, c ___ ___ d ___ ___ ___ ___ ___ ___.

R15
subject — **no one;**
predicate — **can deliver**

S16
Modern and functional are our new office desks. In this sentence the subject, d ___ ___ ___ ___, comes (before, after) the predicate, a ___ ___.

R16
desks; after; **are**

S17
Oats and wheat are basic commodities on the market. The subject in this sentence is _____ and _____. Since there are two parts to the subject, this is called a c ___ ___ ___ ___ ___ ___d subject.

R17
oats; wheat;
compound

S18
Salaries in our firm rose last year and then leveled off. In this sentence the predicate is _____ and _____. This is called a _____ predicate because it is composed of more than _____ part.

R18
rose; leveled;
compound; one

S19
Sue and Mary typed and filed constantly all morning. The subject is _____ and _____; the predicate is _____ and _____. Both the subject and the predicate are c ___ ___ ___ ___ ___ ___ ___.

R19
Sue; Mary;
typed; filed;
compound

S20
Avoid erasures on typed material. The subject in this sentence is not expressed; rather it is u ___ ___ ___ ___ ___ ___ ___ ___ ___ because the sentence is a (command, question).

R20
understood; command

S21
Where am I? This sentence is a q ___ ___ ___ ___ ___ ___ ___ ___. If we reverse the order of the sentence, it will read: ___ _____ _____? In this order the subject is obviously _____; the predicate is _____.

R21
question; **I am where?;**
I; am

S22
Report to your supervisor before lunch. The understood subject is _____.

R22
you

S23
Let us review. A sentence is a group of words that contains a s ___ ___ ___ ___ ___ ___ and a p ___ ___ ___ ___ ___ ___ ___ ___ and expresses a _____ _____.

R23
subject; predicate;
complete thought

● TURN TO Exercise 1

S24
A part of a sentence that is written as though it were a complete sentence is called a sentence f __ __ __ __ __ __ __.

R24 fragment

S25
The efficient typist. What is needed in this fragment to make it a sentence? (A predicate, A subject)

R25 A predicate

S26
Made three carbon copies. What is needed in this fragment to make it a sentence? (A subject, A predicate)

R26 A subject

S27
The efficient typist. Made three carbon copies. How would you write these two sentence fragments as one complete sentence? _____

_____

R27 **The efficient typist made three carbon copies.**

S28
What three necessary characteristics of every sentence can be found in **The efficient typist made three carbon copies.**
a) s __ __ __ __ __ __; b) p __ __ __ __ __ __ __;
c) c __ __ __ __ __ __ __ t __ __ __ __ __ __

R28
a) subject;
b) predicate;
c) complete thought

S29
A clause must contain a _____ and a _____.
The following words are not a clause because they do not contain a _____. **. . . all of our offices.**

R29
subject;
predicate;
predicate

S30
A clause that expresses a complete thought is called an __ __ __ __ __ __ __ __ __ __ __ clause.

R30 independent

S31
A clause that does not express a complete thought is called a _____ clause.

R31 dependent

S32
When we hear from you . . . . This is a(n) _____ clause because it (does; does not) express a complete thought.

R32
dependent;
does not

S33
We will make our decision. . . . This is a(n) _____ clause because it (does; does not) express a complete thought.

R33
independent;
does

S34
When we hear from you, we will make our decision.
This sentence contains a _____ clause and an _____ clause. Such a sentence is called a c __ __ __ __ __ x sentence.

R34
dependent;
independent;
complex

S35 A _____ sentence is a sentence that contains a dependent clause and an independent clause.

R35 complex

S36 **The order was shipped while you were away.**
This is a _____ sentence because it contains an _____ clause and a _____ clause. Underline the dependent clause with one line; the independent clause with two lines.

R36 complex;
independent; dependent;
while you were away;
The order was shipped...

S37 **Organizing his thoughts...** (is; is not) a clause because it (does; does not) contain a subject and a predicate.

R37 is not;
does not

S38 A clause is a group of words that contains a _____ and a _____. A dependent clause is a group of words that contains a _____ and a _____ but does not express a _____ _____.

R38 subject;
predicate;
subject;
predicate;
complete thought

S39 An independent clause is a group of words that contains a _____ and a _____ and expresses a _____ _____. An _____ clause can stand by itself as a sentence.

R39 subject;
predicate;
complete thought;
independent

S40 **Since I didn't feel well.** This is a fragment. It has a subject **I** and a predicate **didn't**. Yet one important essential of a sentence is missing. It does not _____ ___ _____ _____.

R40 express a complete thought

S41 **Since I didn't feel well, I stayed home from work.** This is a (sentence fragment; complete sentence).

R41 complete sentence

S42 In the above sentence, S41, **Since I didn't feel well** is a d_ _ _ _ _ _ _t clause, and **I stayed home from work** is an _____ _____.

R42 dependent;
independent clause

S43 A clause must contain a s_ _ _ _ _ _ _ and a p_ _ _ _ _ _ _ _. The following words are **not** a clause because they do not contain a _____. **...shipped by the fastest way possible**

R43 subject;
predicate; subject

S44
Write the following correctly: **Although our business has increased. Our net profits are substantially the same.**

_____

_____

R44

Although our business has increased, our net profits are substantially the same.

S45

Which of the following is correct:

a) **Because automation is increasing. We must re-examine our own methods.**

b) **Because automation is increasing, we must re-examine our own methods.**

R45

b

• TURN TO Exercise 2

S46

Here is an example of a common error — the writing of two separate sentences as one sentence. **We shall attend the meeting we may be detained, however.** This error is called a _____-_____ sentence.

R46

run-on

S47

A run-on sentence contains too much. It is the opposite of a sentence _____, which contains too little.

R47

fragment

S48

Correct the following run-on sentence by inserting the conjunction **but: Here is your exam paper, do not start until we tell you.**

R48

Here is your exam paper, but do not start until we tell you.

S49

Correct the following run-on sentence by using a period and starting a new sentence: **We must change our bookkeeping practices they are almost obsolete.**

R49

We must change our bookkeeping practices. They are almost obsolete.

S50

It is never permissible to separate two complete sentences by a comma alone. A semicolon may be used when the two sentences are closely allied. Where would you insert the semicolon in this run-on? **Speak carefully before sales executives, they are practical-minded.**

R50

Speak carefully before sales executives; they are practical-minded.

S51

We call two sentences written incorrectly as one a _____-_____ _____.

R51

run-on sentence

• TURN TO Exercises 3 and 4

S52

If the subject of a sentence is singular, the predicate must be s __ __ __ __ __ __ __.

R52

singular

S53

If the subject of a sentence is plural, the predicate must be p __ __ __ __ __.

R53

plural

	S54 Circle your answer: **The chief and his assistant (is, are) ready to leave the office.**
R54 are	**S55** Two subjects connected by **and** make the subject plural. If the two subjects are always identified as one, however, the subject is singular. **Bread and butter (is, are) my favorite food.**
R55 is	**S56** When the word **or** or **nor** is used to connect two subjects, the predicate will agree with the subject that is c __ __ __ __ __ to it.
R56 closer	**S57** **The salesmen or their manager (is, are) able to do the job.** The correct predicate is **is** because the subject that is closer to it is the word _____, which is singular.
R57 manager	**S58** **Neither the desk nor the chairs (seem, seems) in good condition.** The subject closer to the verb is **chairs;** therefore, the correct predicate is the word _____, which is (singular, plural).
R58 seem; plural	**S59** **Either the chairs or the desk (has, have) to be replaced.** Since the subject nearer the verb is **desk,** which is singular, the predicate must be the word _____, which is also _____.
R59 has; singular • TURN TO Exercise 5	**S60** The words **each, everyone, anybody,** and **nobody** are all singular. When they are used as subjects, the predicate must also be _____.
R60 singular	**S61** Circle your answer: **Anybody (is, are) able to succeed with hard work.**
R61 is	**S62** **Each of the posters (has, have) to be redone.** The subject is _____, not p __ __ __ __ __ __. The correct predicate is _____.
R62 each; posters; has	**S63** **Each of the typists (is, are) capable.** The subject is _____, not t __ __ __ __ __ __. The correct predicate is _____.
R63 Each; typists; is	

S64

There are certain expressions like **as well as, accompanied by, together with, in addition to** that do not change a singular subject into a plural subject. **The father, accompanied by his sons, (is, are) coming by plane.** The subject is _____, not s __ __ __. The correct predicate is _____.

R64 father; sons; is (coming)

S65

Mr. Smith, together with his assistants, (is, are) expected at two o'clock. The subject is _____, not _____. The correct predicate is _____.

R65 Mr. Smith; assistants; is (expected)

S66

The news (is, are) good. The subject is _____, which is (singular, plural). The correct predicate is _____.

R66 news; singular; is

S67

A quantity that is the subject may look plural, but if it represents one lump sum, it is singular. Example: **Five dollars (was, were) a lot for a tip.**

R67 was

S68

Circle your answer: **Ten typewriters (was, were) missing.**

R68 were

S69

When the word **number** is the subject of a sentence and is preceded by **the**, use a singular predicate. **The number of bankruptcies (is, are) decreasing. The number** is considered a (singular, plural) subject.

R69 is; singular

S70

When the word **number** is preceded by a, use a plural predicate. **A number of checks (seem, seems) to have been mislaid. A number** is considered a (singular, plural) subject.

R70 seem; plural

S71

Circle your answer: **"Hints To An Executive" (appear, appears) in a magazine this week.**

R71 appears

S72

Words that refer to a group **(committee, jury, class, crowd, mob)** may be either singular or plural depending upon their meaning in the sentence. When the entire group acts as a single unit, the predicate is s __ __ __ __ __ __ __. When the group is thought of in terms of its individual members, the predicate is _____.

R72 singular; plural

S73

Circle your answer: **The committee (is, are) ready to give its report.**

R73 is

S74

Circle your answer: **Smith, Jones and Philips (is, are) a well-known moving firm.**

R74 is

S75
Sometimes the subject will appear after the predicate. **There were three speeches given.** Rewrite this sentence in subject-before-predicate order.

_____

R75
Three speeches were given there.

S76
Circle the subject and the correct predicate in this sentence:
Picked among the candidates (was, were) the new secretary.

R76
subject—**secretary;**
predicate—**was (picked)**

S77
The word **none** may be either singular or plural. Most often it is considered _____ and therefore requires a plural predicate.

R77
plural

S78
Some may be singular or plural. If the noun in the **of** phrase that follows **some** is singular, then **some** is singular. **Some of the work (is, are) too hard.** The noun in the **of** phrase is w __ __ __, which is (singular, plural). The correct predicate, therefore, is _____.

R78
work; singular;
is

S79
Some of the workers (is, are) unsatisfactory. The noun in the **of** phrase is w __ __ __ __ __ __, which is (singular, plural). The correct predicate, therefore, is _____.

R79
workers; plural
are

S80
Fractions used as subjects follow the same rule as **some;** that is, if the phrase following the fraction has a singular noun, the predicate is _____; if the phrase has a plural noun, the predicate is _____.

R80
singular; plural

S81
Choose the correct predicates:
One-third of the mechanics (have, has) arrived.
Fifty percent of the stock (is, are) worthless.

R81
have; is

S82
To review, a singular subject calls for a _____ predicate; a plural subject calls for a _____ predicate.

R82
singular; plural

S83
The only type of sentence in which the subject may be omitted because it is understood to mean **you,** is the c __ __ __ __ __ __ __.

R83
command (imperative sentence)

S84
To make one sentence out of two complete thoughts, you (can, cannot) use a comma **by itself** as the "glue."

R84
cannot

● TURN TO
Exercise 6 and Review

singular - molases
      news.

series - singular or plural.

a series of articles (is) on the TV
     S

There (are) many series of soap operas

a number of men (is) present
     sing

The number of articles (are) overwhelming
     plura

Two tons of coal (is) alot.

seventy miles an hour (is) two fast to drive.
S

There are seventy miles from your house
to my house.

"Safety Hints" (is) a good booklet.
     S
"Fashion Hints" (is) a good column in the paper
     S
                                to read
The Fashion Hints you told me about are
helpful.
Collective Nouns: jury committee, class mob
The jury is giving its decision.
The jury are arguing among themselves.
The mob is large.
The mob were shouting at the singer.

NAME *Lorraine Stone*   CLASS *11*   DATE *Dec 9*

EXERCISE 1 | Identifying the Subject and Predicate

This problem deals with identifying the subject and the predicate of a sentence. In each of the following sentences, underline the subject with one line; underline the predicate with two lines. Remember, ask yourself two questions: 1. Who or what? (The subject) 2. Does what? (The predicate). Disregard all other words.

SCORING: DEDUCT 4 POINTS FOR EACH ERROR.

1. I like this book.

2. This book has been sold to over 200,000 readers.

3. These readers have uniformly expressed their delight with this book.

4. Did you enjoy it?

5. I certainly did enjoy it.

6. George and Harry are co-owners of the restaurant.

7. Mr. Roberts and Mr. Jones are in their office.

8. At the stroke of noon the President and his cabinet met in the East Wing.

9. Have you seen the President and his cabinet in session?

10. Neither Mr. Black nor Mr. Green has sent in his reply.

11. We wish to see either Miss White or Miss Brown.

12. Neither of them is here.

13. She can type and file expertly.

14. The secretary has transcribed and mailed the letter.

15. Has the letter been typed and mailed?

16. There is a simple solution to the problem of unfulfilled obligations.

17. A free and strong America is the objective of our government policies.

18. The men will arise early and depart for the camp at the appointed hour.

19. Before him stood New York—big and beautiful—with its towering buildings, shimmering rivers, and ribbon-like bridges.

20. Give it to me this minute.

21. Ready to greet the new supervisor was his staff of assistants.

22. Waiting at the airport were the accountant and the lawyer.

23. There are more than 50 percent of the offices rented.

24. Near him sat the two partners of the firm.

25. Needed more than economy is efficiency.

NAME   CLASS   DATE

EXERCISE 2   Sentence Fragments

A. This problem deals with recognizing incomplete thoughts. As you know, a sentence must express a complete thought. Below is a list of expressions. Some of them express complete thoughts. In the space provided, mark **C** next to these sentences to indicate that they are <u>complete</u> sentences. The rest of these expressions do not express complete thoughts. Mark **F** next to these to indicate that these expressions are sentence <u>fragments</u>.

SCORING: DEDUCT 5 POINTS FOR EACH ERROR.

1. Running down the street at full speed.   1. _____F_____

2. Despite his lack of experience and maturity.   2. _____F_____

3. We agree.   3. _____C_____

4. Night after night, day after day, till he could hardly speak anymore. 4. _____F_____

5. Mr. Roberts, the most noted authority on aerodynamics in recent years. 5. _____F_____

6. Furtively looking up and down the street, then darting to safety in the shadows, he escaped. 6. _____C_____

7. Where are we going?   7. _____C_____

8. Despite all his protestations to the contrary and his insistence that he was innocent, he was convicted. 8. _____C_____

9. Although we were certain that he was a fine leader and were willing to follow him wherever he would lead. 9. _____F_____

10. When the order arrives and is processed by the receiving department. 10. _____F_____

11. Despite explicit orders to the contrary.   11. _____F_____

12. Nearing the attainment of the production goals set at our last meeting. 12. _____F_____

13. Nearly everyone present, including the President and his aides.   13. _____F_____

14. Nearly everyone was present, including the President and his aides.   14. _____C_____

15. There is no time for further discussion.   15. _____C_____

16. Delivery of one table, four chairs, two desks, and three lamps.   16. _____F_____

17. Your order was received.   17. _____C_____

18. Forgetting all the instructions the foreman had given him in the morning. 18. _____F_____

19. Don't send the letter.   19. _____C_____

20. Where in this entire office?   20. _____F_____

SCORE

B._____

EXERCISE 2   Recognition of Clauses   DEPENDENT AND INDEPENDENT

B. The problem here is to recognize a clause (a group of words with a subject and predicate) and to label it <u>dependent</u> if it cannot stand alone as a sentence, or <u>independent</u> if it can stand alone. In each sentence below a group of words is underlined. In the space to the right, write D if it is a dependent clause; write I if it is an independent clause; write N if it is <u>not</u> a clause.

SCORING: DEDUCT 10 POINTS FOR EACH ERROR.

1. I prefer the typewriter *on the table.*   1. ___ ~~D~~ N
2. *When a letter is typed,* it represents the firm.   2. ___ D
3. He led his sales force *because of his ambition.*   3. ___ ~~D~~ N
4. *Because he was ambitious,* he soon impressed his employers.   4. ___ D
5. *We can offer this guarantee* because of our high quality control.   5. ___ I
6. *Standing behind each man* is a woman who prods him into action.   6. ___ ~~D~~ N
7. *She is a fine bookkeeper* because she is quick with figures.   7. ___ I
8. *Although we have worked hard,* the end is not yet in sight.   8. ___ D
9. *Your order was received in time* despite an unexpected delay.   9. ___ I
10. Because we have years of experience, *we can do the best job.*   10. ___ I

SCORE

C._____

EXERCISE 2   Simple and Complex Sentences

C. A simple sentence is a sentence composed of one independent clause. A complex sentence is a sentence composed of an independent clause and a dependent clause. In the space to the right of each example, write S if it is a <u>simple</u> sentence; write X if it is a <u>complex</u> sentence; write F if it is a sentence <u>fragment</u>.

SCORING: DEDUCT 10 POINTS FOR EACH ERROR.

1. On the last day in April we will hold our meeting.   1. ___ ~~X~~ S
2. Despite our protests, he entered the primary race for the Senate.   2. ___ ~~X~~ S
3. We will expect delivery as soon as possible.   3. ___ S
4. After they deliver the goods, we will bill them.   4. ___ X
5. If anything ever sounded as though it were unwise.   5. ___ F
6. Please try to arrive before 10 o'clock to avoid any delay.   6. ___ ~~X~~ S
7. Though you have a prior engagement, won't you try to attend?   7. ___ X
8. There are several good reasons for our decision and for our unwillingness to participate.   8. ___ ~~X~~ S
9. The merchandise arrived in damaged condition despite the warnings we sent you.   9. ___ X
10. Don't you agree with the Commission's report on unemployment?   10. ___ S

EXERCISE 2 — Proofreading For Sentence Fragments

D. In creating copy for advertising, copywriters occasionally take liberties with the strict rules of grammar in order to emphasize a point. Sometimes, however, they go "overboard" in violating these rules, and any emphasis they hoped for is buried in a morass of misapplied English. We think that this has happened in the advertising copy presented below which is filled with a stream of sentence fragments. Circle any marks of punctuation and capital letters that should be changed.

This material was printed in the OAG Magazine, <u>Air Travel</u>. Remember, just because you see something in print does not mean that it's right!

SCORING: DEDUCT 10 POINTS FOR EACH ERROR.

"I ALWAYS FEEL LIKE I'M SORT OF GIVING A PARTY."

We've hired 15,873 stewardesses.

Since 1933.

So let us tell you something about girls. Makeup can change a face, but it can't change a personality. A girl has to have that special attitude. If she does, you get that special service.

If she doesn't, we both pay.

Sandy Norris is 22. She's from Weslaco, Texas. And after one year on the job, this is what she told us about being a stewardess:

"At first I was bashful.

But then people began thanking me for an enjoyable flight.

I liked that. And I realized how much I wanted everything to go just right.

That I had fun when they did."

We'll keep combing America for girls like Sandy. And as soon as we meet them, we promise to introduce them to you.

Girls who bring a little something extra to their job—That's the American Way.

FLY THE AMERICAN WAY.

AMERICAN AIRLINES.

NAME   CLASS   DATE

EXERCISE 3   Run-on Sentences

This problem deals with recognizing run-on sentences. Some of the following sentences are correct; others are run-on sentences. Wherever there is an error in punctuation or capitalization, cross out the error and write your correction in the space above. If a sentence is entirely correct, mark C in the left-hand margin.

SCORING: DEDUCT 10 POINTS FOR EACH ERROR.

1. Have your representative call. A definite appointment should be made in advance.

2. Maybe later on we will be willing to do as your order man writes. Just now, however, we do not wish to change.

3. Are the letters and articles graded according to difficulty? In our book they are.

4. Mr. James Quinn, a man with considerable experience in office planning, will be ready to help you on March 4.   C

5. At this time, however, we do not wish to change. We are sure you will understand.

6. But read the booklet. Yours will bear your imprint on the front and back covers.

7. She learns all the good points and fortifies herself with facts and evidence about the superiority of York silk and the weak points of others so that when she is ready to buy silk she will want York and no other brand.   C

8. Won't you please take a few moments of your time to tell us the details of the improper shipment. Armed with this information, we will be in a position to ship you the correct items.

9. We are making our plans for next summer. We are interested in your booklet concerning York silk.

10. Try Smilo toothpaste, it will give you the smile of contentedness.

EXERCISE 4 — Sentence Fragments and Run-on Sentences

A. This problem deals with distinguishing a complete sentence from a sentence fragment or a run-on sentence. In the space provided, mark C if the expression is a complete sentence; mark F if it is a sentence fragment; and mark R if it is a run-on sentence.

SCORING: DEDUCT 5 POINTS FOR EACH ERROR.

1. Whenever the attorney had a chance to speak.   1. _F_

2. Ship the books, we will remit within 30 days.   2. _R_

3. Lessons by day, study at night.   3. _F_

4. Because of his initiative, and because he had the proper connections.   4. _F_

5. What will happen next?   5. _C_

6. Continue with your college course, you will graduate at the head of your class.   6. _R_

7. Looking around, sizing up the situation, and foretelling all its ramifications.   7. _F_

8. Oil, steel, and coal in the right proportions.   8. _F_

9. Expect only big things of yourself, and never waver nor doubt that they will come true.   9. _C_

10. Though Miss Blake is young, she is not immature, so I am convinced she can handle the job.   10. _C_

11. Speaking of telephone prices. A new low rate for evening calls is now in practice.   11. _C_

12. Carbon copies are important for checking data, especially in business correspondence.   12. _C_

13. Stay late tonight, you will be paid for overtime.   13. _R_

14. Please check your accuracy, however speed is essential too.   14. _R_

15. Of course we are interested, you would be too.   15. _R_

16. We have written twice, please reply at once.   16. _R_

17. As soon as the incident was reported, rumors started flying; accordingly, the President rushed to clarify the issues to the nation.   _C_

18. Courtesy is contagious, therefore smile often.   18. _R_

19. Help!   19. _C_

20. We followed the directions, but we couldn't assemble the instrument no matter how many different ways we attempted to arrange the elements.   20. _C_

EXERCISE 4 — Sentence Fragments and Run-on Sentences

B. This letter contains a number of sentence fragments and run-on sentences. Proofread this letter, crossing out all mistakes and indicating all necessary changes.

SCORING: DEDUCT 5 POINTS FOR EACH ERROR.

Dear Mr. White:

No two men are alike, One man jumps to a conclusion without careful consideration of all available information. Another man examines each fact, Checks every claim, And profits from the experience of others, Then he makes his decision.

We believe you are the latter type of purchaser, a The man who has to see for himself before he buys. For this reason we are delighted to offer you a Slick Electric Razor on a free home-trial basis. Although you may have used another razor all your life, After seven days with the Slick you will never again want to switch back to your old-type razor.

So mail the enclosed card today, We will ship your sample Slick Razor by return post.

Sincerely,

SCORE

A_____

EXERCISE 5 | The Subject of a Sentence

A. This problem deals with identifying the subject of a sentence and determining if it is singular or plural. In the column headed Subject, write the subject of each sentence. In the column headed Number write S if the subject is singular and P if the subject is plural.

SCORING: DEDUCT 10 POINTS FOR EACH ERROR.

		SUBJECT	NUMBER
1.	A man called at your office.	man	S
2.	A tall, dark, handsome, cultured man called at your office.	man	S
3.	Frank and Mary are staying overtime today.	Frank Mary	P
4.	Macy's and Gimbel's are friendly competitors.	Macy's + Gimbels	P
5.	Efficient supervisors and executives have always been at a premium.	S & e	P
6.	Both the designer and the engineer seem competent workers.	d & e	P
7.	Peaches and cream is my favorite breakfast dish.	P & C	S
8.	A supervisor for all receptionists must be picked today.	supervisor	S
9.	Bread and butter is a staple in the American diet.	B & B	S
10.	Office machinery must be covered and carefully protected.	machinery	S

SCORE

B_____

EXERCISE 5 | The Predicate of a Sentence

B. This problem deals with identifying the predicate. In the column headed Predicate, write the predicate of the sentence. In the column headed Number, write S if the subject is singular and P if the subject is plural.

SCORING: DEDUCT 10 POINTS FOR EACH ERROR.

		PREDICATE	SUBJECT NUMBER
1.	Mr. Smith and his partner will speak at the meeting today.	will speak	P
2.	Either Mary or her friends will be the best models for the new uniform.	will	P
3.	Neither time nor effort should be spared in practicing typing.	spared	S
4.	Neither the desk nor the chairs have arrived at the office.	have arrived	P
5.	Each of the applicants has to fill out a questionnaire.	has	S
6.	Anyone of the export firms is able to handle the shipment.	is able	S
7.	Everybody in the sales force is asked to use the suggestion box.	is	S
8.	Somebody in the executive office is responsible for time studies.	is	S
9.	The news of the sales losses is coming over the ticker tape.	is	S
10.	Each male and each female has equal opportunity for promotion.	has	S

EXERCISE 5　　Identifying Subject and Predicate

C. This problem deals with your ability to pick out subjects and predicates found in a business letter. Underline each subject once and each predicate twice.

SCORING: DEDUCT 5 POINTS FOR EACH ERROR.

Gentlemen:

You In your recent letter you <u>ordered</u> several items for immediate delivery. Our production <u>manager</u> and our consulting <u>engineer</u> <u>have informed</u> me of some delays in retooling machines for your order. <u>We</u> <u>shall expedite</u> this adjustment <u>and put</u> your order into work quickly. The <u>shipping department</u> <u>will</u>, of course, <u>inform</u> you of the shipping date, and <u>Mr. Jones</u> <u>will visit</u> you personally if necessary. Please *You* <u>understand</u> our problems in retooling and accept our assurance of careful attention. Both <u>Mr. Jones</u> and <u>I</u> <u>shall look</u> forward to serving you.

Sincerely,

EXERCISE 6　　Agreement of Subject and Predicate

A. This problem deals with agreement of subject and predicate. In the space provided, write the correct predicate. Remember, first find the subject; then choose its predicate. If you have any trouble, review the Hints on Agreement of Subject and Predicate.

SCORING: DEDUCT 10 POINTS FOR EACH ERROR.

1. Each order (<u>has</u>, have) been received.　　1. _has_

2. Each of the orders (<u>has</u>, have) been received.　　2. _has_

3. Nobody among the secretaries (seem, <u>seems</u>) capable of supervising tests.　　3. _seems_

4. My boss, together with his assistant, (<u>was</u>, were) able to attend the convention.　　4. _was_

5. Mr. Jones, together with his wife, (<u>is</u>, are) planning to take a holiday.　　5. _is_

6. A series of changes in office routines (<u>is</u>, are) expected soon.　　6. _is_

7. News of the price decreases (<u>has</u>, have) reached the customers.　　7. _has_

8. Six tons of coal (<u>was</u>, were) paid for on the last bill.　　8. _was_

9. The number of marriages in the firm (<u>is</u>, are) increasing.　　9. _is_

10. A number of filing clerks and secretaries (has, <u>have</u>) applied.　　10. _have_

SCORE

B_____

EXERCISE 6 — Agreement of Subject and Predicate

B. Choose the correct predicate. Indicate whether the predicate is singular or plural — writing S if it is singular; P if it is plural.

SCORING: DEDUCT 10 POINTS FOR EACH ERROR.

		PREDICATE	NUMBER
1. "Writing Better Letters" (is, are) a good book for secretaries.	1.	is	S
2. "Ideas on Office Improvement" (was, were) put aside for the new typist.	2.	was	S
3. The committee (has, have) decided to issue their report next week.	3.	have	P
4. The jury (was, were) asked by the judge to render its decision.	4.	was	S
5. The faculty of the school (seem, seems) to be against new proposals.	5.	seems	S
6. Pearson, French, Hein and Jackson (is, are) a leading publishing house.	6.	is	S
7. The Providence Producing Company (appear, appears) on the top of the list.	7.	appears	S
8. The members of the ANTA Playhouse Company (is, are) planning a road trip.	8.	are	P
9. A number of checks (was, were) returned marked "No funds."	9.	were	P
10. The number of books available for sale (is, are) low.	10.	is	S

SCORE

C_____

EXERCISE 6 — Agreement of Subject and Predicate

C. In the first space write the subject; in the second, write the predicate.

SCORING: DEDUCT 10 POINTS FOR EACH ERROR.

		SUBJECT	PREDICATE
1. High among the winners (was, were) Jim Taylor.	1.	was	S
2. There (is, are) several ways of making stencil corrections.	2.	are	S
3. There (was, were) three comments in suggestion box.	3.	were	P
4. None of the orders (have, has) been processed yet.	4.	have	P
5. None of the methods of transcription (is, are) beyond criticism.	5.	are	P
6. Some of the firm's investments (seem, seems) to have been affected by the market changes.	6.	seem	P
7. Some of the carbons (have, has) been ruined by careless handling.	7.	have	P
8. Three-fifths of the crop (has, have) to be stored in silos.	8.	has	S
9. Forty percent of the letters (have, has) to be corrected.	9.	have	P
10. Half of the order (appear, appears) to be on its way.	10.	appears	S

NAME   CLASS   DATE

EXERCISE 6 | Agreement of Subject and Predicate

D. This problem deals with agreement of subject and predicate. In the space provided, write the correct predicate. Remember, first find the subject; then choose its predicate. If you have any trouble, review the Hints on Agreement of Subject and Predicate.

SCORING: DEDUCT 4 POINTS FOR EACH ERROR.

1. Each order (has, have) been processed.   1. _has_
2. Each of the orders (has, have) been processed.   2. _has_
3. Anyone (know, knows) what the solution should be.   3. _knows_
4. Walter Clark of Chicago, as well as his entire family, (intend, intends) to spend his summer here.   4. _intends_
5. Either Mr. Burns or Mr. Jones (is, are) the logical candidate.   5. _is_
6. There (is, are) a table and a lamp still unshipped.   6. _are_
7. One million dollars (is, are) a lot of money   7. _is_
8. We feel that neither your office nor your plants (is, are) adequately equipped.   8. _are_
9. The committee (has, have) issued a final decree.   9. _has_
10. Each of the children, in addition to his parents, (is, are) entitled to a free pass.   10. _is_
11. A number of photos (were, was) taken.   11. _were_
12. Anybody with a sound mind (are, is) eligible to enter.   12. _is_
13. I feel that politics (has, have) entered a decade of turmoil.   13. _has_
14. The number of books available for sale (are, is) low.   14. _is_
15. Thirty-six percent of our total production (has, have) been sold.   15. _has_
16. None of the suppliers (has, have) called since our orders were sent.   16. _has_
17. Hundreds of teachers, together with their students, (hail, hails) our product.   17. _hail_
18. Measles (is, are) a contagious disease.   18. _is_
19. This series of figures (is, are) much too confusing.   19. _is_
20. Here (is, are) the list of figures you requested.   20. _is_
21. Any number of consequences (is, are) possible.   21. _are_
22. Nearly one-third of our supply (has, have) been exhausted.   22. _has_
23. Mathematics as well as economics (is, are) required.   23. _is_
24. The members of the jury (is, are) in complete disagreement.   24. _are_
25. The jury and the judge, as well as the general public, (is, are) convinced of the defendant's innocence.   25. _are_

NAME   CLASS   DATE

REVIEW EXERCISE 1 — The Sentence

The letter below contains a number of intentional errors in sentence structure. Cross out all incorrect punctuation and incorrect words. Above each, write the proper form.
SCORING: DEDUCT 5 POINTS FOR EACH ERROR.

Dear Mr. Jones:

On looking over our records this week, we find that
each of your offices has failed to renew its subscription to
<u>Modern Times</u>, ~~And~~ we assure you we regret this very much.
Each of our previous letters express our appreciation of
having you as a subscriber, ~~And~~ explain to you our desire
to have all your offices remain as regular subscribers.

Everyone on our staff ~~are~~ *is* concerned over your failure to renew, ~~was~~ this failure due to something that
somebody in my office ~~have~~ *has* said or done? We would be very
much pleased to hear any suggestions you may have, and
assure you that we will take all steps possible to remedy
any unfortunate situation.

You know "Modern Times" ~~are~~ *is* the finest magazine in
its field, ~~Whether~~ drama, science, current events, or politics ~~are~~ *is* your interest, "Modern Times" ~~have~~ *has* articles of
interest to you, "Modern Times" is read and enjoyed by men
in all walks of life, ~~it~~ *It* is read by doctors, it ~~is read by~~
lawyers, ~~it~~ *and* is read by engineers, the list of readers ~~are~~
just endless.

We do hope that you will reconsider and forward your
renewal so that we may again enter your name on our list of
subscribers and friends. After all, ~~are~~ *is* there anything
more important than loyal friends?

Sincerely yours,

person, place, or thing.

NOUNS

1. the types of nouns   **2. forming the plurals of nouns**

3. possessive nouns

Now that we have studied the sentence, let's turn to the words that make up the sentence. The names of most of these words are probably familiar to you — *nouns, pronouns, verbs, adjectives, adverbs, conjunctions,* and *prepositions.* You undoubtedly met most of these terms in your earlier schooling, but you may have forgotten their *exact* technical meaning. Don't let that worry you! Our purpose is to make you into an expert. We shall start from the very beginning and leave nothing to chance.

You may wonder, "Why must they plague me with technical terms like *nouns* and *verbs* and the like?" And that's a good question. We could have omitted all such terms and given them other, simpler names. We could have called nouns *name words* and called verbs *action words.* But would you really have gained by this? Probably not. More likely you would have become confused by the mixture in your mind of the new terms we would invent and those commonly used terms you would remember from grammar school.

So, we shall use the old familiar terms. If you don't remember them from your grammar-school days, that's no problem. We'll teach you all about them. If you happen to recall the meanings of these terms, all the better. We'll reinforce what you already know and teach you more.

Let's start with the words known as *nouns.*

1. the TYPES of nouns

Nouns are *name* words. We use nouns to *name* persons, places, things, or abstract qualities. Here are some examples:

Person	Place	Thing	Abstract Quality
man	courtroom	chair	truth
typist	school	shorthand	initiative
Smith	lake	book	readiness

You can divide all nouns into two classes: *common nouns* and *proper nouns.* A common noun names a *general* class of people, places, things, or abstract qualities. A proper noun names a *specific* person, place, or thing. Look at these paired examples:

Common Noun: **boy   country   car**
Proper Noun: **John   America   Buick**

The significance of the distinction between common nouns and proper nouns will become apparent when you study capitalization in a later lesson. As you will learn, proper nouns are always capitalized; common nouns are not.

2. forming the PLURAL of nouns

Nouns, as you know, may be either singular or plural.

Singular	*Plural*
book	**books**
child	**children**
alumnus	**alumni**

Do you know how to spell plural nouns correctly? How do you spell the plural of *attorney?* of *solo?* of *brother-in-law?* In business you will have to be able to spell these plural nouns properly at all times. Remember this basic rule: *WHEN IN DOUBT, LOOK IT UP!* Use your dictionary. Most dictionaries include a special note under each noun showing the proper spelling of the plural of that noun. Here is a typical dictionary entry. We have circled the notation that shows you how to spell the plural.

lynx (liŋks), *n.* [*pl.* LYNXES (-iz), LYNX; see PLURAL, II, D, 1], [ME.; L.; Gr. *lynx*], 1. any of a group of wildcats found throughout the northern hemisphere and characterized by a ruff on each side of the face, long legs, a short tail, long, tufted ears, and keen vision: the North American species are the

Extracted from WEBSTER'S NEW WORLD DICTIONARY, College Edition, Copyright 1958 by the World Publishing Co.

Of course, you should not be in doubt so often that you are *constantly* at your dictionary. You should commit to memory the plural forms of most frequently used nouns. To help you do this we have listed some rules to guide you.

These rules for forming plurals are not difficult. All they require is a little of your concentration.

RULE 1.

To form the plural of *most* nouns, simply add *s*.

cigarette	cigarettes
crowd	crowds
desk	desks
group	groups
European	Europeans
paper	papers
piece	pieces
receipt	receipts
town	towns
Mrs. Smith	**the Smiths**

RULE 2.

To form the plural of a noun that ends in the sound *s, sh, x,* or *ch,* add *es.*

box	boxes
bus	buses
bush	bushes
church	churches
gas	gases
glass	glasses
lash	lashes
lunch	lunches
tax	taxes
Mr. Rich	**the Riches**

RULE 3.

To form the plural of a noun that ends in *y* preceded by a *vowel (a, e, i, o, u)*, simply add *s*.

alley	alleys
alloy	alloys
attorney	attorneys
essay	essays
galley	galleys
play	plays
survey	surveys
trolley	trolleys
turkey	turkeys
valley	valleys
Casey	the Caseys

NOTE: Colloquies, soliloquies

RULE 4.

To form the plural of a noun that ends in *y* preceded by a *consonant* (any letter other than *a, e, i, o, u*), change the *y* to *i* and add *es*.

accessory	accessories
baby	babies
company	companies
country	countries
county	counties
laboratory	laboratories
lady	ladies
specialty	specialties
variety	varieties

When a *proper* noun ends in *consonant-y*, just add *s*.

the Henrys   the Kellys   the Murphys

RULE 5.

To form the plural of a noun that ends in *o* preceded by a *vowel*, merely add *s*.

cameo	cameos
embryo	embryos
patio	patios
portfolio	portfolios
radio	radios
ratio	ratios
studio	studios

RULE 6.

a. To form the plurals of many nouns that end in *o* preceded by a *consonant*, add *es*.

cargo	cargoes
echo	echoes
embargo	embargoes
hero	heroes
motto	mottoes
Negro	Negroes
potato	potatoes
tomato	tomatoes
veto	vetoes
volcano	volcanoes

b. To form the plurals of many *musical* terms and some other nouns that end in *o* preceded by a *consonant*, merely add *s*.

banjo	banjos
concerto	concertos
piano	pianos
solo	solos
soprano	sopranos
auto	autos
dynamo	dynamos
halo	halos
memento	mementos
tobacco	tobaccos
zero	zeros

To form the plurals of many nouns that end in the sound of *f*, change the *f* to *v* and add *es*.

calf	calves
half	halves
knife	knives
leaf	leaves
life	lives
loaf	loaves
self	selves
shelf	shelves
thief	thieves
wife	wives

BUT NOTE:

bailiff	bailiffs
chef	chefs
chief	chiefs
dwarf	dwarfs
handkerchief	handkerchiefs
plaintiff	plaintiffs
proof	proofs
roof	roofs
safe	safes

RULE 9.

Certain nouns have special plural forms. Below is a list of the most frequently used ones. Try to learn to recognize these words. If you are not certain of the precise meaning of any of these words, look it up in your dictionary.

Latin
us – i
a – ae
is = es
um = a

Singular	Plural
alumna (female)	alumnae
alumnus (male)	alumni
analysis	analyses
antithesis	antitheses
axis	axes
basis	bases
crisis	crises
datum	data
hypothesis	hypotheses
oasis	oases
parenthesis	parentheses
phenomenon	phenomena
synopsis	synopses
synthesis	syntheses
thesis	theses

RULE 8.

Certain old English nouns have irregular plural forms. You should find these words very familiar.

child	children
foot	feet
gentleman	gentlemen
goose	geese
louse	lice
man	men
mouse	mice
ox	oxen
woman	women

Some nouns have both foreign plural forms and also "Anglicized" plural forms. In the following list we have put the *preferred* spelling of the plural in the middle column.

Singular	Preferred Plural	Acceptable Plural
appendix	appendixes	appendices
criterion	criteria	criterions
formula	formulas	formulae
index	indexes	indices
medium	mediums	media
memorandum	memorandums	memoranda

Many words are composed of two separate nouns that are linked together to form one word. Such words are called *compound* nouns. When a compound noun is written as one *solid* word, without hyphens, form the plural by making the *last* part plural.

blackboard	blackboards
bookcase	bookcases
classmate	classmates
courthouse	courthouses
cupful	cupfuls
grandchild	grandchildren
handful	handfuls
letterhead	letterheads
spoonful	spoonfuls
stepchild	stepchildren
stockholder	stockholders
workman	workmen

When forming the plural of a compound noun that is written with one or more hyphens, make the *principal* or *most important* part plural. Sometimes it's difficult to decide just *which* part is the most important part. So study these examples:

brother-in-law	brothers-in-law
court-martial	courts-martial (or court-martials)
editor-in-chief	editors-in-chief
father-in-law	fathers-in-law
mother-in-law	mothers-in-law
sister-in-law	sisters-in-law

Form the plurals of *numerals*, individual *letters*, and *characters* by adding *'s*.

9	9's	*	*'s
56	56's	#	#'s
h	h's	x	x's

NOTE: These are the *only* instances in which you use an apostrophe to form a plural. Notice also that a number that is *written out* forms its plural in the usual manner, without an apostrophe.

nine	nines	fifty-six	fifty-sixes

You also form in the usual manner the plural of any *word* used simply as a word: It must be done; we will stand for no <u>ifs</u>, <u>ands</u>, or <u>buts</u>.

What is the plural of *Mr.*? of *Mrs.*? of *Miss*? Often a business letter will be addressed to more than one person, and the plurals of these titles can become a problem. Here's how you solve that problem easily.

The plural of *Mr.* (Mister) is *Messrs.*, an abbreviation derived from the French word *Messieurs*. Accordingly, you may write: *Dear Messrs. Smith and Black.* Modern business usage, however, is tending away from this old-fashioned form, and many employers today prefer that you repeat the title of each person: *Dear Mr. Smith and Mr. Black.*

The plural of *Mrs.* is *Mmes.*, an abbreviation derived from the French word *Mesdames*. Accordingly, you may write: *Dear Mmes. Jones and Spencer.* Or you may follow the preferred modern usage and repeat the title: *Dear Mrs. Jones and Mrs. Spencer.*

The plural of *Miss* is *Misses*. Again, it is preferable to repeat the title rather than use the plural term: *Dear Miss Hale and Miss Holsey* rather than *Dear Misses Hale and Holsey*.

Why should you bother to learn these plural forms if they are no longer considered preferable? First, because *your* particular employer may prefer these time-honored forms. Second, because you should be able to recognize them when they appear on letters *received* by your firm. Third, because they are still used widely in *social* correspondence. Fourth, because if you are writing to a firm in which three brothers are partners, you would not write *Dear Mr. Kern, Mr. Kern, and Mr. Kern*. In this instance it is proper to write: *Dear Messrs. Kern*. Of course, it is sometimes less awkward to write *Gentlemen*.

RULE 14.

A few nouns are written the same in both the singular and the plural forms. When one of these nouns is the subject of a sentence, you must look to the meaning of the sentence to determine whether to use a singular or a plural predicate.

corps	Japanese
deer	means (method)
fish (quantity)	series
gross	sheep
head (of cattle)	species

Corps is pronounced *core* in the singular; it is pronounced *cores* in the plural.

Some nouns *look* plural but are really singular in meaning. Always use a singular predicate when one of the following words is the subject of a sentence: *news, measles, mumps, economics, physics, politics, ethics, molasses*. For example:

Politics <u>is</u> a vital field.

Some nouns are *always* plural, never singular. Always use a plural predicate when one of the following words is the subject of a sentence: *scissors, pants* (clothing), *trousers, proceeds* (money), *goods* (merchandise), *thanks, riches, headquarters, premises, auspices*. For example:

The proceeds <u>were</u> turned over to charity.

Turn to Programed Reinforcement S1 through S21

---

3. POSSESSIVE nouns

Another type of noun you will use frequently in business is the *possessive*. A possessive noun is one which shows ownership, authorship, or origin:

The *company's* factory (ownership)
Shakespeare's play (authorship)
The *lamp's* glow (origin)

The rules for the spelling of possessive nouns were quite complicated at one time. In those awful bygone days you had to be a genius to know whether to add *apostrophe s* (*'s*) or just *apostrophe* to the name *Charles* or *Roberts*. Today, fortunately, these complicated rules are no longer required. In fact, the modern rules for forming possessive nouns are extremely simple and will cause you no trouble.

RULE 1

Form the possessive of a noun that does not end in *s* by adding *'s*.

box	box's
children	children's
company	company's
hero	hero's
men	men's
John	John's

Note that it does not matter if the noun is singular or plural. If it does not end in *s*, add *'s*.

RULE 2

Form the possessive of a noun that ends in *s* by adding an *apostrophe* only. Again, note that the rule applies whether the noun is singular or plural.

boxes	boxes'
companies	companies'
grass	grass'
heroes	heroes'
Charles	Charles'
Mr. Roberts	Mr. Roberts'

Why do we use the apostrophe in a possessive noun? We use it for the same reason that we use the apostrophe in a contraction such as *can't* or in an abbreviation such as *gov't*—to indicate that something has been *omitted*.

The apostrophe in the possessive noun indicates that a phrase has been omitted from the sentence—generally, a phrase beginning with *of*. For example:

the company's factory = the factory of the company

Shakespeare's play = the play of Shakespeare

the lamp's glow = the glow of the lamp

Understanding this fact makes it easy for you to decide correctly on the use of the apostrophe in all possessive nouns. To determine whether or not a noun requires an apostrophe — and, if so, where to place it — simply test to see if an *of phrase* can be added in front of the noun in question.

If an *of phrase* can be added, then you place the apostrophe precisely at the end of the word as it would appear in the *of phrase*. For example:

1. **This (companies, companies', company's) policy . . . .**

TEST: The policy of this company . . . .

THEREFORE: This company's policy . . . .
(Apostrophe precisely at end of *company*. Add *apostrophe s* because the noun does not end in *s*.)

2. **These (companies, companies', company's) policies . . . .**

TEST: The policies of these companies . . .

THEREFORE: These companies' policies
(Apostrophe precisely at end of *companies*. No *s* added because the noun already ends in *s*.)

3. **. . . . in two (weeks, week's, weeks') time . . . .**

TEST: . . . . in the time of two weeks . . . .

THEREFORE . . . . in two weeks' time . . . .

Be particularly alert to the need for the apostrophe in this latter type of phrase which refers to a period of time. Other examples of this type:

a moment's hesitation
a few moments' hesitation

a minute's work
ten minutes' work

an hour's delay
four hours' delay

a day's passage
a few days' passage

a week's salary
three weeks' salary

a month's wait
six months' wait

a year's interest
twenty years' interest

Generally, avoid the use of the possessive with nouns that name *inanimate* objects. While such usage is permissible, it is usually considered awkward. The preferred usage is to employ our old friend, the *of phrase*.

AWKWARD: The building's architecture . . . .

PREFERRED: The architecture of the building . . . .

AWKWARD: The airplane's roar....
PREFERRED: **The roar of the air-
                plane....**

Of course, there are some time-honored phrases that involve the possessive form of an inanimate object. There's no need to change these: *a stone's throw; a hair's breadth; an arm's length.*

HINTS ON FORMING POSSESSIVE NOUNS

HINT 1

A problem arises when you want to show joint ownership. How would you write this phrase in possessive form?

The operetta by Gilbert and Sullivan....

Answer: **Gilbert and Sullivan's operetta....**

To show joint possession, write only the *last* name in possessive form.

Smith and Miller's firm....

This means one firm owned jointly by Smith and Miller. Other examples:

Johnson and Johnson's bandages....
Rodgers and Hammerstein's play....

But, when you want to show separate possession of distinct items, write the name of *each* owner in possessive form.

Smith's and Miller's firms are strong competitors. This refers to two firms, one owned by Smith and the other by Miller.

New York's and Chicago's police forces are among the finest. This refers to the police force of each city separately.

HINT 2

To write the possessive form of an abbreviation, place the *apostrophe s* ('s) after the final period.

The U.S.A.'s tariff
The U.N.'s policy
John D. Rockefeller, Jr.'s, fortune
The Wainright Co.'s staff

HINT 3

To form the possessive of a *compound* noun, place the *apostrophe s* ('s) after the *last* word in the noun:

My brother-in-law's inheritance (One brother-in-law)

My brothers-in-law's inheritances (More than one brother-in-law)

HINT 4

Note where the apostrophe is placed in this type of expression:

Smith, our salesman's, record is outstanding.
Alexander the Great's conquests were vast.
Chrysler, the automobile manufacturer's, main plants are in Michigan.

These examples illustrate the use of the possessive in cases where an *explanatory phrase* follows the noun. In such case, you make the last word in the explanatory phrase possessive; you do not make the noun itself possessive.

HINT 5

Often an organization will choose to omit the apostrophe from a plural noun that appears in its official title even though that noun is in the possessive. Always follow the form that appears on the official letterhead or the official listing of the organization.

National Sales Executives Club
National Business Teachers Association
Columbia University Teachers College
Manufacturers Trust Company

Turn to Programed Reinforcement S22 through S30

R1

A. name words

S1

Circle the correct definition of **nouns.**

Nouns are name words.

Nouns are action words.

Nouns are joining words.

Nouns are describing words.

R2

d) abstract qualities

S2

Nouns are name words. Nouns name a) persons, b) places, c) things, or d) abstract qualities. The nouns **truth** and **kindness** are a, b, c, or d? Answer:_____

R3

person

S3

The word **employee** is a common noun that names a p__ __ __ __ __ .

R4

place — **office;**
thing — **package**

S4

In the sentence **He sent a package to the office,** underline a noun naming a thing and circle one naming a place.

S5

In the above examples, you have seen what we call common nouns. They name a general class of persons, places, things, or qualities. The other class of nouns is called proper nouns. They name a specific person, a specific place, or a specific thing. Proper nouns always begin with capital letters. Underline the proper nouns in this sentence: **He was born in Boston near the Bunker Hill Memorial.**

R5

Boston;
Bunker Hill Memorial

S6

In the following sentence pick out the proper nouns that name respectively a) a specific person, b) a specific place, and c) a specific thing: **Frank Baker drove his Pontiac into Manhattan.**

Answers: a)_____ b)_____

c)_____

R6

a) **Frank Baker;**
b) **Manhattan;**
c) **Pontiac**

S7

A proper noun always begins with a _____ letter.

R7

capital

S8

Circle the proper nouns in this sentence.

The President addressed the Congress at the opening session on Thursday.

R8

President;
Congress;
Thursday

S9

Most nouns change from singular to plural simply by adding one letter: _____.

R9

s

S10

Most nouns that end in the sound of **sh, s, x,** or **ch** form their plurals by adding **es.** Write the plurals of **glass, fox, watch, wish.**

_____ _____ _____ _____

R10

glasses; foxes;
watches; wishes

S11

If a noun ends in **y** preceded by a vowel (**a, e, i, o, u**), form the plural by adding **s: survey — surveys.** Write the plurals of **attorney, monkey, turkey, valley.**

_____ _____ _____ _____

R11

attorneys; monkeys;
turkeys; valleys

S12

If a noun ends in **y** preceded by a consonant (any letter other than **a, e, i, o, u**), form the plural by changing the **y** to **i** and adding **es: city — cities.** Write the plurals of **daisy, puppy, university, study.**

_____ _____ _____ _____

R12

daisies; puppies;
universities; studies

S13

If a noun ends in **o** preceded by a vowel, form the plural by adding **s: radio — radios.** Write the plurals of **folio, embryo, cameo, patio.**

_____ _____ _____ _____

R13

folios; embryos;
cameos; patios

S14

Many nouns ending in **o** preceded by a consonant form their plurals by adding **es: tomato — tomatoes.** How would you write the plurals of **potato, hero, cargo, motto?**

_____ _____ _____ _____

R14

potatoes; heroes;
cargoes; mottoes

S15

Musical terms that end in **o** preceded by a consonant form plurals by simply adding **s: piano — pianos.** Write the plurals of **soprano, alto, banjo, solo.**

_____ _____ _____ _____

R15

sopranos; altos;
banjos; solos

S16

Some nouns that end in **f** form their plurals by changing the **f** to **v: knife — knives.** Other such nouns just add **s.** Write the plurals of these correctly: **belief, wife, dwarf, calf.**

_____ _____ _____ _____

R16

beliefs; wives;
dwarfs; calves

S17

Some nouns have special foreign plural forms. How would you write these correctly? **phenomenon, alumnus, thesis, criterion.**

_____   _____
_____   _____

R17
phenomena; alumni;
theses; criteria

S18

Compound nouns are nouns made up of two separate words. If they are written as one word without a hyphen, the plural is formed by making the last part plural. How would you form plurals of these words? **handful, stepchild, courthouse, spoonful.**

_____   _____
_____   _____

R18
handfuls; stepchildren;
courthouses; spoonfuls

S19

If the compound noun is written with a hyphen, make the principal or most important part plural: **brother-in-law — brothers-in-law.** Write the plurals of **sister-in-law, attorney general, editor-in-chief, father-in-law.**

_____   _____

R19
sisters-in-law;
attorneys general;
editors-in-chief;
fathers-in-law

S20

Since plurals of numerals and letters are formed by adding **apostrophe s (6 — 6's),** how would you write this sentence correctly? **Dot the i s, cross the t s, and erase the 8 s.**

R20
**Dot the i's,
cross the t's
and erase the 8's.**

S21

Some nouns form their plurals either by some irregular change (**ox—oxen**) or by no change from the singular (**sheep—sheep**). How would you write the plurals of **deer, series, goose, gross?**

_____ _____ _____ _____

R21
deer; series;
geese; gross

● **TURN TO
Exercises 7 and 8**

S22

If a noun is used to show ownership, authorship, or origin, we show this by using an apostrophe. An apostrophe on a noun therefore shows o __ __ __ __ __ __ __ __ __,
a __ __ __ __ __ __ __ __ __ __, or o __ __ __ __ __ __ .

R22
ownership;
authorship;
origin

S23

If a noun does not end in **s,** possession is shown by simply adding **'s** to the noun. Write these showing possession:
the books of the boy   _____
the hats of the men   _____
the offices of the company   _____
the rest room of the women   _____

R23
boy's books; men's hats;
company's offices;
women's rest room

S24
If the noun that shows possession ends with an **s**, you add only the apostrophe. Write these as possessives.

the sister of the boss _____
the novels of Dickens _____
the monument of the soldiers _____
the salary of two weeks _____

R24
the boss' sister;
Dickens' novels;
the soldiers' monument;
two weeks' salary

S25
To show joint ownership by two or more people, write only the last name as a possessive. For example, **Sally and Bill's car.** Place the apostrophe to show joint authorship in this example: **Rodgers and Hammersteins music.**

R25
Rodgers and
Hammerstein's music

S26
Is this a correct possessive? **The U.S.A.'s laws.** Answer:_____

R26
Yes

S27
The apostrophe is placed after the last word in an explanatory phrase. Which is correct?
A. **Mr. Smith, our President's, health is failing.**
B. **Mr. Smith's, our President's, health is failing.** Answer:_____

R27
A

S28
It is considered by some authorities to be awkward to write a possessive for an inanimate object. Change these examples from the possessive form:
a) **the table's strength** _____
b) **the night's darkness** _____

R28
the strength of the table;
the darkness of the night

S29
Insert apostrophes in any words that should show possession in this sentence:
The union agreement covers mens stores and ladies stores under Mr. Smiths presidency.

R29
men's; ladies'; Smith's

S30
Insert apostrophes where necessary:
Mr. Dickens novels, Gilbert and Sullivans operettas, and G.B.S.s poetry are all Britains products.

R30
Dickens'; Sullivan's
G.B.S.'s; Britain's

• TURN TO
Exercises 9, 10, and Review

EXERCISE 7   Plural Nouns

A. Write the plural form of each of these nouns in the space provided.
SCORING: DEDUCT 1 POINT FOR EACH ERROR.

1. book _____ *books*
2. invoice _____ *invoices*
3. office _____ *offices*
4. mass _____ *masses*
5. tax _____ *taxes*
6. match _____ *matches*
7. facility _____ *facilities*
8. colony _____ *colonies*
9. body _____ *bodies*
10. journey _____ *journeys*
11. attorney _____ *attorneys*
12. studio _____ *studios*
13. hero _____ *heroes*
14. embargo _____ *embargoes*
15. auto _____ *autos*
16. wife _____ *wives*
17. half _____ *halves*
18. chief _____ *chiefs*
19. plaintiff _____ *plaintiffs*
20. proof _____ *proofs*
21. memorandum _____ *memorandum*
22. workingman _____ *workingmen*
23. bookkeeper _____ *bookkeeper's*
24. cupful _____ *cupfuls*
25. grandchild _____ *grandchildren*
26. handful _____ *handfuls*
27. copyright _____ *copyrights*
28. stepchild _____ *stepchildren*
29. father-in-law _____ *fathers-in-law*
30. commander-in-chief _____ *commanders in*
31. **Mr. Hatch** _____ *Mr. Hatch's chief*
32. 26 _____ *26's*

33. twenty-six _____ *twenty-sixes*
34. X _____ *X's*
35. series _____ *series*
36. crisis _____ *crises*
37. veto _____ *vetoes*
38. bus _____ *buses*
39. box _____ *boxes*
40. roof _____ *roofs*
41. laboratory _____ *laboratories*
42. handkerchief _____ *handkerchiefs*
43. basis _____ *basis*
44. shelf _____ *shelves*
45. thesis _____ *thesis*
46. watch _____ *watches*
47. receipt _____ *receipts*
48. company _____ *companies*
49. self _____ *selves*
50. datum _____ *data*
51. radio _____ *radios*
52. stimulus _____ *stimulus*
53. valley _____ *valleys*
54. alumnus _____ *alumni*
55. criterion _____ *criteria*
56. Mrs. _____ *Mmes.*
57. zero _____ *zeros*
58. letterhead _____ *letterheads*
59. census _____ *censuses*
60. deletion _____ *deletions*
61. analysis _____ *analyses*
62. court-martial _____ *courts-martial*
63. piano _____ *pianos*

(continued)

64. medium _mediums_
65. bureau _bureaus_
66. Miss _misses_
67. if _ifs_
68. five _fives_
69. Mr. _Messrs._

70. scissors _scissors'_
71. agency _agencies_
72. C.P.A. _C.P.A.'s_
73. Jones _Jones'_
74. spoonful _spoonfuls_
75. gas _gases_

SCORE

B_____

EXERCISE 7 — Plural Nouns

B. Below are listed 20 words. Some are singular; some are plural. Check in the appropriate column and write the opposite form in the other column.

SCORING: DEDUCT 5 POINTS FOR EACH ERROR.

	Singular	Plural
1. test	✓	tests
2. column	✓	columns
3. lighters	lighter	✓
4. children	child	✓
5. ladies	lady	✓
6. attorney	✓	attorneys
7. knife	✓	knives
8. shelves	shelf	✓
9. phenomenon	✓	phenomena
10. alumnus	✓	alumni
11. datum	✓	data
12. alloys	alloy	✓
13. volcanoes	volcano	✓
14. cupful	✓	cupfuls
15. brother-in-law	✓	brothers-in-law
16. species	✓	✓
17. sheep	✓	✓
18. politics	✓	none
19. zero	✓	zeros
20. company	✓	companies

NAME _____ CLASS _____ DATE _____

EXERCISE 8 — Plural Nouns

A. This problem deals with recognizing improperly spelled plural nouns. In the following paragraph, 14 plural nouns are improperly spelled. Cross out each incorrectly spelled noun and write the correct form above it.

SCORING: DEDUCT 6 POINTS FOR EACH ERROR.

Industries

valleys

~~Industrys~~ of all sorts have flourished in the central ~~vallies~~ of the Acme Mountains. Each

Tomatoes

year, cargoes of ~~tomatos~~ and potatoes are shipped from the valleys in large quantities. The

is

area is famous for its fine ~~tobaccos~~, which ~~are~~ bought by all the large cigar ~~companys~~. In

facilities

addition to these agricultural products the region has fine ~~facilitys~~ for steel ~~foundrys~~ and

radios *pianos*   *attorneys*

for the manufacture of ~~radioes~~ and ~~pianoes~~. The Caseys', who are ~~attornies~~ and steel men,

alloy *data*   *formula*

made fortunes in ~~alloyes~~, ~~datas~~ for which came from their own ~~formulaes~~.

NAME _____ CLASS _____ DATE _____

EXERCISE 8 — Plural Nouns

B. This problem deals with recognizing plural nouns. Choose the proper predicate in each of the following sentences. Remember, if the subject is singular, use a singular predicate. If the subject is plural, use a plural predicate.

SCORING: DEDUCT 5 POINTS FOR EACH ERROR.

1. The data (has, have) been entered in the account book. 1. *has*
2. Our most successful media (is, are) radio and TV. 2. *is*
3. Our curriculum (include, includes) courses in many fields. 3. *includes*
4. The bases for my contention (is, are) twofold. 4. *is*
5. (Were, was) the memoranda left on my desk? 5. *was*
6. The alumni (is, are) fully behind the dean. 6. *are*
7. The stimulus (has, have) been measured in electrical units. 7. *have*
8. The fathers-in-law (has, have) met for the first time. 8. *have*
9. The crisis in his illness (is, are) finally past. 9. *is*
10. The series of revisions (is, are) complete, at last. 10. *is*
11. Riches (is, are) something to be thankful for. 11. *are*
12. Proper ethics (was, were) the backbone of the new concern. 12. *were*
13. What (are, is) the major criterion in judging a letter? 13. *is*
14. The theses the philosopher expounded (was, were) stimulating. 14. *were*
15. How many international crises (has, have) there been lately? 15. *have*
16. The latest phenomena in the electronics industry (seems, seem) to be concerned with transistors. 16. *seem*
17. Three handfuls of rice (was, were) thrown at the couple. 17. *were*
18. What new formulae (were, was) presented by him? 18. *were*
19. Parentheses (present, presents) occasional punctuation problems. 19. *presents*
20. An editor realizes that plot synopses (is, are) important. 20. *is*

NAME   CLASS   DATE

EXERCISE 9   Possessive Nouns

A. This problem deals with writing the possessive of nouns. Below is a list of 20 possessive phrases. Rewrite them using the correct possessive form.
SCORING: DEDUCT 5 POINTS FOR EACH ERROR.

1. the clothes of the ladies
1. *ladies' clothes*

2. the ties of the men
2. *men's ties*

3. the books of the boy
3. *boy's books*

4. the wool of the sheep
4. *sheep's wool*

5. the report of the boss
5. *boss' report*

6. the meeting of the directors
6. *directors' meeting*

7. the statement of the Vice-Presidents
7. *Vice-Presidents' state.*

8. the poetry of Burns
8. *Burns' poetry*

9. the finances of the firm
9. *firm's finances*

10. the letters of the secretaries
10. *secretaries' letters*

11. the store of John
11. *John's store*

12. the association of the teachers
12. *teachers' association*

13. the children of my brother-in-law
13. *brother-in-law's children*

14. the policy of R. H. Macy
14. *R. H. Macy's policy*

15. the home of Dickens
15. *Dickens' home*

16. the editorials of the *New York Times*
16. *New York Times' editorials*

17. the engine of the old bus
17. *old bus' engine*

18. the daughter of my boss
18. *boss' daughter*

19. the notes of the typists
19. *typists' notes*

20. the motor of the tape recorder
20. *tape recorder's motor*

NAME   CLASS   DATE

EXERCISE 9   Possessive Nouns

B. This problem deals with possessive nouns. Each of the following sentences contains one or more possessive nouns from which the apostrophe has been omitted. In the space provided, rewrite these possessive nouns properly.

SCORING: DEDUCT 5 POINTS FOR EACH ERROR.

1. The chairmans report included details on the proposed workmens cafeteria.
2. The camp directors view was that drastic changes had to be made in Johns outlook.
3. At the sales meeting it was agreed that new desks should be installed in the salesmens office.
4. Yesterdays techniques cannot succeed in today's market.
5. You have one weeks time to accept or reject this companys offer.
6. The managers, at last Wednesdays meeting, agreed to rebuild the executives recreation hall.
7. The new sales managers plan was discussesd at the boards last meeting.
8. Roberts trouble is that he takes nobodys advice.
9. We agree with Mr. Johnsons plan for improving our office forces morale.
10. We asked Charles opinion, but he refused to discuss Smiths plan.
11. Miller and Jones is one of the citys finest firms.
12. Miller and Jones policies are in complete agreement with the District Attorneys suggested code of conduct.
13. Browns and Whites stores compete in the ladies' garments line.
14. Green and Blacks store handles a complete line of mens items.
15. A committee to support the U. S. s policy in Europe sent a flood of telegrams to Senator Bass office.
16. The A.A.A.s vehicle policy is under the I.C.C.s direction.
17. My sister-in-laws child left college after two years' work.
18. Frederick the Wises policies are comparable to the fiscal policies of the Farmers National Alliance.
19. The sales managers convention dealt with the new organizations policies.
20. The Tribunes point of view is that a secretarys contributions sometimes exceed those of the employer.

1. _chairman's_
2. _director's John's_
3. _salesmen's_
4. _Yesterday's_
5. _week's company's_
6. _managers' Wednesday's_
7. _manager's board's_
8. _Robert's nobody's_
9. _Johnson's force's_
10. _Charles' Smith's_
11. _Jones'_
12. _Jones' attorney's_
13. _Brown's White's_
14. _Black's men's_
15. _Bass' U.S.'s_
16. _AAA's ICC's_
17. _sister-in-law's_
18. _Wise's Farmers'_
19. _managers'_
20. _Tribune's secretary's_

NAME   CLASS   DATE

EXERCISE 10   Nouns—Plural and Possessive

This problem tests what you have learned about the spelling of possessive nouns and plural nouns. Fill in the form of the noun called for in each column — singular possessive, plural, and plural possessive.

SCORING: DEDUCT 4 POINTS FOR EACH ERROR.

Singular	Singular Possessive	Plural	Plural Possessive
1. book	book's	books	books'
2. child	child's	children	children's
3. tax	tax's	taxes	taxes'
4. Smith & Smith	Smith & Smith's	Smith's	Smith's
5. wife	wife's	wives	wives'
6. ratio	ratio's	ratios	ratios'
7. body	body's	bodies	bodies'
8. criterion	criterion's	criteria	criteria's
9. attorney	attorney's	attorneys	attorneys'
10. workingman	workingman's	workingmen	workingmen's
11. radio	radio's	radios	radios'
12. memorandum	memorandum's	memorandums	memorandums'
13. brother-in-law	brother-in-law's	brothers-in-law	brothers-in-law's
14. hero	hero's	heroes	heroes'
15. stockholder	stockholder's	stockholders	stockholders'
16. roof	roof's	roofs	roofs'
17. journey	journey's	journeys	journeys'
18. letterhead	letterhead's	letterheads	letterheads'
19. committee	committee's	committee's	committees'
20. county	country's	counties	countries'
21. boss	boss's	bosses	bosses'
22. medium	medium's	mediums	mediums'
23. lady	lady's	ladies	ladies'
24. ox	ox's	oxen	oxen's
25. attorney general	attorney general's	attorneys general	attorneys generals'

REVIEW EXERCISE 2   Nouns

The following passage contains a number of errors in the use of possessive and plural nouns. Whenever you locate such an error, cross out the incorrect form and write the correct form above it.

SCORING: DEDUCT 5 POINTS FOR EACH ERROR.

Dear Reader:

In the world's most famous museum, the Louvre in
Paris, hangs a painting by America's celebrated artist,
James McNeill Whistler. This painting's formal title is
"An Arrangement in Gray and Black," but it is better known
by the simple name, "Whistler's Mother." Many studies have
been made in an effort to explain the basises of this
portrait's almost universal appeal.

criteria

But what criterions can the art critic use in judging a painting? The critic is not like a scientist; he
cannot set up a controlled experiment wherein a number of
stimuli   *data*
stimulus are shot into a subject and datums collected on the
subject's reaction. No, the art critic must rely on his
inner emotions and sensitivity when he analyzes a painting.
analysis
His analyses of a painting is a very personal thing.

If you looked at "Whistler's Mother," what would you
see? Would you recognize the source of this portrait's
greatness? Would you, like most of us, be left wondering
what makes this painting a masterpiece?

(continued)

Dr. Felix A. Roberts has come forward to help you. Dr. Roberts' new book, <u>Art for the Layman</u>, has just been published. For a limited period only, this fine book is being made available to you at a very special discount price.

In this books Table of Contents are listed such interesting topics as: Criterions of Evaluation; Mediums for Communicating Art to the Masses; The Artists Studio; The Analysis of Expression through Color.

criteria   *media*

After you have read this fine volume, you will find new meaning in such great works as "Whistlers Mother." New horizons of appreciation will be opened to you.

Send for your copy today. Don't delay. Make out your check, payable to the Art Lovers' Book Club, and mail it at once.

Cheque

Very truly yours,

PRONOUNS

1. the forms of pronouns

2. possessive pronouns

3. the relative pronouns

4. pronouns and their antecedents

5. clarity in using pronouns

The pronoun is the efficient man's tool. It is a shortcut by which you can save time and space. How? The job of the pronoun is to stand in place of a noun. Since many nouns are long words and most pronouns are short, you can shorten statements by skillfully using pronouns. Compare the length of the following sentences:

WITHOUT PRONOUNS
The Coca Cola Bottling Company announced that the Coca Cola Bottling Company intends to double the sale of the Coca Cola Bottling Company's product.

WITH PRONOUNS
The Coca Cola Bottling Company announced that it intends to double the sale of its product.

1. the FORMS of pronouns

Pronouns take different forms, depending upon how they are used in a sentence. You have used these different forms automatically for most of your life, so they should cause no difficulty now.

	Singular	Plural
First Person (The person speaking)	I	WE
Second Person (The person spoken to)	YOU	YOU
Third Person (The person or thing spoken about)	HE, SHE, IT	THEY

These forms — called *personal pronouns* — are familiar to you, aren't they? Then let's move on to our major concern — the proper *use* of pronouns.

2. POSSESSIVE pronouns

You learned in the previous lesson that the possessive form of a noun is generally formed by adding an apostrophe-s (*'s*). For example:

firm	firm's
author	author's
John	John's
America	America's

Now look at the possessive form of these pronouns:

Person	Singular	Plural
First:	my, mine	our, ours
Second:	your, yours	your, yours
Third:	its, his, her, hers	their, theirs

What is the first thing you noticed about these possessive pronouns? That's right! You noticed that *none* is written with an apostrophe. If you learn nothing else about possessive pronouns, learn this one simple rule: The possessive pronouns *yours, hers, its, ours,* and *theirs* are written *without apostrophes.*

As an added warning, remember: The word *its* is a pronoun. The word *it's* is *NOT* a pronoun. *It's* is a contraction for the words *it is.*

For example:
It's illegal to sell liquor on Sunday.
(*It is* illegal to sell liquor on Sunday.)
The book lay on its side.
(The book lay on the book's side.)
It's going to be a cold winter.
The firm is proud of its history.
The officers say that it's not going to be sold.
How can your company increase its sales?

3. RELATIVE pronouns: Who, Whom, Which, That

The pronouns *who, whom, which,* and *that* are used to *relate* one thought to another. For this reason they are called *relative* pronouns.

Look at these examples. Do you see how the relative pronoun in each sentence *relates* one thought to another?

Here is the man who will be our next president.

The book, which had fallen, was soon found.
Shorthand is the subject that I like best.

When should you use *who, whom, which,* or *that?* The answer is simple:

1. Use *who* or *whom* to refer to a person (In a later lesson you'll learn how to select between *who* and *whom.*)
2. Use *which* to refer to an animal or a thing
3. Use *that* to refer to a person, an animal, or a thing

At one time there were complicated rules controlling the choice of *which* or *that.* Fortunately, today they may be used interchangeably to refer to animals or things.

Turn to Programed Reinforcement S1 through S10

4. pronouns and their ANTECEDENTS

England expects every man to do (her) (their) (his) duty.

How do you know which pronoun to use? Let's work this problem through together. You remember that the function of the pronoun is to replace a noun. We call the noun

56

that is replaced by the pronoun the *ante-cedent* of that pronoun. (*Cede* means *to go* and *ante* means *before*. An *antecedent* goes before the pronoun.)

David says he is tired. (*David* is the antecedent of *he*.)

Mary knows she cannot succeed. (*Mary* is the antecedent of *she*.)

We have heard from our salesmen. They write that they cannot fill the quota. (*Salesmen* is the antecedent of *they*.)

Since a pronoun must stand in place of its antecedent, it should be as identical to the antecedent as possible. If the antecedent is singular, the pronoun must be singular. If the antecedent is plural, the pronoun must be plural. This is called agreement in number. If the antecedent is masculine, the pronoun must be masculine. This is called agreement in *gender*.

Now, let us return to our problem sentence:

England expects every man to do (her) (their) (his) duty.

First, what is the antecedent? Right! The antecedent is *man*. The antecedent *man* is clearly masculine, so we can eliminate *her* from our choice. Our problem is reduced to:

England expects every man to do (their) (his) duty.

The final step is to determine whether the antecedent is singular or plural. The antecedent *man* is singular. Therefore, we should use the singular pronoun *his*.

Our sentence should read:

England expects every man to do his duty.

Once you learn to recognize antecedents, you will never have trouble choosing the proper pronouns. The problem of agreement of a pronoun with its antecedent is very much like a problem you have already studied and mastered — the agreement of a

subject and its predicate. Right now, go back to the section in Lesson 1 on agreement of subject and predicate and review all the Hints given there. Only when you have fully refamiliarized yourself with that topic should you proceed with the Hints given below on agreement of pronouns with their antecedents.

HINTS on AGREEMENT of PRONOUNS with their ANTECEDENTS

HINT 1.

Try this sentence. It should be easy.

Jack and Jill are on (his, their) way.

Obviously, *their* is correct. The antecedent of *their* is *Jack and Jill*. Always use a plural pronoun to represent two or more antecedents connected by *and*.

Mr. Johnson and Miss Smith are on their way here.

The Acme Company and the Ajax Company are merging their assets.

Now look at this sentence.

The Secretary and Treasurer rendered (his, their) report.

If the positions of Secretary and Treasurer are held by two different men, *their* is obviously correct. If the two positions are held by one one man, *his* is correct. If, however, two men hold the two posts, the sentence would be better written as follows: **The Secretary and the Treasurer rendered their report.** The inclusion of the second *the* clearly tells the reader that two men are involved.

HINT 2.

When two antecedents are connected by *or* or *nor*, have the pronoun agree in number with the *nearer* antecedent.

1. **Neither Johnson nor Smith knows his business.** (*Smith* is the nearer antecedent. *Smith* is singular. Therefore, use *his*.)

2. **Either Miss Smith or Miss Black will get her wish.** (*Miss Black* is the nearer antecedent. *Miss Black* is singular. Therefore, use *her*.)

3. **Neither the boys nor the girls are ready for their lessons.** (*Girls* is the nearer antecedent. *Girls* is plural. Therefore, use *their*.)

4. **Neither Mr. Smith nor his sons have done their best.** (*Sons* is the closer antecedent. *Sons* is plural. Therefore, use *their*.)

Note: In a sentence like this, where one antecedent is singular and the other is plural, always place the plural antecedent *last*.

HINT 3.

The following words or groups of words are always singular: *anybody, anyone, each, every, everybody, everyone, many a, nobody, no one, somebody, someone.* When used as an antecedent, therefore, each of these expressions calls for a *singular* pronoun. Naturally, if one of these expressions is the *subject* of a sentence, it calls for a singular *predicate* too.

Nobody is eager to risk his life.

Many a soldier has displayed his courage under fire.

Everyone does his work efficiently.

We have selected each of the men on the basis of his merit.

Note that *of the men* in the last sentence does not alter the requirement that a singular pronoun be used. *Each* is the antecedent. You may disregard the *of* phrase that follows it.

Each of our competitors has reduced his sales.

Each of the factories is operating at its fullest capacity.

HINT 4.

Which pronoun do you use in the following sentence?

Everyone in the class did (his) (her) homework.

Is *everyone* masculine or feminine? It could be either. In such case, where the sex of the antecedent is unknown, use a *masculine* pronoun.

For example:

Not a person left his seat before the last curtain.

One of the students left his books.

Of course, if the context of the sentence clearly indicates that the pronoun refers to a *feminine* antecedent, use a *feminine* pronoun.

Each student at Vassar College must attend her classes regularly.

Since Vassar is a girls' school, we know that *each student* calls for a feminine pronoun.

None of the airline stewardesses failed her flight examination.

Neither of the waitresses does her job well.

Now let's try this sentence.

Each man and woman in the audience enthusiastically showed (his, her) approval.

Here you specifically refer to a masculine *and* a feminine antecedent, *man and woman.* In this instance, to avoid confusion, you must use *both* the masculine *and* the feminine pronoun.

Each man and woman in the audience enthusiastically showed his or her approval.

Since this is clearly an awkward sentence, you would be wise to rephrase the sentence into a less awkward construction.

Enthusiastic approval was shown by every man and woman in the audience.

Awkward: The host or hostess should always personally greet his or her guests.

Better: Guests should be personally greeted by the host or hostess.

HINT 5.

When locating the antecedent, disregard a phrase beginning with *as well as, in addition to, and not.*

1. John, as well as his brothers, is on his way. (The antecedent is *John*. Disregard *brothers*.)

2. The boys, in addition to John, are on their way. (The antecedent is *boys*. Disregard *John*.)

3. John, and not his brothers, is on his way. (The antecedent is *John*. Disregard *brothers*.)

HINT 6.

Words like *committee, jury, class, crowd,* and *army* may be either singular or plural depending upon their meaning in the sentence. Each of these words refers to a group of people. When you are referring to that group as a single unit, use a singular pronoun.

The committee is holding its meeting.

The class is in its room.

When you refer to the individuals that make up the group, however, use a plural pronoun.

The committee were called at their homes one at a time.

The jury brought in their split verdict.

HINT 7.

You have already learned to recognize the relative pronouns — *who, which,* and *that.* The relative pronoun is often followed by a predicate verb that must agree in number with the antecedent of the relative pronoun. But recognizing the *real* antecedent may sometimes require all your reasoning skill. If you think through the problem carefully, however, you will come up with the correct answer. For example, try this sentence:

She is one of those girls who (is, are) conscientious in following directions.

In this sentence what word does *who* relate to, *one* or *girls*? Look at the sentence carefully and you will see that a statement is being made about a broad characteristic of *those girls. Who*, therefore, relates to the plural word *girls* and requires the plural verb *are.*

She is one of those girls who are conscientious.

Let's examine another example:

She is the one girl of all the applicants who (is, are) able to do the job.

Who shows the ability to do the job in this sentence — *all the applicants* or the *one girl*? Clearly *who* relates to *one girl*; it is therefore a singular subject and takes the singular predicate *is.*

5. CLARITY in using pronouns

When using pronouns in your writing, be sure that the meaning of each pronoun is clearly understood. Look at this sentence:

The manager told Brown that the meaning of his report was unclear.

Whose report is unclear—the manager's? or Brown's? From this sentence you cannot tell because the *reference* of the pronoun is ambiguous. Here's how this sentence could be improved.

The manager told Brown that the meaning of Brown's report was unclear.

This sentence, though better, is awkward; so let's rephrase it:

The meaning of Brown's report was unclear, the manager told him.

Turn to Programed Reinforcement S11 through S34

	S1 A pronoun is a part of speech that takes the place of a n ___ ___ ___.
R1 noun	**S2** Pronouns may be in the first person, the second person, or the third person. **I** is the _____ person; **you** is the _____ person; **they** is the _____ person.
R2 **I** — first person; **you** — second person; **they** — third person	**S3** **I** is a pronoun that is in the first person singular. _____ is the first person plural pronoun.
R3 We	**S4** The second person plural of the singular pronoun **you** is _____.
R4 you	**S5** **Company's** is the p ___ ___ ___ ___ ___ ___ ___ ___ ___ form of the noun **company.**
R5 possessive	**S6** Pronouns also have possessive forms. The first person singular is **my, mine. You** and **yours** are in the _____ person; h ___ ___, h ___ ___, h ___ ___ ___, and i ___ ___ are in the third person singular possessive.
R6 second; his; her; hers; its	**S7** Possessives of nouns must have an apostrophe. This is not true of pronouns. Circle the correct form: a) **yours, your's;** b) **ours, our's;** c) **theirs, their's.**
R7 a) yours; b) ours; c) theirs	**S8** The possessive pronoun **its** does **not** have an apostrophe. Which is correct? a) **The dog hurt it's tail.** b) **The dog hurt its tail.** Answer: _____.
R8 b	**S9** You should remember that **it's** is a contraction that always means **it is. It's** is not a possessive. Circle the correct form: a) **(It's, Its) time to punch the clock.** b) **The company and (its, it's) affiliates amalgamated.**
R9 a) It's; b) its	**S10** A relative pronoun generally relates to a previous word in the sentence. Circle the relative pronoun in this sentence. Underline the word it relates to. **This is the machine that I want repaired.**
R10 that; machine • TURN TO Exercise 11	**S11** The word that a pronoun refers to is called the ante ___ ___ ___ ___ ___ t of that pronoun.
R11 antecedent	

S12
Circle the relative pronoun and underline its antecedent in this sentence. **I saw the worker who repaired the typewriter.**

R12 who; worker

S13
Who is a relative pronoun that refers to a person. _____ and _____ are relative pronouns that refer to things.

R13 which; that

S14
If the antecedent that a pronoun relates to is singular, the pronoun must be s __ __ __ __ __ __ __. If the antecedent is plural, the pronoun must be _____.

R14 singular; plural

S15
Our firm expects all employees to do (his, their) best work. Employees is the antecedent of the pronoun. a) **Employees** is (singular, plural). b) The pronoun that agrees with **employees** is (his, their).

R15 a) plural; b) **their**

S16
Let us change the above sentence somewhat. **My manager expects every man to do (his, their) best.** The antecedent to the pronoun is _____ which is (singular, plural). Therefore, the correct pronoun is _____.

R16 man; singular; **his**

S17
A pronoun and its antecedent must agree not only in number (singular or plural), but also in gender (masculine or feminine). Circle the correct word. **The coach wants every boy to exert (his, her, their) utmost at the game.**

R17 his

S18
If the antecedent consists of two nouns connected by **and,** the pronoun must be p __ __ __ __ __ in number. Circle the correct word. **The Merit Company and the Vitality Company will make (his, its, their) decision known today.**

R18 plural; **their**

S19
When two antecedents are connected by **or** or **nor,** the pronoun will agree in number with the (nearer, farther) antecedent.

R19 nearer

S20
Underline the nearer antecedent and circle the correct pronoun in this sentence: **Neither the father nor the sons will do (his, their) share of the work.**

R20 sons; their

S21
Either the parents or the girl will give her speech on the platform. This sentence is awkward and would be improved if the p __ __ __ __ __ antecedent were placed after the s __ __ __ __ __ __ __ antecedent. Then the pronoun before **speech** would have to be _____.

R21 plural; singular; **their**

S22

This is a partial list of words that are always singular: **anybody, anyone, each, everybody, everyone, nobody, no one, somebody, someone.** When used as an antecedent, each of these expressions calls for a (singular, plural) pronoun.

R22
singular

S23

Circle the correct pronoun.

a) Nobody wants to give (his, their) complete fortune to unworthy causes.

b) Everybody did (his, their) practice typing at home.

R23
a) **his;** b) **his**

S24

If a phrase (a group of words) comes between the singular antecedent and the pronoun, it does not alter the fact that the pronoun is still singular. **Each of the executives has (his, their) duties cut out for (him, them).**

a) Underline the group of words after the antecedent that you should ignore in determining the number of the pronoun.

b) Circle the correct pronouns.

R24
a) **of the executives;**
b) **his, him**

S25

Where the sex of the antecedent is unknown, you should use the **(masculine, feminine)** pronoun.

R25
masculine

S26

Everyone in the office gave (his, her, their) donation to United Charities. Assuming both sexes are represented in the office, circle the correct pronoun.

R26
his

S27

If the antecedent refers to females only, the pronoun should be f _ _ _ _ _ _ _ . Circle the correct pronoun: **Each of the salesgirls at Nieman Marcus did (his, her, their) shopping at the home store.**

R27
feminine; **her**

S28

You learned that phrases like **together with, accompanied by, in addition to,** and **as well as** do not make a singular word plural. Circle the correct pronoun: **John, accompanied by his brothers, did (his, their) best to stop the walkout.**

R28
his

S29

You learned that words like **committee, jury, crowd,** and **army** are usually singular but may be plural if you are referring to the individuals in the group. Circle the correct pronouns: **The committee is holding (its, their) meeting. The committee received individual letters at (its, their) home(s).**

R29
its; their

S30

Sometimes the true antecedent of a relative pronoun will be found in the phrase following the subject. **He is one of those workers who (do, does) (his, their) best work all the time.** Underline the true antecedent. Circle the correct answers.

R30
workers; do their

S31

It is important to avoid the use of pronouns that are not clearly understood. In this sentence which pronoun is not clear? **The man told his friend that he was late.**

R31
he

S32

You have learned that a pronoun takes the place of a n_____; that each pronoun is singular or p_____ and is in the first, second, or _____ person.

R32
noun; plural; third

S33

Circle the correct answers in this review sentence: **(It's, Its) clear that (ours, our's) is the machine (who, that) is superior.**

R33
It's; ours; that

S34

Circle the correct pronouns in this review sentence: **Our government expects each of its citizens to do (his, their) best because neither the President nor the members of Congress (is, are) able to do (his, their) work alone.**

R34
his; are; their

● TURN TO
Exercises 12, 13, and Review

EXERCISE 11 — Possessive Pronouns

A. This problem deals mainly with the possessive forms of pronouns. In the space provided, write the proper word. Remember, you do not write possessive pronouns with apostrophes.

SCORING: DEDUCT 6 POINTS FOR EACH ERROR.

1. The book fell on (its) (it's)side.
2. (Its) (It's) going to be a cold winter.
3. The package on top is (ours) (our's).
4. They claimed the package was (theirs) (there's) (their's).
5. These men are certain (their) (they're) correct.
6. Mr. Jones is a man (who) (that) can get his own way.
7. Victory is (our's) (ours).
8. The pact must stand or fall on (its) (it's) merits.
9. (Yours) (Your's) truly,
10. Here is the man (that) (which) I told you about.
11. This car of (ours) (our's) is similar to (yours) (your's) (yours').
12. This work of (hers) (her's) is extremely clear in (its) (it's) analysis of (there) (their) accounting department.
13. (Its, It's) not clear whether the package is (yours, your's) or (theirs, their's, theres, there's).
14. Tell me (whose, who's) letter is more accurate, mine or (hers, her's).
15. The company hurt (its, it's) reputation, (its it's) sad to say.

1. _its_
2. _It's_
3. _ours_
4. _theirs_
5. _they're_
6. _who_
7. _ours_
8. _its_
9. _Yours_
10. _that_
11. _ours yours_
12. _hers its their_
13. _It's yours theirs_
14. _whose hers_
15. _its it's_

EXERCISE 11 — Possessive Nouns and Pronouns

B. This problem deals with the proper use of possessive nouns and pronouns. Wherever a possessive noun or pronoun is incorrectly spelled, cross it out and write the correct form above it.

SCORING: DEDUCT 10 POINTS FOR EACH ERROR.

Dear Mr. Byrnes:

Thank you for your order of a year's supply of Danity Perfumes which your buyer, Mr. Stoll, gave us yesterday. ~~Your~~'s *Yours* is an unusually large order and this, combined with Mr. Stoll's extreme courtesy, is appreciated. ~~Our~~'s *Ours* is a small firm, and an order the size of yours is very encouraging.

(continued)

We know that our line of perfumes will meet the perfume needs of a number of your departments.

You will find Danity Perfume's are an especially good item for your Womens' Toiletry Department. In addition, it's success has been proven in the Debs' Department of many stores.

If we can be of any further service, please call upon us.

Very truly yours',

EXERCISE 11 · Personal Pronouns

C. This problem deals with the various forms that pronouns take. Fill in the missing pronouns in the following table.

SCORING: DEDUCT 10 POINTS FOR EACH ERROR.

	SINGULAR	PLURAL	SINGULAR POSSESSIVE	PLURAL POSSESSIVE
FIRST PERSON	I	we	my / mine	our / ours
SECOND PERSON	you	you	your / yours	your / yours
THIRD PERSON	he / she / it	they	its / his / her / hers	their / theirs

66

EXERCISE 12 — Pronouns—Antecedents and Number

In this problem you are to identify pronouns and their antecedents. In the column marked Pronoun write the pronoun. In the column marked Antecedent write the antecedent. In the column marked Number write **S** if the antecedent is singular; write **P** if the antecedent is plural.

SCORING: DEDUCT 6 POINTS FOR EACH ERROR.

		PRONOUN	ANTECEDENT	NUMBER
1.	The present equipment deserves all the praise given it.	it	equipment	S
2.	Mr. Jones is certain of his grounds.	his	Mr Jones	S
3.	The Acme Laundry knows it can count on continued community support.	it	laundry	S
4.	The boy's rackets were hung on their sides.	their	boy's	P
5.	Mr. Jones can protect the firm if he acts quickly.	he	Mr Jones	S
6.	Our firm is proud of its record.	its	firm	S
7.	Somebody forgot his glasses.	his	somebody	S
8.	Each of the players has his part.	his	each	S
9.	Mr. Jones and Mr. Smith are on their way to the meeting.	their	Mr. J & Mr. S	P
10.	Mr. Jones, as well as Mr. Smith, is on his way to the meeting.	his	Mr. J	S
11.	Each man must do his very best.	his	each	S
12.	The committee has been in its meeting room for hours.	its	committee	S
13.	Neither the desk nor the table is worth its price.	its	table	S
14.	Mr. Roberts, in addition to the entire staff, will offer his resignation.	his	Mr. Roberts	S
15.	Neither Mrs. Jones nor the boys have saved their money.	their	boys	P

NAME   CLASS   DATE

EXERCISE 13 — Agreement of Pronoun and Antecedent

This problem deals mainly with the agreement of a pronoun with its antecedent. In the spaces provided, write the proper pronouns.

SCORING: DEDUCT 4 POINTS FOR EACH ERROR.

1. Smith and Jones has grown till (it, they) is the largest firm in (its, it's, their) field.
2. If somebody does an outstanding job, (he, they) will be rewarded for (his, their) efforts.
3. The memoranda (is, are) in (its, their) proper place.
4. Every girl in that class knows (his, her, their) lessons.
5. The crisis (is, are) over but has left (its, their) mark.
6. Now is the time for all good men to come to the aid of (his, their) country.
7. Each good man should come to the aid of (his, their) country.
8. No one in this world is certain of (his, their) future; yet each must plan as best (he, they) can.
9. If a man does a valiant deed, (he, they) shall be honored wherever (he, they) goes.
10. Somebody tried to force (his, their) way through the crowd.
11. If Miss Smith or Miss Jones orders at once, (she, they) will receive the merchandise by return post.
12. Either Mr. Dunlap or Mr. Firestone left (his, their) lighter.
13. Every man, woman, and child owed (his, their) life to the Coast Guard.
14. James Randall is one man who realizes (his, their) own value.
15. James is one of those men who realize (his, their) own value.
16. Acme Lumber, in addition to Zenith Lumber, is launching (its, their) annual campaign.
17. The President, but not his Cabinet, is on (his, their) way.
18. All the members (has, have) received (his, their) invitations.
19. Each of the books (has, have) been autographed on (its, their) cover.
20. This is one of those problems that (is, are) not easily solved on (its, their) bare facts.
21. Neither Mary nor Madeline (was, were) able to do (his, her, their) special report on time.
22. None of the manufacturers (is, are) willing to make (his, their) contribution yet.
23. Mr. James, accompanied by his sons, (was, were) able to make (his, their) entrance at the appropriate moment.
24. He is one of those men who (is, are) always complaining about (his, their) tasks.
25. He is different from any of those executives who (remain, remains) calm when (he, they) (is, are) harassed.

Answers (handwritten):
1. it, its
2. he, his
3. are, their
4. her
5. is, its
6. their
7. his
8. his, he
9. he, he
10. his
11. she
12. his
13. his
14. his
15. their
16. its
17. his
18. have their
19. has its
20. are their
21. was her
22. are their
23. was his / all their
24. is his
25. remains calm he is

NAME   CLASS   DATE

REVIEW EXERCISE 3 — Pronouns

The letter below includes many intentional errors. Cross out each incorrect word and write the correct word above it. Pay particular attention to the use of possessive pronouns and to the agreement of a pronoun with its antecedent.

SCORING: DEDUCT 5 POINTS FOR EACH ERROR.

Dear Miss Johnson:

We were extremely pleased to be invited by P.C.L. to attend ~~it's~~ [its] annual convention. I know that each of the members of our staff felt it ~~their~~ [his] personal duty and pleasure to attend. Mr. Smith, as well as Mr. Johnson, send[s] ~~their~~ [his] special thanks to you for the invitation.

I was especially thrilled by the talks given by Professor Poole and Dean Brown. ~~Their's~~ [Theirs] is an unusual combination of talents. I noticed that during ~~there~~ [their] talks every member of the audience ~~were~~ [was] glued to ~~their~~ [his] seats. It's a rarity in this day and age to meet men who have such complete command of ~~his~~ [their] English and ~~his~~ [their] subject matter.

I also wish to congratulate you on the fine job done by your banquet committee. Every table decoration, every knife, every fork ~~were~~ [was] in ~~their~~ [its] proper places. The banquet speakers, especially Miss Green, did ~~her~~ [their] work exceptionally well. By the way, Miss Green is the woman ~~which~~ [whom] I told you about at lunch last week. I'm very much pleased that talent such as ~~her's~~ [hers] was recognized by your committee. She is one of those women who ~~is~~ [are] reliable and can be trusted to do ~~her~~ [their] work to ~~it's~~ [its] fullest extent. Neither Mr. Smith nor Mr. Johnson ~~were~~ [was] disappointed in ~~their~~ [his] expectations.

In closing, let me say that I believe wholeheartedly in the work of this organization of ~~your's~~ [yours]. Since ~~ours'~~ [ours] is a small firm, we are especially proud to be members. You will probably be pleased to know that neither Mr. Smith nor any of ~~his~~ [their] associates ~~has~~ [have had] had a word of criticism of your organization.

Sincerely,

LESSON 4

Verbs are the words in a sentence that pack the wallop. They give a sentence punch. They supply action.

The purpose of business communication is to promote decisive action. Well-chosen verbs in a business letter are the dynamos that generate the desired action. No matter what your position in business may be—executive, secretary, or teacher—verbs are the tools that will get things done for you. They are tools that you must use with facility and ease if you are to be a success in the business world.

Are you skilled in the use of these verb-tools? Can you, at this moment, state the precise difference between the proper use of the verbs *lie* and *lay* or *sit* and *set*? The correct use of such verbs is governed by a relatively few simple rules. You can master these rules with a little application. You *must* master them if you are to be a success in the business office.

to be" — is, are, was, were, be, being, been or any verb that can be replaced by any part of verb "to be".

1. the TYPES of verbs: action and linking

You probably remember from grammar school that a verb is a word that expresses *action*. Do you remember, however, that a verb may also be a word that merely *links* one part of the sentence to another but does not express action? Compare the two types of verbs below.

Action verbs: **run, hit, fly, explode, lie, sleep, sit.**

Linking verbs: **is, are, will be, seem, appear, taste, sound, look.**

Can you tell the difference between these types of verbs? You probably noticed that the action verbs depict an occurrence that you can easily picture in your imagination. On the other hand, the linking verbs refer to occurrences that are much more difficult to picture. Compare these two sentences:

1. **The automobile swerved off the road.**

2. **It seems a good idea.**

In your imagination you can probably picture the car *swerving*, but can you picture something *seeming*? Note that the linking verb *seems* can be replaced by the word *is*. This is true of all linking verbs. They do little more than stand in place of the word *is*.

> **It seems a good idea.**
> **It is a good idea.**

Another name for *linking verbs* is *state-of-being verbs*. In this course we shall call them simply *linking verbs*.

Many verbs may be either action verbs or linking verbs depending upon how they are used in a sentence. Compare the use of the verb *taste* in the following sentences:

1. **The gourmet tasted the soup with obvious delight.**

2. **Candy tastes sweet.**

In the first sentence *taste* is an action verb. It depicts the action of the gourmet in sampling the soup. You can almost picture him as he brings the spoon to his lips. In the second sentence, however, *taste* is a linking verb. It merely links the quality of sweetness to the subject *candy*. The word *is* could replace the word *tastes*.

> **Candy tastes sweet.**
> **Candy is sweet.**

Learn to recognize the distinction between action verbs and linking verbs, for you will have to apply it in later lessons. For the moment, remember these two points:

1. All forms of the verb *to be* are linking verbs. (Below is a list of all forms of the verb *to be*. You need not memorize this list; however, you should become familiar with these forms.)

is	is being	shall be	has been	shall have been
am	am being	will be	have been	will have been
are	are being	should be	had been	should have been
was	was being	would be		would have been
were	were being			

2. Verbs such as *become, seem, appear, prove, grow, remain, feel, taste, sound, look,* and *smell* are linking verbs when they can be replaced by the word *is*.

> **Candy tastes (is) sweet.**
> **Stone appears (is) solid.**
> **Velvet feels (is) soft.**
> **Buttermilk smells (is) sour.**

Turn to Programed Reinforcement S1 through S6

2. the SIMPLE tenses

Verbs change their form depending upon the time of the event they depict. We call the different forms a verb may take by the name *tenses.*

You undoubtedly know the three simple tenses: *the present tense, the past tense,* and *the future tense.* Certainly, in your daily conversation you have employed these tenses properly — perhaps without even realizing you were doing so. You would never say **I will go to the bank yesterday.** You realize, of course, that when you refer to an action that occurred *yesterday,* you must use the *past* tense of the verb *to go.* You would properly say **I went to the bank yesterday.**

Using the simple tenses is easy enough. You have used them correctly since you were an infant. Just as a review, here is an outline of the proper use of the three simple tenses:

1. The past tense refers to a *definite* past event or action.

> **I went to the movies yesterday.**
> **I sold the books last year.**

2. The future tense applies to events that will take place at a future time. You form the future tense by placing *will* or *shall* before the verb.

While many authorities permit the use of *will* or *shall* interchangeably, there are certain rules governing their proper use that you should learn just to be absolutely correct. These rules can be simply stated as follows:

a) To express ordinary future, use *shall* with the first person pronouns *I* and *we;* use *will* for all other pronouns *(you, he, she, it, they).* For example: **I shall see you tomorrow. They will be at the theatre in an hour.**

b) Reverse this rule to show great determination or emotion—using *will* with *I* and *we;* and using *shall* for all other pronouns. For example: **I will see you tomorrow, no matter what you say! They shall be at the theatre in an hour, even if I have to carry them.**

A simple way to remember these uses of *will* and *shall* is by memorizing this little sentence:

> **The king roared: "I will that you and he shall do it."**

The king's will must be done—so in this sentence you tie together *I will, you shall,* and *he shall* to show determination. By memorizing this sentence, you'll always be able to remember how to use *will* or *shall* correctly.

Should and *would* are treated exactly like *shall* and *will.* Use *should* in those instances where *shall* is correct. Use *would* in those instances where *will* is correct.

> **I would like to see you immediately.** (Determination)

> **I should like you to visit me when you can.** (Ordinary future)

3. The present tense is used to denote three types of actions:

a) It describes action going on at the present time.

> **I am satisfied.   He is here.**

b) It describes action that is continued or habitual.

> **I see him every day.   We sell hardware.**

c) It is used to denote a general truth.

> **Cats are animals.   Candy is sweet.**

That's all there is to the present tense.

Should / Shall

would / will

73

Future—I or we use "shall"
you
he   } use will
she
(it, they)

strong determination
I will   she shall
we will   "

part of verb "to be"
unfinished action
ends in ing.

3. the PROGRESSIVE form

ending in ing.

The progressive form is used to refer to an *unfinished* action.

1. I am working on the books right now.
This means that you are at work on the books at present and have not finished them yet. Your work is unfinished.

2. I was studying when John came in.
This means that your studying was interrupted by John. You were not through studying. Your studying was unfinished.

In <u>Sentences 1 and 2</u> each verb is in the <u>progressive form</u> because the action it denotes is still progressing—is *unfinished*. Did you notice that these verbs end in *ing*? The *ing* ending is the sign of the progressive form. In addition, did you notice that each progressive verb is preceded by a form of the verb *to be*? This too is essential to the progressive form.

> **1. am working**
>
> **2. was studying**

<u>The name we give to a verb to which</u> *ing* <u>is added is the</u> *present participle. Working* <u>is the present participle of the verb</u> *work*; *studying* is the present participle of the verb *study*. The *ing*-verb is called a participle because it is *part* of the progressive form.

Learn these three things about the progressive form:

1. Use the progressive to show action that is, was, or will be unfinished;
2. Form the progressive verb by adding *ing* to the simple verb; and
3. Place a form of the verb *to be* before the progressive verb.

Occasionally you will have to decide whether to use a simple tense or the progressive form. Here's an easy way to solve this problem. Merely ask yourself one question: *Is or was the action finished?* If finished, use the simple tense. If unfinished, use the progressive.

1. I (walked, was walking) down the street yesterday when the wind blew my hat off.
Ask: Was the action finished?
Answer: *No.* It was interrupted by the hat incident.
Therefore: Use the progressive form.
I was walking down the street when the wind blew my hat off. (Past Progressive)

2. He (writes) (is writing) out the report at this very moment.
Ask: Is the action finished?
Answer: *No.* He is still working on the report.
Therefore: Use the progressive form.
He is writing out the report at this very moment. (Present Progressive)

3. We (swam) (were swimming) at the lake every day last summer.
Ask: Was the action finished?
Answer: *Yes.* It was completed by the end of last summer.
Therefore: Use the simple tense.
We swam at the lake every day last summer. (Simple Past)

4. They (worked) (were working) feverishly until dawn.
Ask: Was the action finished?
Answer: *Yes.* This is tricky. Dawn did not interrupt their work. It merely marked the moment when they stopped work.
Therefore: Use the simple tense.
They worked feverishly until dawn. (Simple Past)

5. I (listened) (was listening) to the radio when the accident occurred.
Ask: Was the action completed?
Answer: *No.* It was interrupted by the accident.

74

Therefore: Use the progressive form.

I was listening to the radio when the accident occured. (Past Progressive)

6. I shall be swimming in the pool by the time you arrive. (Future Progressive)

By now you should know exactly why *shall be swimming* is correct, and not *shall swim.* Why?

Turn to Programed Reinforcement S7 through S13

---

4. the PERFECT tenses

Let's turn to the final tenses you are going to study — the *perfect* tenses.

They are called the perfect tenses because they always denote action that is *perfect*ed — that is, completed. In the progressive forms that you have just learned, an action is uncompleted when another action occurs. In the perfect tenses the reverse is true — an action is always completed *before* another action occurs.

The form of the verb that is used in all perfect tenses is called the *perfect participle* because this verb form is *part* of all perfect tenses. For example, *brought* is the perfect participle of the verb *bring*:

Present Perfect **has (or have) brought**

Past Perfect **had brought**

Future Perfect **shall (or will) have brought**

Remember, the perfect participle is simply the name given to that form of a verb that is used in all three perfect tenses. Now let's explore the three perfect tenses in detail.

A. THE PAST PERFECT:

I had shipped the order by the time the message arrived.

This means that I had completed the shipment of the order before another event occurred. The other event was the arrival of the message. *Had shipped* is called the *past perfect tense.* It is past perfect because it denotes an action that was completed before another event, *also in the past,* occurred. Remember this: Use the *past* perfect tense to show action that was completed before another event in the *past* occurred.

The sign of the past perfect is the word *had* before the verb.

He had left by the time I arrived.

They had hidden the prizes before the company sat down for dinner.

It had stopped raining by noon.

He had finished college before the war was over.

Occasionally you will be faced with a choice of using either the simple past tense or the past perfect tense. Both refer to events completed in the past, but they are easily distinguished. Remember, the *past* perfect always refers to an action completed *before another event in the past.*

1. We (printed) (had printed) the edition before the censorship order arrived.

Ask: Did one event occur before another occurred?

Answer: *Yes.* The books were printed *before the order arrived.*

Therefore: Use the past perfect.

We had printed the edition before the censorship order arrived.

2. We (suspected) (had suspected) his statements even before we received the police report.

Ask: Did one event occur before another occurred?

Answer: *Yes.* We *had suspected* before we received the report.

Therefore: Use the past perfect.

We had suspected his statements even before we received the police report.

Future (*shall or will* + *has*
Perfect *have* + *main*
had *verb*

3. **Spring (arrived) (had arrived) early last year.**

Ask: Did one event occur before another occurred?

Answer: *No.* There is only one event — the arrival of spring.

Therefore: Use the simple past.

Spring arrived early last year.

4. **Did he know that you (heard) (had heard) from the home office?**

Ask: Did one event occur before another occurred?

Answer: *Yes. You had heard* before *he did know.* Even though this sentence is in the form of a question, treat it as though it makes an affirmative statement. Remember, you learned to do this in determining the subject and predicate of a sentence back in Lesson 1. Treat this sentence as though it reads: *You had heard from the home office before he did know that.*

Therefore: Use the past perfect tense.

Did he know that you had heard from the home office?

B. THE FUTURE PERFECT:

By this time tomorrow I shall have finished my exams.

This means that my exams will be completed by a definite moment in the future. As you probably guessed, *shall have finished* is in the *future perfect* tense.

Remember this: Use the future perfect tense to show action that will be completed by a definite time in the future. The sign of the future perfect is the words *shall have* or *will have* before the verb.

By the time the message arrives, John will have left.

By June 30 our firm will have completed its expansion plans.

I shall have finished my report by noon tomorrow.

Since the future perfect is not used too frequently in business material, we won't bother you with any of the complications that it may cause. You should, however, be able to cope with it when it does come up. So, right now, reread this little section on the future perfect.

C. THE PRESENT PERFECT:

John has filed only one report so far.

This means that John filed a report and will probably file more. The *so far* tells us there will probably be more reports. *Has filed* is called the *present perfect* tense. It is present perfect because it refers to an action that was completed in the past but is part of a series of actions that continues into the present. The sign of the present perfect is the word *has* or *have* before the verb. Let's look at some more examples to make this clearer.

1. **He has shopped in our store many times.**
Has shopped indicates that you expect him to shop some more at your store. If you don't expect him back — let's suppose he had just moved to Pago-Pago — you would say **He shopped in our store many times.** By using the simple past tense *shopped,* you show that the action is completed once-and-for-all. It is not part of a continuing series.

2. **John and Jane's bickering has gone on for years.**
Has gone indicates that it is still going on. If the bickering had finally stopped — let's say that Jane divorced John and moved to Alaska — then you would say **John and Jane's bickering went on for years.**

3. **The Smiths have traveled to this park year after year.**

2 actions, 1 completed by a certian time, or event in the future.

Do the Smiths intend to come back again? Certainly. *Have traveled* indicates they expect to continue to do so. If they didn't expect to return any more you would say **The Smiths traveled to this park year after year.**

Does the present perfect seem clearer to you now? Good. Let's see how you do with a few problems that we'll work through together.

1. Mr. Jones (came) (has come) to see us on numerous occasions.
Which is right, *came* or *has come*? The answer depends on what we mean. If Mr. Jones still comes to see us, then use *has come*. **Mr. Jones has come to see us on numerous occasions.** But if Mr. Jones doesn't like us any more and doesn't visit us any more, use *came*. **Mr. Jones came to see us on many occasions.**

2. The boys (spoiled) (have spoiled) their little sister.
If she is still being spoiled: **The boys have spoiled their little sister.** If she is no longer being spoiled: **The boys spoiled their little sister.**

3. Our offices (were) (have been) on the same corner for years. If they still are on that corner, use *have been*. **Our offices have been on the same corner for years.** If they have been moved elsewhere: **Our offices were on the same corner for years.**

Note: A common error many people make is to substitute the present tense for the present perfect tense. Note these examples — and avoid making the error.

Incorrect: **I am in this office for three months.**
Correct: **I have been in this office for three months.**
Incorrect: **I am living in this house since September.**
Correct: **I have been living in this house since September.**

5. SUMMARY of tenses

You have now studied all the tenses that you need know. Let's review the ground you have covered. In studying one tense at a time, you can easily lose track of the overall picture. Does the following outline help you get a better view of all the tenses?

TENSE	REFERS TO:	EXAMPLE
Simple Past	A completed past action	arrived
Past Perfect	A completed past action that came before another completed past action.	had arrived
Simple Future	A future action	will / shall } arrive
Future Perfect	A future action that will be completed by a definite time in the future.	will / shall } have arrived
Simple Present	An action going on in the present	arrive
Present Perfect	A completed action that is part of a continuing series of such actions.	has / have } arrived
Progressive	An action that is or was uncompleted.	is / was } arriving

Turn to Programed Reinforcement S14 through S22

6. verb FORMS

Look at how the verb *swim* changes depending upon its tense. In the present tense you use *swim*: **I swim every day that I can.** In the past tense you use *swam*: **I swam every day last summer.** In the perfect tense you use *have swum*: **I have swum every day this summer.**

These three forms – *swim, swam, have swum* – enable you to write all simple and perfect tenses of the verb *swim*. You have already learned how to do this.

1. *Swim* is the present tense. To form the future tense, place *shall* or *will* before *swim*: **He will swim again next summer. They shall swim this afternoon.**

2. *Swam* is the past tense. This is the *only* tense where *swam* is correct: **I swam yesterday.**

3. *Swum* is used in all the perfect tenses. As you have learned, it is called the *perfect participle* because *swum* is part of the three perfect tenses as follows:

   a) *Has swum* or *have swum* is the present perfect: **He has swum for hours.**

   b) *Had swum* is the past perfect: **He had swum for hours before he came out.**

   c) *Will have swum* or *shall have swum* is the future perfect: **In an hour I shall have swum my race.**

So, by knowing only three forms of the verb *swim*, you can form all simple and perfect tenses. This is true of all verbs. By knowing only *three* words you can write any simple or perfect tense.

Take another example – the verb *drink*.

1. **Drink** { Present Tense   I **drink** milk.
Future Tense   I **will drink** milk.

2. **Drank**   Past Tense   I **drank** all the milk.

3. **Drunk** { Present Perfect   I **have drunk** milk for years.
Past Perfect   I **had drunk** only milk till I was eighteen.
Future Perfect   I **shall have drunk** a full quart by the time I finish this glass.

Here is another example – the verb *see*.

1. **See** { Present Tense   I **see** him.
Future Tense   I **shall** see him.

2. **Saw**   Past Tense   I **saw** him.

3. **Seen** { Present Perfect   I **have seen** him....
Past Perfect   I **had seen** him....
Future Perfect   I **shall have seen** ....

Here is a final example – the verb *go*.

1. **Go** { Present Tense   I **go.**
Future Tense   I **will** go.

2. **Went**   Past Tense   I **went.**

3. **Gone** { Present Perfect   I **have gone** ....
Past Perfect   I **had gone** ....
Future Perfect   I **will have gone** ....

To review, the above examples show that you can form any simple or perfect tense by knowing only three forms:

1. The present tense;
2. The past tense;
3. The perfect participle.

Now let us turn to choosing the proper forms of some other verbs.

7. REGULAR and IRREGULAR verbs

Most verbs are what we call *regular* verbs. By this we mean that they form the past tense by merely adding *d* or *ed* to the present tense, and they form the present perfect tense by placing the word *has* or *have* before the past tense. For example, the following are some regular verbs:

Present	Past	Present Perfect
receive	received	has or have received
like	liked	has or have liked
allow	allowed	has or have allowed
follow	followed	has or have followed

There are many so-called irregular verbs, however, which do not form their past and perfect tenses in this regular manner. You have already studied four irregular verbs — *swim, drink, see, go.* Some books on English list a hundred or more irregular verbs and tell you, "Memorize these!" Such books are actually making the task more difficult than it need be. While irregular verbs do not follow the pattern of regular verbs, we can still find other patterns within them. For example, there is obvious similarity among:

drink	drank	has drunk
sink	sank	has sunk
shrink	shrank	has shrunk

To enable you to master irregular verbs in record time, we have divided them into families. When studying these families, read them *aloud.*

SAY:

sing	sang	has sung
ring	rang	has rung
spring	sprang	has sprung

By reading these word-groups aloud, your mind will *hear* the pattern within each family. You will learn *by ear* — the simplest, most indelible way. Remember, the key to saving yourself hours of work is to *say* the words in each family aloud and let your mind *hear the pattern.*

To help you learn to *hear* the perfect tenses correctly, we have used the *present perfect* tense in which *has* is placed before the perfect participle. Remember that *have* would also be correct in the present perfect tense; *had* in the past perfect; and *shall have* or *will have* in the future perfect.

I. Present	Past	Perfect
bring	brought	has brought
buy	bought	has bought
fight	fought	has fought
seek	sought	has sought
teach	taught	has taught

II. Present	Past	Perfect
begin	began	has begun
swim	swam	has swum
ring	rang	has rung
sing	sang	has sung
spring	sprang	has sprung
sink	sank	has sunk
shrink	shrank	has shrunk
drink	drank	has drunk
run	ran	has run

III. Present	Past	Perfect
blow	blew	has blown
grow	grew	has grown
know	knew	has known
throw	threw	has thrown
fly	flew	has flown
draw	drew	has drawn
withdraw	withdrew	has withdrawn
wear	wore	has worn
swear	swore	has sworn
tear	tore	has torn
show	showed	has shown

IV. Present	Past	Perfect
bend	bent	has bent
lend	lent	has lent
spend	spent	has spent
deal	dealt	has dealt
feel	felt	has felt
keep	kept	has kept
sleep	slept	has slept
sweep	swept	has swept
weep	wept	has wept
mean	meant	has meant
leave	left	has left
lose	lost	has lost

V. Present	Past	Perfect
break	broke	has broken
choose	chose	has chosen
freeze	froze	has frozen
speak	spoke	has spoken
steal	stole	has stolen
forget	forgot	has forgotten

VI. Present	Past	Perfect
strive	strove	has striven
arise	arose	has arisen
take	took	has taken
mistake	mistook	has mistaken
shake	shook	has shaken
write	wrote	has written
typewrite	typewrote	has typewritten
underwrite	underwrote	has underwritten
eat	ate	has eaten
fall	fell	has fallen
forbid	forbade	has forbidden
give	gave	has given
hide	hid	has hidden

Present	Past	Perfect
come	came	has come
become	became	has become
bleed	bled	has bled
lead	led	has led
flee	fled	has fled
get	got	has got
meet	met	has met
bind	bound	has bound
stand	stood	has stood
win	won	has won
hold	held	has held
stick	stuck	has stuck
strike	struck	has struck
string	strung	has strung
have	had	has had
say	said	has said
make	made	has made
do	did	has done
go	went	has gone

Turn to Programed Reinforcement S23 through S31

VII. The verbs in this group are irregular because they don't change at all. As you can see, they are the same in the present, past, and perfect tenses.

Present	Past	Perfect
bid	bid	has bid
burst	burst	has burst
cost	cost	has cost
cut	cut	has cut
forecast	forecast	has forecast
hurt	hurt	has hurt
let	let	has let
put	put	has put
quit	quit	has quit
spread	spread	has spread
thrust	thrust	has thrust

VIII. There is very little rhyme, and even less reason, in this group. Say the words aloud till they sound familiar.

8. INFINITIVES

You've probably come across the word *infinitive* before. Like so many other terms that seem complicated, this one is really quite easy. An *infinitive* is simply a verb with the word *to* before it: *to love, to have loved; to see, to have been seen; to be, to have been.*

Take the infinitive *to see.* You may use any of the following forms:

To see Paris is exciting. *— verb*

To have seen Paris is to have fulfilled a dream.

To be seen in Paris is chic.

To have been seen in Paris is something to talk about.

Let us remember then that infinitives may be used in different forms to express different ideas.

Infinitives to + verb
to run
to sit

The pronoun used after an infinitive is exactly the same as the pronoun used after any other verb. For example: **The manager plans to visit him and me.** (*Him* and *me* are objects of the infinitive *to visit*.) **The boss says he wants to see me in the office.** (*Me* is object of the infinitive *to see*.) You've probably heard the expression *to split an infinitive*. Maybe you have heard it without knowing what it means. It simply means that a word has been placed between *to* and the verb, thereby splitting the infinitive. This is generally not considered perfect English.

Wrong: **I wish to frequently visit you.** To avoid such an awkward expression, you need merely keep the infinitive *to visit* unsplit: **I wish to visit you frequently.**

Wrong: **I have to sadly leave you.**

Right: **Sadly, I have to leave you.**

never split an infinitive

---

9. PARTICIPLES, dangling and otherwise

When you add *ing* to the verb, you have what is called a *present* participle. Sometimes the present participle is used as the progressive form of the verb that we described earlier in this lesson. For example: **I was working when you came in.** *Working* is the present participle, and *was working* is the progressive form.

Sometimes the present participle is used in a phrase that describes the subject of a sentence. Here is an example of such a *participial phrase*: **Working steadily, John finished his job by noon.** Do you see how the participial phrase *working steadily* describes the subject *John?* Your problem is to be certain that the subject being de-

scribed is very clearly identified. Otherwise some most peculiar sentences will result, like these:

Walking down the street, the building came in sight.

Now buildings can't walk! Of course a man was doing the walking, and a man should be expressed as the subject of the sentence, like this:

Walking down the street, the man saw the building.

Examine this example: **Climbing the trees and swinging in the branches, the old lady noticed the monkeys.** Our old lady is not that agile! The climbing and swinging were done by the monkeys. The sentence should read: **Climbing the trees and swinging in the branches, the monkeys were noticed by the old lady.**

So remember that when a participial phrase begins a sentence, the person doing the "*ing-ing*" must be stated clearly *immediately after* the phrase. Otherwise you have the error known as a *dangling participle*.

Other examples: Wrong: **Lighting a match, the fire was started.** Right: **Lighting a match, he started a fire.**

Don't dangle any participles yourself. It might prove embarrassing!

---

10. verbs and OBJECTS of verbs

You know that a sentence must contain a noun or pronoun as its subject and a verb as its predicate; but you can combine a noun and a verb and still not have a meaningful sentence. *The secretary mailed....* Though this expression contains a subject-

Object of a Verb — who or what after a verb.

intransitive verb — verb does not require an object. eg I slept. They met. He walks.

noun *secretary* and a predicate-verb *mailed*, it is incomplete by itself. It lacks an explanation of *what* was mailed.

What is needed is an *object* of the verb *mailed* — a word that will tell us what was mailed. For example: *The secretary mailed the invoice. Invoice* is the object of the verb *mailed* because it tells us what was mailed.

object

To find the object of a verb, you merely ask yourself *Whom?* or *What?* after the verb. *The secretary mailed . . . . What?* The invoice. *Invoice* is the object of the verb *mailed. The President gave . . . . What?* A speech. *Speech* is the object of the verb *gave. John loves . . . Whom?* Mary. *Mary* is the object of John's affections.

Of course, many verbs do not require objects to complete the meaning of a sentence. For example: *The President speaks.* Here the verb *speaks* is complete without an object. Or: *The plaster shook. The group met.* A verb that needs an object to make sense is called a *transitive* verb since the action *transfers* to the object. *Frank put the letter on the table. Put* is transitive; *letter* is its object. A verb that does not take an object is called an *intransitive* verb. Its action is complete in itself. *Frank sleeps on the couch every afternoon. Sleeps* is intransitive. It does not take an object.

must have object

Turn to Programed Reinforcement S32 through S58

people *hens lay* *peace*

11. lie and lay—sit and set— rise and raise

You should learn the difference between verbs that require objects and verbs that do not. Once you have done so, you can easily master the proper use of such confusing verbs as *lie* and *lay, sit* and *set, rise* and *raise.*

Verb requires an object transfer action from subject to object — transitive verb.

82

A. LIE AND LAY

Probably no two words in the English language are more frequently confused than *lie* and *lay.* Yet *lie* and *lay* have entirely different meanings:

　To lie means *to recline.*
　To lay means *to place.*

An easy way to remember their different meanings is this little trick: There is an *i* in both *lie* and *recline.* There is an *a* in both *lay* and *place.*

As with all irregular verbs, the best way to learn the different tenses of *lie* and *lay* is to say them aloud: *SAY:*

Present	Past	Perfect
lie	lay	has lain
lay	laid	has laid

Another trick: Note that there is an *n* in both *recline* and *lain.*

Here are some sentences using *lie.*
Present Tense: **I lie on the grass.**
Past Tense: **I lay on the grass yesterday.**
Perfect Tense: **I have lain on the grass every afternoon this week.**

Here are some sentences using *lay.*
Present Tense: **I lay the book on the table.**
Past Tense: **I laid the book on the table yesterday.**
Perfect Tense: **I have laid the book on the table as you requested.**

There is another trick that makes distinguishing between *lie* and *lay* easy. *To lie* never needs an object to complete its meaning. It is always intransitive. *To lay* always needs an object to complete its meaning — it is always transitive. Observe these examples.

1. **I lay the book on the table.**
　Lay what? *The book.*

2. **I lie on the grass.**
　Lie what? No answer. *Lie* does not take an object.

3. I laid the carpeting yesterday.
Laid what? *The carpeting.*

4. I lay in bed all day yesterday.
Lay what? No answer. *Lay,* the past tense of *lie,* does not take an object.

5. They have laid their cards on the table.
Have laid what? *Their cards.*

6. He has lain in a hospital bed for over a month.
Has lain what? No answer. *Lain* does not take an object.

Let's try some problems using this method.

7. The workmen have (laid, lain) the linoleum in the kitchen.
Have (laid, lain) what? *The linoleum.* Therefore, *laid* is correct since *laid* always takes an object.
The workmen have laid the linoleum in the kitchen.

8. The books have (laid, lain) on the shelves for years.
Have (laid, lain) what? No answer. Therefore, use *lain* since *lain* never takes an object.
The books have lain on the shelves for years.

If you understand the difference between *lie* and *lay,* you will easily master the distinction between *sit* and *set* and between *rise* and *raise.* If you have any doubts about *lie* and *lay,* however, go back and restudy this lesson before you proceed further.

B. SIT AND SET

To sit means *to be seated.* (people)
To set means *to place.* (place)
Again, say the different tense forms aloud. *SAY:*

Present	Past	Perfect
sit	sat	has sat
set	set	has set

needs an object set it

EXAMPLES:

The director sits at the head of the table.
The director sat at the head yesterday.
The director has sat at the head at every meeting.
He sets the book on the desk.
He set the book on the desk yesterday.
He has set the book on the desk.

Again, *sit* never takes an object to complete its meaning. It is intransitive. *Set* is transitive and always needs an object to complete its meaning. It requires a word to tell us what was set.

Grandpa used to (sit, set) in his chair by the hour.
(Sit, set) what? No answer. Therefore, use *sit* since *sit* never takes an object.
Grandpa used to sit in his chair by the hour.

C. RISE AND RAISE

To rise means *to get up.* (people)
To raise means *to lift.*
Remember, say the different tense forms aloud. *SAY:* — must have an object

Present	Past	Perfect
rise	rose	has risen
raise	raised	has raised

EXAMPLES:

I rise early every morning.
I rose early yesterday.
I have risen early every morning this week.

We raise the flag each morning.
We raised the flag at dawn this morning.
We have raised the flag every morning this summer.

Once more, *rise* never takes an object to complete its meaning. It is intransitive. *Raise* is transitive and always needs an object to complete its meaning. It requires a word to tell us what was raised.

1. **After he fell, he (rose, raised) himself from the floor.**

   (Rose, raised) what? *Himself*. Therefore, use *raised* since *raised* always takes an object.

   He raised himself.

2. **The balloon (rose, raised) from the ground.**

   (Rose, raised) what? No answer. Therefore, use *rose* since *rose* never takes an object.

   The balloon rose from the ground.

Now, here's a trick to tie all you have learned together. You have learned that all forms of the verbs *lie, sit,* and *rise* do not require objects to complete their meaning — that is, they are all intransitive. Just remember that *intransitive* begins with an *i*, and *lie, sit,* and *rise* also have *i's*. Whenever there is no answer to the question *what* after the verb, you know that the verb is intransitive and that it must be a form of the verbs, *lie, sit,* or *rise*.

---

12. GERUNDS and PARALLEL CONSTRUCTION

Sometimes a word ending in *ing* looks like a verb, but is really a noun. For example: *Swimming is fun.* For the word *swimming,* you could substitute *baseball* or any other noun, couldn't you? Such a noun coming from the *ing* form of a verb is called a *gerund*.

Logic and common sense would indicate the error in the following sentence: WRONG: **I like swimming, boating, and to hike.** In this sentence you are using as the objects of the verb *like* two gerunds (*swimming* and *boating*) and one infinitive (*to hike*). Of course, you should use the *same* form throughout. Either use all gerunds (**I like swimming, boating, and hiking**) or use all infinitives (**I like to swim, to boat, and to hike**). In other words, don't mix the types of verbs or gerunds used in a series, but rather keep them the same — what we call parallel structure.

Let's look at another example: WRONG: **I like to read, to paint, and playing the piano.** How would you correct this? It's easy! Either **I like to read, to paint, and to play the piano**; or **I like reading, painting, and playing the piano.**

---

13. IF I WERE... *impossibility or a wish*

There is one peculiarity of the verb *to be* that you should master. It is proper for you to say *"I were"* and *"he were"* in two instances:

a) to express a situation that you know to be contrary to fact:

If I were king, I would free all men from servitude.

If I were you, I would not talk so much.

If Mr. Jones were here, your demands would be quickly met.

Remember, you use this form only if the situation is *known* to be false. Note this sentence, for example:

If he was at the party, I didn't see him. You don't know for sure that he was not there, so you use the regular past tense, *if he was*. But if you know that he is not at the party, then you might say: **If he were at this party, it would be really lively.**

b) To express a wish:

I wish I were king.

I wish he were here now.

We wish we were able to answer your question more fully.

Would that I were king.

Turn to Programed Reinforcement S44 through S63

verb forms — end in "ing" & work like a noun.

84

	S1 Circle one: A verb is a word that generally expresses A) action; B) the name of a place; C) a description.
R1 A) action	**S2** Verbs are of two types, action verbs and l__ __ __ __ __ g verbs.
R2 linking	**S3** A linking verb like **seems** expresses state of being, not action. It may be replaced by the verb _____.
R3 is	**S4** Verbs relating to the senses may often be either linking or action verbs depending on the way they're used. Circle the verb that expresses action: A. **The boy tasted the cake.** B. **The cake tasted good.**
R4 A. **tasted**	**S5** In the sentence **The flower smells sweet**, the verb **smells** is a linking or non-action verb. Write the entire sentence substituting **is** for the linking verb. _____
R5 **The flower is sweet.**	**S6** In the following group of verbs, two are always action verbs; the others are usually linking verbs. Circle the two action verbs: **appear, become, seem, write, feel, speak.**
R6 **write; speak** • **TURN TO Exercise 14**	**S7** Circle one: The tense of a verb is related to A) person; B) degree; C) time.
R7 C) time	**S8** There are three simple verb tenses: the p __ __ __ __ __ __ __ , the p __ __ __ , and the f __ __ __ __ __ .
R8 present; past; future	**S9** Consider the verb **to be.** In the first person singular the present tense would be **Now I _____ here.** The past tense would be **Yesterday I _____ here.** The simple future tense would be **Tomorrow I _____ here.**
R9 **am; was; shall be** or **will be**	**S10** In the future tense **shall** and **will** are sometimes confused. For ordinary future we use _____ with the first person (**I**) and _____ with the second and third person (**you, he, etc.**).
R10 shall; will	**S11** When you express strong emotion with the use of **shall** and **will,** you reverse the normal procedure. You then say **I_____ leave the room!** and **You _____ do as I say!**
R11 **will; shall**	

S12

The **ing** ending to a verb indicates usually that it is the progressive form. In the sentence **I am reading now,** the progressive form deals with **(finished, unfinished)** business.

R12
unfinished

S13

The simple tense and the progressive form often seem interchangeable. The progressive form, however, should be used when the action is unfinished. Circle the correct sentence:
A. **I was typing when the ribbon broke.** B. **I typed when the ribbon broke.**

R13
A
• TURN TO Exercise 15

S14

In the **perfect** tenses the verbs always need the help of **h ___ s h ___ ___ e** or **h ___ d.**

R14
has; have; had

S15

The past perfect tense describes an action that was completed before another action in the past. Circle the past perfect verbs in these two sentences:
A. **He had just left the office when the storm broke.**
B. **The accountant had checked the books before the bookkeeper arrived.**

R15
A. **had left;**
B. **had checked**

S16

Since the past perfect tense, consisting of **had** and the perfect participle, always precedes another action in the past, what tense is the other verb in the sentence:
Mr. Smith learned that the salesman had reported the error.
Answer: _____ tense.

R16
learned is past tense

S17

The future perfect tense is used to show action that will be completed by a definite time in the future. It contains **shall have** or **will have.** Circle the future perfect tense: **I shall have completed the book by the time he arrives.**

R17
shall have completed

S18

The present perfect tense always uses the helping verb h ___ ___ ___ or h ___ ___ .

R18
have; has

S19

The present perfect tense is used to describe a past action that is part of a series of actions that continues through the present. Circle the present perfect tense: **Frank has worked here since 1960 when he was graduated from college.**

R19
has worked

S20

Circle the correct sentence:
A. **She has been a good secretary, and still is!**
B. **She was a good secretary, and still is!**

R20
A.

S21

Identify the tenses in each sentence and circle the correct sentence:

A. **I am in this office for a year already.**

Answer: _____ tense

B. **I have been in this office for a year already.**

Answer: _____ tense

R21
A. Present tense — incorrect;
B. Present perfect — correct

S22

Let's review. In this sentence there are three verbs. Circle them and indicate the tense of each:

Mr. Jones had expected the promotion, but Mr. Smith arrived and nothing has been the same since.

Answer: _____ tense; _____ tense;

_____ tense

R22
had expected — past perfect;
arrived — past tense;
has been — present perfect
● **TURN TO Exercise 16**

S23

You need know only three forms of any verb: the present tense, the past tenses, and the perfect tense (perfect participle). Write these forms of the verb **drink**:

Present: _____; Past _____; Perfect: **has** _____.

R23
present tense — **drink**;
past tense — **drank**;
perfect tense — **has drunk**

S24

I brought the list to the manager who had begun the inventory.
The tense of **brought** is _____;
had begun is _____.

R24
past; past perfect

S25

Fill in the appropriate verbs:

Present tense	Past tense	Perfect tense
_____	drew	_____
tear	_____	_____
_____	_____	has flown

R25
draw, drew, has drawn;
tear, tore, has torn;
fly, flew, has flown

S26

Present tense	Past tense	Perfect tense
_____	_____	has grown
spring	_____	_____
_____	shrank	_____

R26
grow, grew, has grown;
spring, sprang, has sprung;
shrink, shrank, has shrunk

S27

Verbs may form their past and perfect tenses in a regular or an ir _ _ _ _ _ _ _ manner.

R27
irregular

S28

The verb **walk** (present — **walk**; past — **walked**; perfect participle — **walked**) is an example of a _____ verb.

R28
regular

		S29 In a regular verb, the past tense and the perfect p _ _ _ _ _ _ _ _ are identical.
R29 participle		**S30** Write the correct verbs in these sentences: A. **I (awoke) early in the morning yesterday.** Answer: _____ B. **The fire has (blow) out.** Answer: _____ C. **He had (see) many things on his trip.** Answer: _____
R30 A. **awoke**; B. **blown**; C. **seen**		**S31** Write the correct verbs in these sentences: A. **He has (choose) a few samples.** Answer: _____ B. **The pipe (burst) in the factory.** Answer: _____ C. **The dinner has (cost) me more in the past.** Answer: _____
R31 A. **chosen**; B. **burst**; C. **cost** • TURN TO Exercises 17, 18, and 19		**S32** A sentence may be incomplete if the receiver of the action is not stated. **The secretary typed a letter. Letter** is the "receiver" of the action. It is the o _ _ _ _ _ of the verb _____.
R32 object; **typed**		**S33** To find the object of a verb, ask yourself **what** or _____ after the verb.
R33 **whom**		**S34** In the sentence **The clerk mailed** . . . what question will lead to the object? Answer: _____.
R34 what		**S35** A verb that takes an object is called a **transitive** verb. A verb that does not need an object is called an i _ _ _ _ _ _ _ _ _ _ _ verb.
R35 intransitive		**S36** Circle the transitive verbs in these sentences: A. **He put the mail on the desk.** B. **The sun shines on the window.** C. **Lay the envelope on the desk.**
R36 **put; lay**		**S37** Circle two objects of verbs in this sentence: **He complimented his assistant and bought a present for her.**
R37 **assistant; present**		**S38** A verb preceded by the word **to** is called an i _ _ _ _ _ _ _ _ .
R38 infinitive		**S39** An infinitive may be used like almost any other part of speech. **To listen is important. To listen** is used as s _____ of the verb **is.**
R39 subject		

88

S40 I like to listen to good music. The infinitive **to listen** in this sentence is used as o _ _ _ _ _ of the verb **like.**

R40 object

S41 An infinitive may also be followed by objects. Circle the objects of the infinitive in this sentence: **I plan to visit my friends and my relatives in the country.**

R41 friends; relatives

S42 What word splits the infinitive here: **I want to clearly state my intentions.**

R42 clearly

S43 An **ing** form of a verb, if it is used as part of the progressive form, is called a **present** p _ _ _ _ _ _ ple. Circle the present participle in this sentence: **I am waiting for the operator.**

R43 participle; **waiting**
● **TURN TO Exercise 20**

S44 A verb form ending in **ing** and used as a noun, as in the sentence **Hiking is healthful,** is called a g _ _ _ _ _ d.

R44 gerund

S45 Since a gerund is really a noun that is derived from a verb, it may be used as a subject or object in a sentence. **He enjoyed writing to his friends.** In this sentence the gerund is _ _ _ _ and it is a(n) _ _ ject.

R45 **writing;** object

S46 **Listening is an underdeveloped activity.** In this sentence the gerund is _ _ _ _ and it is a(n) _ _ _ ject.

R46 **listening;** subject

S47 **Filing is tedious work.**
In this sentence **filing** is a g _ _ _ _ _ _.
She was filing the letters. In this sentence filing is a p _ _ _ _ _t p _ _ _ _ _ _ ple.

R47 gerund; present participle

S48 Circle the noun that **walking** modifies in this sentence: **Walking down the street, the man saw the store.**

R48 **man**

S49 If the participle does not clearly relate to the noun that it modifies, it is called a **dangling participle.** Circle the dangling participle here: **Walking along the street, the store came in sight.**

R49 **walking**

S50 In this sentence, **Walking along the street, the store came in sight,** circle the word that **walking** seems to modify.

R50 **store**

S51

Is this a dangling participle construction?
Speaking softly, the audience listened to the lecturer.
Answer: _____.

R51

Yes (unless the audience was speaking softly, and not the lecturer).

S52

Is this a dangling participle construction?
Knowing the result, he quickly phoned his broker. Answer: _____

R52

No

S53

Circle the word that is incorrectly used here: **To swim, to hike, to play, and boating are enjoyable.** What word(s) would correct this sentence?   Answer: _____

R53

boating;
to boat

S54

Show two different ways you could change this sentence to correct the lack of parallel structure. **Speaking, listening, and to take notes are student activities.**

Answer: A. _____, _____, and _____

Answer: A. _____, _____, and _____

R54

A. **speaking, listening, and taking;**

B. **to speak, to listen, and to take**

S55

To lie means **to recline**; **to lay** means **to place.** What are the three parts of the verb **to lie**?
Present _____ Past _____ Perfect _____.
What are the three parts of the verb **to lay**?
Present _____ Past _____ Perfect _____.

R55

present, lie;
past, lay;
perfect, has lain

present, lay;
past, laid;
perfect, has laid

S56

Circle the verb that is intransitive: **to lie** or **to lay.**

R56

to lie

S57

Circle the correct forms:
A. I wish (**to lie, to lay**) down on the couch.
B. He has (**laid, lain**) on the grass for an hour.

R57

A. **to lie;**
B. **lain**

S58

Circle the correct forms:
A. He (**lay, laid**) the carpet on the floor.
B. I want to (**lay, lie**) the law down.

R58

A. **laid;**
B. **lay**

S59

Set is a transitive verb; that means it needs an object to complete its meaning. Circle the object of **to set: I want you to set the table for two.**

R59 table

S60

Sit is intransitive, requiring no object. Which is correct? **Grandma likes to (sit, set) in her rocking chair.**

R60 sit

S61

Rise is intransitive; it never takes an object. Which is correct? **The salesman's speech will (raise, rise) the consumers' spirits.**

R61 raise

S62

When we want to show something contrary to the fact, we say **were** rather than **was.** Circle the correct verb: **If I (were, was) an angel, I would have wings.**

R62 were

S63

Rewrite these sentences correctly:
Since I'm often busy, I frequently let matters lay around for many days. If I was less busy, by working diligently the work could be cleared up in a few hours.

_____

_____

_____

_____

_____

_____

_____

_____

R63

Since I'm often busy, I frequently let matters **lie** around for many days. If I **were** less busy, by working diligently I could clear up the work in a few hours.

● TURN TO
Exercise 21 and Review

EXERCISE 14 — Recognizing Action and Linking Verbs

A. This problem deals with recognizing the difference between action and linking verbs. Below is a list of verbs. In the space next to each verb mark A if it is an action verb; mark L if it is a linking verb; mark E if it could be either.

SCORING: DEDUCT 4 POINTS FOR EACH ERROR.

1. explode _____ A
2. spend _____ A
3. had been _____ L
4. sleep _____ A
5. lie _____ A
6. were _____ L
7. seem _____ L
8. walk _____ A
9. would have been _____ L
10. looks _____ ~~A~~ E
11. was _____ L
12. recline _____ A
13. rested _____ A
14. mail _____ A
15. becoming _____ E
16. thinks _____ A
17. tastes _____ E
18. attack _____ A
19. receives _____ A
20. feels _____ E
21. taste _____ E
22. smell _____ E
23. touch _____ A, L
24. appear _____ E
25. desire _____ A

EXERCISE 14 — Recognizing Action and Linking Verbs

B. This problem deals with distinguishing between action and linking verbs. Below is a list of sentences. Find the verb (predicate) of each sentence and write it in the space provided. In the other space provided, write A if the verb is an action verb; write L if the verb is a linking verb.

SCORING: DEDUCT 5 POINTS FOR EACH ERROR.

		Predicate Verb	*Action or Linking*
1.	This booklet will show our entire line of clothing.	1. show	A
2.	We feel certain of your success.	2. feel	L
3.	Did you feel the texture of the cloth?	3. feel	A
4.	The meal tasted wonderful.	4. tasted	LA
5.	I tasted the soup.	5. tasted	A
6.	This business becomes tedious after a few weeks.	6. becomes	L
7.	The situation looks promising.	7. looks	L
8.	He will be there.	8. will be	L
9.	He looked me straight in the eye.	9. looked	A
10.	Lie down before dinner.	10. lie	A
11.	Mr. Smith looked for his papers.	11. looked	A
12.	The exam looked very easy to everyone.	12. looked	A
13.	The dinner smells delicious.	13. smells	A
14.	I can smell the food from here.	14. smell	A
15.	Don't those pies taste delectable?	15. taste	A
16.	Did you taste them?	16. taste	A
17.	I can feel the cold in my bones.	17. feel	A
18.	I don't feel well.	18. feels	L
19.	He feels bad about losing his job.	19. feels	L
20.	His infected thumb feels the pain intensely.	20. feels	A

EXERCISE 15 — The Simple Tenses

A. This exercise deals with the use of the simple tenses. Here are five sentences. You are to change the verb to the indicated tense. Fill in the blanks.

SCORING: DEDUCT 7 POINTS FOR EACH ERROR.

1. a. Present: **I work.**
   b. Past: They _worked_
   c. Simple future: We _shall work_
   d. Emphatic future: You _shall work_

2. a. Present: **He sells.**
   b. Past: You _have sold_
   c. Simple future: I _shall sell_
   d. Emphatic future: They _shall sell_

3. a. Present: **They hear.**
   b. Past: We _heard_
   c. Simple future: You _will hear_
   d. Emphatic future: I _will hear_

4. a. Present: **You say.**
   b. Past: He _said_
   c. Simple future: They _will say_
   d. Emphatic future: She _shall say_

5. a. Present: **She is.**
   b. Past: He _was_
   c. Simple future: They _will_
   d. Emphatic future: It _shall_

EXERCISE 15 — The Progressive Form

B. This problem deals with the proper use of the progressive form. In the space provided, write the proper verb for each of the following sentences. Remember, ask yourself: Is or was the action completed?

SCORING: DEDUCT 10 POINTS FOR EACH ERROR.

1. They (work) when the bell rang. 1. _were working_
2. Mrs. Smith (see) Mr. Jones in his office at this very minute. 2. _is seeing_
3. Last year we (sell) hundreds of desks. 3. _sold_
4. While we (talk) the manager arrived. 4. _were talking_
5. Miss Johnson (type) the letter right now. 5. _is typing_
6. We (send) all our customers the new price list last month. 6. _sent_
7. Weren't you (visit) the home office when the explosion occurred? 7. _visiting_
8. We (know) you can do a perfect job. 8. _know_
9. They (leave) when the order was delivered. 9. _were leaving_
10. Yesterday we (file) the invoices that were received last week. 10. _filed_

SCORE

A_____

EXERCISE 16   The Perfect Tenses

A. This problem deals with the proper use of the past perfect. In the space provided, write the proper verb for each of the following sentences. Remember, ask yourself: Did one event occur before another event, also in the past, occurred?

SCORING: DEDUCT 10 POINTS FOR EACH ERROR.

1. The mail (arrive) before we opened the office.
2. Our department (ship) the order before we received your wire.
3. We (see) him walking in the street yesterday.
4. Your officers (be) very courteous to us during the entire party yesterday.
5. The inspector found that the crowd (be) dispersed before he arrived.
6. We saw the puff of smoke right after we (hear) the explosion.
7. As the bell rang, I (finish) my assignment.
8. By the time the bell rang, I (finish) my assignment.
9. My boss (dictate) five letters by noon.
10. Napoleon (conquer) Italy before his thirtieth birthday.

1. _had arrived_
2. _had shipped_
3. _had seen_
4. _had been_
5. _had been_
6. _had heard_
7. _finished_
8. _had finished_
9. _had dictated_
10. _had conquered_

SCORE

B_____

EXERCISE 16   The Perfect Tenses

B. This problem deals with the proper use of the present perfect. In the space provided, write the proper verb for each of the following sentences. Remember, ask yourself: Is this action part of a series of actions that continues up to the present?

SCORING: DEDUCT 6 POINTS FOR EACH ERROR.

1. Ever since I entered the room, the clerk (do) nothing.
2. The baby (cry) since its mother left the room.
3. We (be) here for the past hour.
4. We (go) to the office many times last week.
5. The present governor (be) in office for seven years.
6. Since you left this office, there (be) very little activity.
7. I (be) in this office since 9 A.M.
8. The clerk (stay) on the job since 1942.
9. The printer (proofread) this paper before he left last night.
10. I (work) on this job since graduating.

1. _has done_
2. _has cried_
3. _have been_
4. _have gone_
5. _has been_
6. _has been_
7. _have been_
8. _has stayed_
9. _had proofread_
10. _have worked_

SCORE

A_____

EXERCISE 17   Regular Verbs

A. This problem deals with the way regular verbs change depending upon tense. Fill in the missing verbs in this table.

SCORING: DEDUCT 5 POINTS FOR EACH ERROR.

Present Tense	Past Tense	Present Perfect Tense
1. work	worked	has worked
2. sign	signed	has signed
3. order	ordered	have ordered
4. reply	replied	has replied
5. return	returned	has returned
6. complain	complained	have complained
7. expect	expected	has expected
8. interfere	interfered	have interfered
9. convene	convened	has convened
10. adjourn	adjourned	have adjourned

SCORE

B_____

EXERCISE 17   Regular Verbs

B. This problem involves working with regular verbs. In the space provided, fill in the proper form of the verb for each of the following sentences.

SCORING: DEDUCT 6 POINTS FOR EACH ERROR.

1. Our firm (distribute) advertising leaflets for twelve years so far.
2. By this time next week we (eliminate) this bottleneck.
3. We hereby (acknowledge) receipt of your order.
4. The Board (submit) the dispute to arbitration last week.
5. We (expect) your reply by next Monday.
6. Miss Johnson (leave) with her escort when she was called to the phone.
7. We (describe) the project in our next letter.
8. We (accumulate) too large an inventory last year.
9. By this time last year we (accumulate) too large an inventory.
10. The members of the committee (bicker) among themselves at last night's meeting.
11. Yesterday we (invite) the Mayor to attend our banquet.
12. So far, twelve people (answer) our questionnaire.
13. The clerk (work) here since 1960.
14. Last night she (type) in the office until midnight.
15. Was he (allow) to see your accounts?

1. has distributed
2. shall have eliminated
3. acknowledge
4. submitted
5. shall expect
6. was leaving
7. shall describe
8. accumulated
9. had accumulated
10. bickered
11. invited
12. have answered
13. has worked
14. typed
15. allowed

EXERCISE 18

Irregular Verbs I

This problem deals with irregular verbs. On each line is printed the present tense of an irregular verb. Write the past tense and the present perfect tense of each of these verbs. Have you studied the irregular verbs carefully and recited them aloud?

SCORING: DEDUCT 2 POINTS FOR EACH ERROR.

Present	Past	Past Perfect *had*
1. I am	I _was_	I _had been_
2. You blow	You _blew_	You _have blown_
3. It breaks	It _broke_	It _had broken_
4. It bursts	It _burst_	It _had burst_
5. They cost	They _cost_	They _have cost_
6. You deal	You _delt_	You _have delt_
7. We drive	We _drove_	We _have driven_
8. I forbid	I _forbade_	I _have forbidden_
9. We fly	We _flew_	We _have flown_
10. They go	They _went_	They _have gone_
11. I hide	I _hid_	I _have hidden_
12. She knows	She _knew_	She _has known_
13. I lead	I _led_	I _have led_
14. You mistake	You _mistook_	You _have mistaken_
15. We pay	We _paid_	We _have paid_
16. He reads	He _read_	He _has read_
17. You seek	You _sought_	You _have sought_
18. I shrink	I _shrank_	I _have shrunk_
19. We sing	We _sang_	We _have sung_
20. You speak	You _spoke_	You _have spoken_
21. I spend	I _spent_	I _have spent_
22. They stand	They _stood_	They _have stood_
23. We take	We _took_	We _have taken_
24. She teaches	She _taught_	She _has taught_
25. We tear	We _tore_	We _have torn_
26. You throw	You _threw_	You _have thrown_
27. I typewrite	I _typewrote_	I _have typewritten_
28. He wears	He _wore_	He _worn_
29. I withdraw	I _withdrew_	I _have withdrawn_
30. You write	You _wrote_	You _have written_

EXERCISE 19   Irregular Verbs II

This problem deals with the correct forms of irregular verbs. In the space provided, write the correct form of the indicated verb in each of the following sentences. Have you recited the irregular-verb families so often that you know these verbs by ear?

SCORING: DEDUCT 2 POINTS FOR EACH ERROR.

1. I (awake) at the crack of dawn yesterday.
2. By the time he arrived, she had (become) very tired.
3. The general had (awake) by the time I called.
4. I (bid) $50 for the vase at yesterday's auction.
5. They were (bind) to each other by a common interest.
6. The tire had (blow) out.
7. Her heart had been (break) by the cad.
8. We will (build) a factory on the river.
9. Yesterday the pipe (burst) with a roar.
10. He was (choose) to accompany you.
11. He has (come) a long way.
12. By noon it had already (cost) me my entire salary.
13. It was (cut) across the top.
14. They were (deal) with in short order.
15. He has (do) no wrong.
16. This convention has (draw) a huge crowd.
17. He had (drink) too much water.
18. We discovered that prices had (fall).
19. Father (forbid) their leaving the house.
20. Planes have (fly) millions of miles.
21. The weather department has (forecast) clearing skies.
22. By morning the water had (freeze).
23. He has (get) too big for his breeches.
24. The prize was (give) to the bookkeeper.
25. All the members had (go) before the bell sounded.
26. Our nation has (grow) to enormous power.
27. He has not (hear) of your product.
28. The invoice was (hide) under a pile of paper.
29. He had (hurt) himself.
30. Have you (keep) up with the news?
31. Had I (know) of the detour, I would have chosen a different road.
32. He has (lose) his opportunity.
33. He has (lend) a fortune to the firm.
34. He (mean) what he said.

1. _awoke_
2. _become_
3. _awakened_
4. _bid_
5. _blended_ bound
6. _blown_
7. _broken_
8. _build_
9. _burst_
10. _chosen_
11. _come_
12. ~~had~~ cost
13. _cut_
14. _delt_
15. _done_
16. _drawn_
17. _drunk_
18. _fallen_
19. _has forbidden_ (forbade)
20. _flown_
21. _forcast_
22. _frozen_
23. _gotten_
24. _given_
25. _gone_
26. _grown_
27. _heard_
28. _hiden_
29. _hurt_
30. _kept_
31. _known_
32. _lost_
33. _lent_
34. _meant_

(continued)

35. He had (meet) most of them before.   35. _met_
36. I had (mistake) you for him.   36. _mistaken_
37. Your account was (overdraw).   37. _overdrawn_
38. He has (prepay) the postage.   38. _prepaid_
39. Have you (read) the contract?   39. _read_
40. We had (put) the matter before the board.   40. _put_
41. Had he (quit) the race by the end of the first mile?   41. _quit_
42. The race had been (run) before noon.   42. _run_
43. He had (see) many examples, but could follow none.   43. _seen_
44. They have (seek) the answer in vain.   44. _sought_
45. The building had (shake) under the force of the earthquake.   45. _shaken_
46. Had he (show) you how to operate it?   46. _shown_
47. The profits (shrink) last week to half their former level.   47. _shrank_
48. She has (sing) the song before royalty.   48. _sung_
49. The ship had (sink) to the bottom.   49. _sunk_
50. I (sleep) until noon yesterday.   50. _slept_
51. Had he (speak) to you about it?   51. _spoken_
52. We (spend) many hours discussing the problem last night.   52. _spent_
53. The coil had (spring) from its covering.   53. _sprung_
54. Our company has (stand) for the finest quality for 100 years.   54. _stood_
55. The two pieces had (stick) together.   55. _stuck_
56. Catastrophe had (strike) the city.   56. _struck_
57. All year long he had (strive) for the top.   57. _striven_
58. He was (swear) to secrecy.   58. _sworn_
59. The river had (sweep) all in its path.   59. _swept_
60. I (swim) at the lake last week.   60. _swam_
61. They have (take) more than their fair share.   61. _taken_
62. Had I (teach) the course, I would have (teach) it differently.   62. _taught_
63. Has he (tear) up those papers?   63. _torn_
64. I had (think) he was much taller.   64. _thought_
65. The President has (throw) out the first ball.   65. _thrown_
66. Cyrano (thrust) home with his sword.   66. _thrust_
67. His aunt (undertake) his obligations last week.   67. _undertook_
68. The company had (underwrite) all his debts.   68. _underwrote_
69. Yesterday I (typewrite) the entire copy.   69. _typewrote_
70. He has (wear) a hole through his sleeve.   70. _worn_
71. They have (weep) for days.   71. _wept_
72. Has he (win) his bet?   72. _won_
73. The Acme Co. has (withdraw) its bid.   73. _withdrawn_
74. Has she (write) to you in the past few weeks?   74. _written_
75. They (write) a letter to you last week.   75. _wrote_

EXERCISE 20 — Infinitives, Dangling Participles, Parallel Structure

A. This problem deals with the proper use of infinitives, participles, and parallel structure in sentences. If the sentence is correct as it is, mark **C** in the space provided. If it is incorrect, use the space above the sentence to indicate the changes that have to be made.

SCORING: DEDUCT 10 POINTS FOR EACH ERROR.

1. I intend to strongly complain about the errors in my bill.   1. _____
2. I was supposed to have gone to the party last night.   2. C
3. He wants to see Frank and me and to carefully explain what to do.   3. _____
4. Typing at top speed, the letter was finished on time by the typist. *who was*   4. _____
5. We want to carefully proofread the manuscript.   5. _____
6. Reading the paper at lunch, the news upset him. *when he was*   6. _____
7. Knowing the answer, he raised his hand.   7. C
8. You must be sure to fully reply to this letter.   *conversing* 8. _____
9. Reading broadens a person, writing sharpens him, and to converse stimulates him.   *to putter*   9. _____
10. On a vacation we should plan to rest, to dream, and puttering in the garden.   10. _____

EXERCISE 20 — Was and Were

B. This problem deals with the proper use of was and were. In the space provided, fill in the proper word.

SCORING: DEDUCT 10 POINTS FOR EACH ERROR.

1. If I (was, were) you, I would change my mind.   1. *were*
2. I wish I (was, were) President.   2. *were*
3. He (was, were) not here yesterday.   3. *was*
4. If he (was, were) to disappear into thin air, I could not be more pleased.   4. *were*
5. I don't know if he (was, were) at the meeting.   5. *was*
6. (Was, Were) I you, I would do the same.   6. *Were*
7. If I (was, were) the manager of this firm, I would do things differently.   7. *were*
8. Since the report turned out to be false, I (was, were) relieved.   8. *was*
9. Here is how I would act if I (was, were) in your shoes.   9. *were*
10. I certainly wish it (was, were) cooler.   10. *were*

101

SCORE

A_____

EXERCISE 21   Verbs—and their Objects

A. This problem deals with the objects of verbs. Each of the following sentences contains a verb and its object. In the space provided, rewrite the verb and the object of that verb. Remember, to find the object, just ask yourself: Whom? or What? after the verb.

SCORING: DEDUCT 10 POINTS FOR EACH ERROR.

		Verb	*Object of Verb*
1.	John loves Mary.	1. loves	Mary
2.	Smith sent me to the factory.	2. sent	me
3.	Our firm makes the finest clothing.	3. makes	clothing
4.	We appreciate your letter of September 20.	4. appreciate	letter
5.	We hear the important events of the day on the radio.	5. hear	events
6.	We will send our representatives next week.	6. send	representatives
7.	Will you mail your remittance by return post?	7. mail	remittance
8.	We are enclosing a copy of the contract form.	8. enclosing	copy
9.	We discussed the entire matter with him.	9. discussed	matter
10.	They advised him against the contract.	10. advised	him

SCORE

B_____

EXERCISE 21   Verbs—Lie and Lay

B. This problem deals with the proper use of lie and lay. In the space provided, fill in the correct word. Remember: to lay means to place; to lie means to recline.

SCORING: DEDUCT 10 POINTS FOR EACH ERROR.

1.	The book (lay, laid) on the shelf for months.	1. lay
2.	(Lay, Lie) down before dinner.	2. Lie
3.	The President (lay, laid) down our basic foreign policy.	3. laid
4.	It has (laid, lain) on a shelf for years.	4. laid
5.	He will (lie, lay) the carpet tomorrow.	5. lay
6.	Will you (lay, lie) down for a few moments' rest?	6. lie
7.	He (lay, laid) the foundations for a solid business.	7. laid
8.	They had (laid, lain) the goods on top of the table.	8. laid
9.	The goods have (laid, lain) on the table for weeks.	9. laid
10.	He had (laid, lain) his cards on the table and was ready to suffer the consequences.	10. laid

(laid - if you have object)

EXERCISE 21 | Verbs – Sit-Set and Rise-Raise

C. This problem deals with the proper use of *sit* or *set* and *rise* or *raise*. In the space provided, fill in the correct word.

SCORING: DEDUCT 10 POINTS FOR EACH ERROR.

1. (Sit, Set) down in that chair.
2. They have (sat, set) in their rocking chairs for years.
3. Can you (raise, rise) to the situation?
4. (Set, Sit) the table down carefully.
5. Will you (raise, rise) your hand if you agree.
6. We must try to (raise, rise) above such petty bickering.
7. Can you (sit, set) by doing nothing?
8. He would have (raised, rose) prices had he foreseen the inflation.
9. Prices (raise, rose) due to the inflation.
10. (Sit, Set) the piano in the corner.

1. *Sit*
2. *sat*
3. *rise*
4. *Set*
5. *raise*
6. *rise*
7. *sit*
8. *raised*
9. *rose*
10. *Set*

raise - object

EXERCISE 21 | Verbs – Transitive and Intransitive

D. This problem deals with the proper use of *lie* or *lay*; *sit* or *set*; and *raise* or *rise*. In the space provided, fill in the proper word.

SCORING: DEDUCT 6 POINTS FOR EACH ERROR.

1. Have you been (sitting, setting) here all afternoon?
2. Prices had not (raised, risen) not so fast as expected.
3. The journal has (laid, lain) on the shelf for years.
4. They were so tired they just (sat, set) right down on the ground.
5. The plane will (rise, raise) beyond the clouds in a few moments.
6. (Rise, Raise) the curtains and we will see better.
7. The accountant (lay, laid) the checkbook on the table.
8. Will you (lie, lay) down for a nap?
9. A number of rockets have (rose, risen) beyond the stratosphere.
10. He has (set, sat) in the same spot for hours.
11. The blame was (laid, lain) at his doorstep.
12. Will you (rise, raise) a fuss if they don't agree?
13. (Sit, Set) down at the table before the guests arrive.
14. Regulations have been (laid, lain) down by the Board.
15. Have they (sat, set) long enough to be rested?

1. *sitting*
2. *risen*
3. *laid*
4. *sat*
5. *rise*
6. *Raise*
7. *laid*
8. *lie*
9. *risen*
10. *sat*
11. *laid*
12. *raise*
13. *Sit*
14. *laid*
15. *sat*

REVIEW EXERCISE 4 — Verbs

This problem deals with the proper use of verbs. In the following letter many verbs are in italics. If the italicized verb is correct, place a C above it. If the verb is incorrect, cross it out and write the correct form above it. Pay particular attention to the use of proper tenses and to irregular verbs.

SCORING: DEDUCT 5 POINTS FOR EACH ERROR.

Dear Mr. Robinson:

I *was* very disappointed that you *do* [did] not send your representative to *watch* the test of our new Starfire car model last week. We are positive that he would *be* [have been] astounded by the way the Starfire *performed*, as *was* [were] the hundreds of others who *was* [were] there. Did he *forgot* [forget] the date of this demonstration test?

If he had *attended,* he would *be seeing* [have seen] a new concept in automotive design and engineering. The Starfire *was* an all-new car. It *had* [was] a new engine, new streamlining, new controls.

Until the new line of Starfires *were* [was] unveiled last week, the automobile industry *has* [had] been lagging behind other industries in the use of plastics. The Starfire *has* changed this.

At last week's demonstration tests, the Starfire *accelerated* to 90 miles per hour in under 25 seconds.

I needn't tell you how *astonished* the representatives of other firms *were* when they *had seen* [saw] this spectacular performance. I'm sure that many of them *had* already told you about it themselves.

Until you have *seen* the Starfire and *drove* [driven] in it, you will be missing the thrill of your life. If I *was* [were] you, I would make arrangements to *attendance* [attend] the next demonstration, which will be *holded* [held] next Thursday at four o'clock at the Grand Plaza Arena. We *know* [shall] that by six o'clock next Thursday you *are* [will have been] convinced that your going to the demonstration *were* [was] one of the wisest moves of your life.

Moreover, Mr. Robinson, I am pleased to *inform* you that your firm *have* [has] been chosen to enjoy a particular distinction at next week's demonstration. I am *forbid* [forbidden] to disclose anything further, but I can *forecast* with certainty that you will be *freezed* [frozen] with surprise.

(continued)

known

You have *know* our firm for many years, Mr. Robinson. You have *seed* us become the

seen

spent

leader in our field. You know that during the past three years we have *spended* many mil-

build *build*

lions of dollars to *built* the Starfire and that we will *spend* many millions more to improve

striven

held

it. We have *stroved* to *shaken* off the shackles of conservative thinking that have *hold* the

strived *shake*   *undertaken*

automotive industry back for years. We have *undertook* a difficult task these past three

sitting   *lying*

years. While others were *setting* in their easy chairs, or *laying* around relaxing, our re-

striving

search men were *stroving* for perfection.

wrought   *sprung*

The Starfire has been *brung* into being by this devotion to a concept. It has *sprang*

into being out of the minds and energy of America's top automotive engineers. In the same

way that the jet plane *shrunk* the highways of the air, so shall the Starfire *shrink* the high-

ways on land.

We feel that with the Starfire we have *laid* the groundwork for all new automobiles.

set

We have *setted* new standards in the field of transportation. *Won't* you find out for yourself

all about the all-new Starfire?

Sincerely,

Friday Test on Verbs.

modifies a noun or pronoun .

ADJECTIVES

1. comparison of adjectives   2. adjectives after linking verbs

3. using adjectives   4. articles   5. repeating the article

An old Chinese proverb says: "A picture is worth a thousand words." In writing sentences, you paint pictures with adjectives. An adjective is a word that describes a noun or pronoun. Adjectives give color to an otherwise drab subject.

Compare these two classified advertisements. Which woman will win the job?

1. **WOMAN,** college education, looking for job as secretary in theatrical field.

2. **ATTRACTIVE,** energetic young woman, with college education and experience, desires challenging position as secretary to overburdened executive in theatrical field.

By using adjectives in a colorful, forceful manner, Woman No. 2 has created a positive image of herself in the prospective employer's mind. Remember this example when you apply for your job upon completion of your education. You can paint a positive, colorful portrait of yourself by the skillful use of adjectives.

1. COMPARISON of adjectives

I usually er

The *simple* form of an adjective describes a *single* item or a single *group* of items.

fine book, pretty girls, fast cars, long letters

Adjectives, however, have an added power. They give you the ability to compare one item with others. If you are comparing *two* things, you add *er* to most *simple* adjectives to form what we call the *comparative.*

This is a finer book than that one.

Jane is prettier than Mary.

Sports cars are faster than stock cars.

These letters are longer than those.

Remember, use the *comparative* form only when comparing *two* items.

When you compare *three* or *more* items, add *est* to the simple adjective. We call this form the *superlative*.

This is the finest book I ever read.
Jane is the prettiest of the three girls.
This is the fastest sports car in the world.
This is the longest letter we have received.

Is the difference between the comparative and the superlative clear in your mind? To repeat: You use the *comparative* form only when comparing *two* items. You use the *superlative* when comparing *three or more*.

Why is the following sentence incorrect?

Wrong: He is the taller of the three boys.

If the answer is not obvious to you, you should review this lesson.

Not all adjectives, however, form their comparatives and superlatives by adding *er* and *est*. It would be very awkward for a suitor to whisper in his damsel's ear: **"You are the beautifulest girl in the world."** Long adjectives such as *beautiful* would become tongue-twisters if we were to add *er* or *est*. So, instead of adding *er* or *est* to the end of such an adjective, we simply place the word *more* or *most* in front of it.

To form the *comparative* of long adjectives we say:

more beautiful	**more grateful**
more difficult	**more durable**

To form the *superlative* we say:

most beautiful	**most grateful**
most difficult	**most durable**

Note, however, that the rule about comparatives and superlatives still applies.

More beautiful compares only *two*.
Most beautiful compares *three or more*.

By now you are probably wondering: How do I know when to add *er* or *est* and when to prefix the adjective with *more* or *most*? The best we can offer you is a rule of thumb. To most adjectives of *one* syllable add *er* or *est*. To most adjectives of more than two syllables add *more* or *most*.

Study the list of adjectives below. Note particularly the spelling of the different forms of these adjectives.

Simple	Comparative	Superlative
short	**shorter**	**shortest**
long	**longer**	**longest**
sad	**sadder**	**saddest**
happy	**happier**	**happiest**
lovely	**lovelier**	**loveliest**
lazy	**lazier**	**laziest**
dry	**drier**	**driest**
attractive	**more attractive**	**most attractive**
difficult	**more difficult**	**most difficult**

A few adjectives form their comparatives and superlatives in a different manner. Don't let that worry you. Not only are there very few of these irregular adjectives, but also you are familiar with most of them already.

Simple	Comparative	Superlative
bad	**worse**	**worst**
good	**better**	**best**
little	**less**	**least**
many **much**	**more**	**most**
late	**later** **latter**	**latest** **last**
far	**farther** **further**	**farthest** **furthest**

2. adjectives after LINKING VERBS

Do you remember the linking verbs you learned about in Lesson 4 — verbs that express a *state of being* rather than an action? Linking verbs include all forms of the verb *to be* (for example: *am, was, shall*

108

be, should have been) and also verbs like *feel, seem,* and *appear* when they are used in such a manner that they could be replaced by the verb *is.* (For example: **Candy tastes sweet. Candy is sweet.**)

What is the adjective in this sentence: **We have a heavy schedule.** Right. It is *heavy.* What is the adjective in this sentence: **Our schedule is heavy.** If you again said *heavy,* you are right. Even though *heavy* is separated from the noun it modifies (*schedule*) by the linking verb *is, heavy* is still an adjective and still modifies *schedule.* Pick out the adjectives in these paired examples:

This is a long day.
This day is long.
He stated a forceful argument.
His argument is forceful.

Of course the adjective in the first pair is *long*; in the second pair, it is *forceful.* Remember that an adjective is still an adjective even if it is separated from its noun by a linking verb. You'll learn more about the significance of this in a later lesson.

Turn to Programed Reinforcement S1 through S14

3. USING adjectives

A. Comparison with a Group

What is wrong with this sentence?
Wrong: I am smarter than any person in my class.

I am in my class. I cannot be smarter than myself. I must therefore exclude myself from the rest of the group by the use of the word *other* or the word *else* as follows:

Right: I am smarter than any other person in my class.

Right: I am smarter than anyone else in my class.

Do you see the point? It is subtle, but logical.

B. This and That

These is the plural of *this. Those* is the plural of *that.*
This book is perfect.
These books are perfect.
That mountain is farther than it looks.
Those mountains are farther than they look.

this kind of
that kind of

You may have trouble with these words where the noun that is modified sounds plural but is really singular—nouns such as *kind, sort,* and *type.* Be sure to write *this kind* or *that kind*—NOT, *these kind* or *those kind.* Write *those kinds* or *these kinds* since *kinds* is plural.

those kinds of
these kinds

C. Less and Fewer

Less should be used to refer to items measured in bulk.
Fewer should be used to refer to items counted separately.
Less coal was mined this year.
Fewer men applied for the job than we anticipated.

D. Them

The word *them* is a pronoun, not an adjective. NEVER use *them* to modify a noun or another pronoun.
Right: Those books are mine.
(NOT: Them books are mine.)
Right: That kind is no good.
(NOT: Them kind is no good.)
In Lesson 8 you will learn when to use *them.* For the present learn when *not* to use it.

3 or more *only 2*

E. One Another and Each Other

Do you know what's wrong with this sentence?

Wrong: The two men knew one another.
One another always refers to three or more persons or things. In our sentence there are only two men. So we must use *each other* which is the proper form when there are only two persons or things.

Right: **The two men knew each other.**
Right: **The three men knew one another.**

F. Placement of the Word ONLY

The three sentences below show how we can completely change our meaning by merely moving the word *only*.

Only Bob was accused of lying. This means that no one else was accused.

Bob was only accused of lying. This means that he was accused, but not convicted.

Bob was accused of lying only. He was not accused of anything else.

From these sentences learn this rule of good English. Always place the word *only* as close as possible to the word it modifies so that its meaning is absolutely clear.

Right: **I paid only eight dollars.**
Wrong: **I only paid eight dollars.**
Right: **I filed my application only a day late.**
Wrong: **I only filed my application a day late.**

G. First and Last

When using the word *first* or the word *last* to modify a number, always place it *directly before* the number.

usually in front of a number.

The first eight pages have been typed.
NOT: The eight first pages.
The last six people arrived late.
NOT: The six last people arrived late.

Turn to Programed Reinforcement S15 through S28

110

H. Misrelated Expressions

Sometimes an entire phrase will be used to modify a noun. Here is an example of such an *adjective phrase:* **The desk with the steel legs is sturdy.** The adjective phrase *with the steel legs* describes the noun *desk.* You should always place an adjective phrase as close as possible to the word it modifies. Failure to do so can result in strange sentences like these:

Wrong: **They delivered the piano to the woman with mahogany legs.**
Right: **They delivered the piano with mahogany legs to the woman.**

Wrong: **I bought a fan for my friend that was reconditioned.**
Right: **I bought a fan that was reconditioned for my friend.**

You have already met the dangling participle that leads to a similar problem:

Wrong: **Serving lunch, a banana peel tripped the waitress.**
Right: **Serving lunch, the waitress tripped on a banana peel.**

distance *(greater depth)*

I. Farther — Further; Farthest — Furthest

Sometimes these forms of the adjective *far* are used incorrectly. The words *farther* and *farthest* should be used when an actual physical distance is thought of. An easy way to remember is to think of the *a* in *space* and the *a* in *farther* and *farthest.*

Our car will travel farther on less gas.
Alaska is the farthest state from Florida.

Use *further* and *furthest* in all other situations.

Study this chapter further.
If we delve further, we will find the solution.

J. Later and Latter

Later is the comparative form of the adjective *late* and refers to time.

I shall be there later.

The speech was given later than I had expected.

Latter means the second of two; it is usually used as the opposite of *former*, which means the first of two.

The latter part of the book is the more interesting.

Jones and Smith were both successful — the former through luck; the latter through hard work.

K. Capitalizing Proper Adjectives

Proper adjectives are adjectives that are derived from proper nouns — the names of specific people, places, or things. Words like *American, Asiatic,* and *Victorian* are capitalized just like the proper nouns from which they come.

Some proper adjectives, however, are no longer thought of in connection with the original proper noun. Here are a few of such adjectives that are not capitalized: *morocco binding, oriental rug, jersey wool.*

An interesting area is the study of trademarks that have become so common in everyday use that they have passed into the public domain and have lost their status as trademarks — and thereby their capital letters. Here are just a few examples: *aspirin, escalator, cellophane, shredded wheat, thermos bottle.* There are hundreds of others.

L. Unique

This jewel is unique. Since *unique* means *one of a kind,* nothing can be *more unique* or *most unique. Unique* is already a superlative; it cannot be compared.

M. Compound Adjectives

You have already met the word *compound* which means the uniting of two or more elements. You have studied compound subjects, compound predicates, compound sentences, and compound nouns. Now meet the *compound adjective;* for example: *well bred, up to date, well known, high grade.* The question is: When are compound adjectives hyphenated and when aren't they? Do you write *up-to-date* or *up to date?* The answer is simplicity itself. Compound adjectives are generally hyphenated when they immediately *precede* the noun they describe; they are usually not hyphenated when they come *after* the noun. Look at these examples:

Our up-to-date styles can't be surpassed.
Our styles are known to be up to date.
We sell first-class products.
The products we sell are first class.
A high-grade executive is hard to find.
We are looking for an executive who is high grade.

Compound adjectives are often formed by joining a numeral with words of measure like *inch, foot, mile, pound, month, quart.* Your basic rule still pertains:

a three-foot ruler	**a ruler three feet long**
a five-mile walk	**a walk of five miles**
a four-year period	**a period of four years**

Note that in the hyphenated adjectives that precede the noun the unit of measure is always singular: **A five-pound cake.** NOT: **A five-pounds cake.**

There are a few compound adjectives that are *always* hyphenated regardless of their position in a sentence.

A hyphen is used in all compound adjectives formed with *self.*

He is a self-made man.
This truth is self-evident.

[handwritten: alway hyphened.]
[handwritten: self - 9: self-made]
[handwritten: anti -]
[handwritten: pro -]
[handwritten: ex -]

A hyphen should be used in numerical adjectives from twenty-one through ninety-nine.

We celebrated our twenty-fifth anniversary.
He was elected on the thirty-second count.
This attempt was his one hundred and twenty-ninth.

[handwritten: definate - the]
[handwritten: indefinate - an, a.]

4. ARTICLES

There are three words that we call *articles* — **a, an, the.** You've used these words all your life, so you should have little trouble with them.

Whether to use *a* or *an* depends upon the sound of the next word. When the next word begins with a *consonant* sound, you use *a*. A consonant sound is the sound of any letter in the alphabet except *a, e, i, o, u.*

a boy	**a happy boy**
a man	**a young man**

Note that you say: *a happy boy.* On the other hand you say: *an honest man.* Why? Because in the word *honest*, the *h* is silent. Since the word *honest* does not begin with a consonant *sound*, use *an*.

an hour	**a house**
an honor	**a hotel**

You use **an** wherever a word begins with a *vowel* sound. The vowels are **a, e, i, o, u.**

an apple	**an incident**
an event	**an orange**
an umbrella	

Note that while you should say *an umbrella*, you also say *a university.* Why? Because the *u* in *university* sounds like the *y* in *you.* Remember, it is the *sound* that counts, not the spelling.

a union	**an ulcer**
a usurer	**an undertaking**

5. REPEATING the article

Occasionally, you will be faced with a problem of whether to repeat the article when you are listing a series of things. For example:

The red and (the) white coats are on sale.
Should you use the extra *the*? This depends upon what you mean. If each coat is part white and part red, then omit the extra *the*: **The red and white coats are on sale.** For the sake of clarity, you might better use hyphens here to express your meaning: **The red-and-white coats are on sale.** If, however, there are two types of coats — one all white and the other all red — then add the extra *the*: **The red and the white coats are on sale.**
Do you see this subtle distinction?

The President and the Chairman arrived. (Two men.)

The President and Chairman arrived. (One man holding both positions.)

The steel and the plastic cabinets are in place. (Some cabinets are all steel; some, all plastic.)

The steel and plastic cabinets are in place. (Cabinets of part steel and part plastic.)

Turn to Programed Reinforcement S29 through S52

		S1	An adjective is a word that describes a _____.
R1	noun ? pronoun	**S2**	Circle one: Adjectives as a rule make sentences more A. colorful; B. brief; C. grammatical.
R2	A. colorful	**S3**	Circle three adjectives in this sentence: **A red tie and green socks do not go with conservative clothing.**
R3	**red; green; conservative**	**S4**	Circle three adjectives in this sentence: **The young applicant gave five answers to the revised questionnaire.**
R4	**young; five; revised**	**S5**	**Smiling prettily, she curtsied. Prettily is not an adjective because the word it modifies (smiling) is not a n ___ ___ ___; it is a ___ ___ ___ ___.**
R5	noun; verb	**S6**	Adjectives may be used to compare one item with others. When we compare two things, we use the c ___ ___ ___ ___ ___ ___ ___ ___ ___ form.
R6	comparative	**S7**	The comparative form of an adjective generally adds the letters _____ to the simple form.
R7	er	**S8**	Circle the simple adjective and underline the comparative adjective: **The modernized factory is busier than it has been in years.**
R8	simple adjective — **modernized;** comparative — **busier**	**S9**	The superlative form of the adjective generally ends with the letters ___ ___ ___.
R9	est	**S10**	Circle two superlative form adjectives in this sentence: **John is the strongest and fastest boy in the warehouse crew.**
R10	**strongest; fastest**	**S11**	Some adjectives of more than one syllable would sound awkward with the addition of **er** for the comparative or **est** for the superlative form. The word **beautiful** is compared by having the word m ___ ___ ___ precede it in the comparative form and m ___ ___ ___ in the superlative form.
R11	more; most		

S12
Circle any comparative forms; underline any superlatives: **The longest runway today is too short for the larger, more powerful jets planned for the future.**

R12
comparatives —
larger; more powerful;
superlative —
longest

S13
Write the comparative and superlative of the following simple adjectives:
lovely _____ _____
attractive _____ _____
bad _____ _____

R13
lovely, lovelier, loveliest;
attractive, more attractive,
most attractive;
bad, worse, worst

S14
Circle the adjectives in these two sentences: **Here is a solid desk. This desk is solid.** In the second example, **solid** is still an adjective even though it is separated from its noun by a l__ __ __ __ __ __ verb.

R14
solid; solid; linking

● TURN TO Exercise 22

S15
In the sentence **He is more personable than any executive,** what word has been incorrectly omitted before the word **executive?** Answer: _____.

R15
other

S16
The word **kind** or **type** when preceded by **this** or **that** is perfectly correct. When we use the plural **kinds** or **types,** we must change **this** to _____ and **that** to _____.

R16
these; those

S17
Circle the incorrect adjective in this sentence. **I like these kind of scissors.**

R17
these

S18
Circle the incorrect adjective in this sentence. **Let us stock those type of stencils.**

R18
those

S19
Less and **fewer** are adjectives that are sometimes confused. We say **less money** but **fewer checks.** We use **less** when items are not counted separately; we use **fewer** when items can be counted s__ __ __ __ __ __ __ __ y.

R19
separately

S20
Circle the correct sentence:
A. Fewer receptionists are available than before.
B. Less typists are unemployed today.

R20
A.

S21
This sentence contains a flagrant error where a pronoun is used instead of an adjective. Circle the improper word. **Them notes were taken at the last conference.** The proper word is _____.

R21
them;
these or those

	S22 Rewrite this sentence correctly: **Them kind is not any good.**
R22 **That** kind (or **This** kind)	**S23** **Each other** refers to _____ people or things; **one another** refers to _____ or more.
R23 two; three	**S24** Misplaced modifiers can change the meaning of a sentence. In the sentence **Only Bob worked on Saturday,** the word **only** refers to the noun _____.
R24 Bob	**S25** In the sentence **Bob only worked on Saturday,** the word **only** refers to the verb _____.
R25 worked	**S26** In the sentence **Bob worked only on Saturday,** circle the word that **only** refers to?
R26 Saturday	**S27** Circle the misplaced adjective: **The three last days have been trying.**
R27 last	**S28** Circle the misplaced adjective: **The six first people at the concert were relatives.** What word should this adjective precede? _____
R28 **first** should precede **six.** • TURN TO Exercises 23 and 24	**S29** A group of words describing a noun is called an adjective phrase. Such a phrase should be placed next to the noun it describes. Circle the group of words that is misplaced: **The cabinet belongs to the housewife with the formica top.** Underline the word this circled phrase should follow.
R29 with the formica top should follow **cabinet**	**S30** Do the same in this sentence: **I gave the pen to the typist with the ball point.**
R30 with the ball point should follow **pen**	**S31** **Farther** and **further** are adjectives sometimes confused. The **a** in **space** is related to the **a** in f __ __ __ __ __ __.
R31 farther	**S32** Circle the correct answer: **He threw the ball the (farthest, furthest).**
R32 farthest	**S33** Circle the correct answer: **I want no (farther, further) questions.**
R33 further	

S34 Later and latter are adjectives sometimes confused. Remember that later refers to t _____ , and latter refers to p _____ tion.

R34 time; position

S35 Circle the correct answer: **I shall see you (later, latter).**

R35 later

S36 Latter is the second of two as opposed to f _____ which is the first of two. Circle the correct answer: **The former answer is wrong; the (latter, later) is correct.**

R36 former; latter

S37 Proper adjectives are derived from proper names. When they are thought of in connection with the original proper name they are (capitalized, not capitalized).

R37 capitalized

S38 Change the capitalization of proper adjectives where necessary: **The american soccer team wore Jersey wool sweaters.**

R38 American; jersey

S39 Do the same with this sentence: **The victorian age was marked by ornateness like Oriental designs tooled on Moroccan leather.**

R39 Victorian; oriental; moroccan

S40 **This is the most unique plan.** Since **unique** means **one and only,** circle the incorrect word in the sentence.

R40 most

S41 A compound adjective like **well made** or **high grade** is usually hyphenated when it comes (before, after) the noun modified.

R41 before

S42 Circle the compound adjective in this sentence. **This account is up to date.** It (is, is not) hyphenated because it comes (before, after) its noun.

R42 up to date; is not; after

S43 Circle the compound adjective in this sentence. **He has an up-to-date showroom.** It is hyhenated because it comes _____ its noun.

R43 up-to-date; before

S44 A numerical compound adjective from **twenty-first** to **ninety-ninth** is always hyphenated when spelled out. Circle the correct answer: **This anniversary is his (twenty fifth, twenty-fifth).**

R44 twenty-fifth

S45 Compound adjectives involving the word **self** — for example, **self-evident** — are (always, sometimes, never) hyphenated.

R45 always

R46
half-inch ruler;
three-mile run;
four-pound fish

R47
vowel

R48
vowel; consonant

R49
a unique; a usual;
an unusual; an error;
an honest

R50
sound

R51
two

R52
noun; comparative;
superlative; two

● TURN TO
Exercises 25, 26, and Review

S46 Here are compound adjectives combining a numeral with words like **inch, mile, foot.** Insert hyphens where necessary: **half inch ruler; three mile run; fish of four pounds; four pound fish.**

S47 The article **an** rather than **a** is used in **an antique** because **antique** begins with a v __ __ __ __ sound.

S48 You should write **an understatement** because the **u** has a v _____ sound. You write **a union** because here the **u** has a c __ __ __ __ __ __ __ __ sound.

S49 Insert **a** or **an:** _____ unique problem: _____ usual offer; _____ unusual offer; _____ error; _____ honest mistake.

S50 You should write **an honor** because **honor** begins with the s __ __ __ __ of a vowel.

S51 The article **the** repeated in the sentence **The President and the Treasurer spoke,** means that (one, two) people are involved.

S52 As a review, an adjective modifies a n __ __ __ __. It may be compared by changing the simple form to the c __ __ __ __ __ __ __ __ __ __ when comparing two; to the _____ when comparing more than __ __ __.

117

SCORE

A_____

EXERCISE 22   Recognizing Adjectives

A. This problem deals with recognizing adjectives. Underline the adjective in each of the following sentences with one line. Then, underline the word each adjective modifies with two lines.

SCORING: DEDUCT 5 POINTS FOR EACH ERROR.

1. He picked up the heavy case.
2. She prepared a light supper.
3. The colored lights were dimmed.
4. It was a very efficient system.
5. We have complete records.
6. Our latest records show a deficit.
7. We sent an order for farm machinery.
8. He slowly walked to his first class.
9. These are first-class goods.
10. Here is our new catalogue.
11. Send me your final approval.
12. Where is my brown hat?
13. Forgive my late reply.
14. The table has a smooth finish.
15. We went horseback riding.
16. It's a very smooth-riding car.
17. This is an easy problem.
18. This problem is easy.
19. I am hungry.
20. He feels hungry.

SCORE

B_____

EXERCISE 22   Degrees of Adjectives

B. This problem deals with the choice of the comparative or the superlative adjective. In the space provided, write the proper form of the adjective in parentheses. Remember, use the comparative when comparing two; use the superlative when comparing three or more.

SCORING: DEDUCT 10 POINTS FOR EACH ERROR.

1. Although Mr. Smith and Mr. Jones are bright, Mr. Roberts is the (wise).   1. _wisest_
2. Which of this pair has the (bright) colors?   2. _brighter_
3. Though our Raleigh plant is large, the Durham plant is (large).   3. _larger_
4. New York is the (exciting) of the two cities.   4. _more exciting_
5. New York is the (exciting) city in the world.   5. _most exciting_
6. She is the (tall) girl in the whole office.   6. _tallest_
7. The left sleeve is (long) than the right.   7. _longer_
8. Of all our forty-three offices, the (large) is in Los Angeles.   8. _largest_
9. Test this one, then that one, and choose the (good).   9. _better_
10. Which of the twins is the (pretty)?   10. _prettier_

EXERCISE 22   Degrees of Adjectives

C. This problem deals with the three forms an adjective may take—simple, comparative, and superlative. On each line of the following table is written one of the three adjective forms. Fill in the other two forms. Pay special attention to proper spelling. Nothing less than perfect spelling is acceptable.

SCORING: DEDUCT 5 POINTS FOR EACH ERROR.

	Simple	Comparative	Superlative
1.	pretty	prettier	prettiest
2.	busy	busier	busiest
3.	familiar	more familiar	most familiar
4.	many, much	more	most
5.	little	less	least
6.	late	later	last
7.	hot	hotter	hottest
8.	good	better	best
9.	dark	farther	farthest
10.	sad	sadder	saddest
11.	difficult	more difficult	most difficult
12.	bad	worse	worst
13.	unusual	more unusual	most unusual
14.	lovely	lovelier	loveliest
15.	friendly	friendlier	friendliest
16.	important	more important	most important
17.	afraid	more afraid	most afraid
18.	wealthy	wealthier	wealthiest
19.	happy	happier	happiest
20.	dry	drier	driest

EXERCISE 23 | Comparison with a Group

A. This problem deals with the comparison of a member of a group with the rest of the group. Of the following ten sentences, two are correct and eight are incorrect. If the sentence is incorrect, indicate the necessary corrections.

SCORING: DEDUCT 10 POINTS FOR EACH ERROR.

1. My son is smaller than any boy in his class. *the smallest / other*

2. John is bigger, smarter, and more handsome than any of his classmates. *biggest smartest, most hansome*

3. Mr. Smith is shrewder than anyone in his department. *the shrewdest*

4. Who is fairer than any girl in her group? *the fairest*

5. Mr. Jones is more popular than anyone. *most popular*

6. Henry is better than any child in his school. *best / other*

7. Of all the tenants, Mr. Smith is least objectionable.

8. He is taller than any pupil in his class. *tallest*

9. More level-headed than any man in his company, John was promoted. *The most level - headed*

10. This is the best and most efficient of any other system used today.

NAME   CLASS   DATE

EXERCISE 23   This and That

B. This problem deals with the proper use of this and that, these and those. In the space provided next to each sentence, write the proper word. Remember, this and that are singular; these and those are plural.

SCORING: DEDUCT 10 POINTS FOR EACH ERROR.

1. (This) (These) forms of designs are very effective.   1. _These_
2. (That) (Those) make of cars sells very well.   2. _That_
3. Our firm makes (this) (these) style of trousers.   3. _this_
4. (That) (Those) kind of book is for adults.   4. _That_
5. Where do you buy (this) (these) type of shoes?   5. _this_
6. I don't associate with (that) (those) kind of people.   6. _that_
7. I don't associate with (that) (those) people.   7. _those_
8. (This) (These) type of table is very sturdy.   8. _this_
9. Do you like (that) (those) kind of pants?   9. _that_
10. Would you call (this) (these) forms the best for us?   10. _these_

EXERCISE 23   Less and Fewer

C. This problem deals with the proper use of less and fewer. In the space provided, write the correct word, either less or fewer. Remember, use less to refer to quantities measured in bulk; use fewer to refer to items counted separately.

SCORING: DEDUCT 10 POINTS FOR EACH ERROR.

1. They delivered (less) (fewer) coal than we had ordered.   1. _less_
2. They delivered (less) (fewer) tons of coal than we had ordered.   2. _fewer_
3. There were (less) (fewer) than ten customers today.   3. _fewer_
4. We can do the same amount of work with (less) (fewer) secretaries.   4. _fewer_
5. Your firm has sent (less) (fewer) orders than anticipated.   5. _fewer_
6. There is (less) (fewer) unemployment than anticipated.   6. _less_
7. This air conditioner uses (less) (fewer) electricity than any other model.   7. _less_
8. This air conditioner uses (less) (fewer) kilowatts of electricity than any other model.   8. _fewer_
9. This typewriter weighs (less) (fewer) than twenty pounds.   9. _less_
10. (Less) (Fewer) than ten people showed up.   10. _fewer_

NAME   CLASS   DATE

EXERCISE 24   Each Other—One Another

A. This problem deals with the proper use of each other and one another. In the space provided, write the correct expression. Remember, each other refers to two; one another refers to three or more.

SCORING: DEDUCT 20 POINTS FOR EACH ERROR.

1. The two men spoke to (each other) (one another).
2. The committee members spoke to (each other) (one another) until it was time to convene.
3. We are acquainted with (each other) (one another), he and I.
4. The men in the mob prodded (each other) (one another) to greater violence.
5. The two airmen helped (each other) (one another) survive in the jungle.

1. *each other*
2. *one another*
3. *each other*
4. *one another*
5. *each other*

NAME   CLASS   DATE

EXERCISE 24   Only

B. This problem deals with placement of the word only. In each of the following sentences, only is improperly placed. Indicate the proper placement of the word only. Remember, only should be placed directly before the word it modifies.

SCORING: DEDUCT 10 POINTS FOR EACH ERROR.

1. The President only signed the first bill. *only*

2. He only saw *only* three familiar faces.

3. I only met him *only* twice.

4. We only filed our applications *only* one day late.

5. This hat only cost three dollars.

6. He only leaves early *only* on Fridays.

(continued)

7. He was only convicted of a misdemeanor.

8. He only promotes *only* the younger, alert employees.

9. We have only seen him *only* once.

10. It only is eleven o'clock. *only*

SCORE

C_____

| EXERCISE 24 | First and Last |

C. This problem deals with the proper placement of the words **first** and **last**. In only one of the following five sentences is the word **first** or **last** properly placed. Write **C** in front of that sentence. Indicate the necessary changes to correct the other sentences. Remember, place the word **first** or **last** directly in front of the number it modifies.

SCORING: DEDUCT 20 POINTS FOR EACH ERROR.

1. We enjoyed the two *last* last weeks.

2. I don't understand the *first* eight first pages.

3. We haven't heard from him for the last three days. ✓

4. We have read all but the *last* eight last pages.

5. Only the *first* six first people were admitted.

EXERCISE 25 — Placement of Modifiers

A. This problem deals with the proper placement of modifiers. Each of the sentences below is incorrect because of a misplaced modifier. Rewrite these sentences correctly in the space provided. Remember, place the modifier as close as possible to the word it modifies.

SCORING: DEDUCT 12 POINTS FOR EACH ERROR.

1. People cannot fail to notice vast changes in business methods who are in touch with business offices.

   People who are in touch with business offices, cannot fail to notice vast changes in business.

2. We saw the new building walking down East Shore Drive.

   Walking down East Shore Drive we saw the new building.

3. The soldier saddled his horse who was wearing a new uniform.

   The soldier, who was wearing a new uniform, saddled his horse.

4. Take the book to the man with the beautiful leather binding.

   Take the book, with the beautiful leather binding to the man.

5. The dog ran toward his master wagging his tail.

   The dog, wagging his tail ran toward his master.

6. Take the table to the shop with its four legs to be mended.

   Take the table, with its four legs to be mended, to the shop.

7. He watched the parade pass by standing at the corner.

   While standing at the corner he watched the parade pass by.

8. The men took the chair to the woman with all four legs painted black.

   The men took the chair with all four legs painted black, to the woman.

SCORE

B_____

EXERCISE 25   Farther and Later

B. This problem deals with the proper use of the adjectives farther-further and later-latter. Remember that farther refers to physical space, and that later is used only when time is involved. In the space provided, fill in the proper word.

SCORING: DEDUCT 12 POINTS FOR EACH ERROR.

1. He threw the ball (farther, further) than I.
2. He sat in the chair (farthest, furthest) from the chairman.
3. I will go to the (farthest, furthest) place in the world for you.
4. (Further, farther) than that, I cannot go in compromising with you.
5. The (later, latter) we meet tonight, the less time we will have.
6. The (later, latter) part of the sermon contained some powerful points.
7. The former speaker introduced the guest; the (later, latter) spoke at length.
8. The two men spoke. The former said: "It is (later, latter) than you think."

1. _farther_
2. _farthest_
3. _farthest_
4. _Further_
5. _later_
6. _latter_
7. _latter_
8. _later_

SCORE

C_____

EXERCISE 25   Capitalizing and Hyphenating

C. This problem deals with capitalizing and hyphenating adjectives. Remember that most adjectives derived from proper nouns are capitalized. Compound adjectives have hyphens if they come before the nouns they modify. In the space provided, fill in the proper word.

SCORING: DEDUCT 10 POINTS FOR EACH ERROR.

1. The (American, american) Indian created (well-made, well made) tools.
2. The (Victorian, victorian) age occurred in the '80's.
3. A (Persian, persian) rug may be very valuable.
4. He heard (Martial, martial) music on the radio.
5. He was a (well-intentioned, well intentioned) worker who made mistakes.
6. The fact that he cannot perform the work is (self-evident, self evident).
7. A (first-rate, first rate) mechanic is difficult to get.
8. The battalion put up a (last-ditch, last ditch) effort.
9. This pie is obviously (home made, home-made).
10. In this office we need workers who are (well-disciplined, well disciplined).

1. _American_
2. _Victorian_
3. _Persian_
4. _martial_
5. _well-intentioned_
6. _self-evident_
7. _first-rate_
8. _last-ditch_
9. _home made_
10. _well disciplined_

SCORE

A_____

EXERCISE 26   Using Articles

A. This problem deals with choosing a or an. In the spaces provided, write either a or an, which-ever is correct.

SCORING: DEDUCT 20 POINTS FOR EACH ERROR.

1. _a_ man wearing _an_ unusual jacket left _a_ package.

2. _a_ humorist is _a_ human being with _a_ peculiar sense of humor.

3. _An_ understanding of all operations in our plant is _a_ necessity for _a_ foreman.

4. _An_ hour before dawn is _an_ inhuman hour for _a_ human being to be awakened.

5. _a_ union leader should be _an_ honest man, for to lead _a_ union is _an_ under-taking of great responsibility.

SCORE

B_____

EXERCISE 26   Repeating the Article

B. This problem deals with repeating the article. Indicate any necessary corrections.

SCORING: DEDUCT 20 POINTS FOR EACH ERROR.

the
1. The secretary and vice-president met at noon.

2. He was elected to be both the vice-president and ~~the~~ secretary.

3. The car has a blue and ~~a~~ white finish.

an
4. We have in stock two cabinets, a chromium and aluminum one.

5. She wore a red and ~~a~~ green sweater.

NAME   CLASS   DATE

EXERCISE REVIEW 5   Adjectives

The letter below includes many intentional errors. Cross out all errors and indicate the necessary changes in the space above them.

SCORING: DEDUCT 5 POINTS FOR EACH ERROR.

Dear Mr. White:

Have you heard about our sale on phonograph records? This sale is ~~the most~~ excitinger *more* and spectacularer ~~most~~ *more* than any sale in *other* this city's history.

~~Only~~ during the two first weeks *only* we have sold no less than 10,000 records in each of our two stores. You might be interested to know that the South Street store has sold the ~~greatest~~ number of records even though the store is *greater* ~~furthest~~ from the heart of town. This is a extremely *farther* unusual development.

We would be very grateful if you would visit our store. You can't miss it, walking down Sixth Avenue toward Elm. Mr. Johnson, our manager, and his assistant, Mr. Roberts, are very ~~anxious~~ to see you. I'm sure you three *eager* will enjoy chatting with ~~each~~ other. *one an*

Perhaps you will explain to these men why they have ~~least~~ sales than the South Street store. We want you to *less fewer* give them a honest opinion. See if you can help them catch up and surpass the South Street store during the three *last* ~~last~~ weeks of the sale.

Sincerely,

adverbs - modify adjectives, verbs or adverbs.

they tell when,
how,
how much (many)
where.

adverbs - adjective + ly.

LESSON 6

ADVERBS

1. forming adverbs

2. choosing between adverbs and adjectives

3. using adverbs

You already know what words we use to give color to nouns or pronouns. That's right, *adjectives!* Now let's discuss those words that we use to give color to verbs — words we call *adverbs.* Adverbs are jacks-of-all-trades. Not only do they modify verbs, they also can modify adjectives and they can even modify other adverbs.

The ship sailed swiftly. The adverb **swiftly** modifies the verb **sailed.**

Broadway is an extremely wide street. The adverb **extremely** modifies the adjective **wide.**

The old man walked very slowly. The adverb **very** modifies the adverb **slowly.**

An *adverb* is a word that tells you *how, when, where,* or *how much.*

The book was printed carefully. Printed *how?* **Carefully.**

The order was shipped promptly. Shipped *when?* **Promptly.**

The officials came here. Came *where?* **Here.**

They were very pleased. Pleased *how much?* **Very.**

1. FORMING adverbs

You form most adverbs from adjectives by merely adding *ly*:

Adjective	Adverb
swift	swiftly
careful	carefully
familiar	familiarly
sole	solely

In spelling, remember that the *ly* adverb ending is simply attached to the existing word in most cases. Adjectives that end with *e* or *al* fall into the same category — just attach the *ly.*

separate + ly = separately

scarce + ly = scarcely

authoritative + ly = authoritatively

accidental + ly = accidentally

cordial + ly = cordially

official + ly = officially

129

adverb — action verb
ajective — linking

When the adjective ends in *y*, to form the adverb change the *y* to *i* and add *ly*.

Adjective	Adverb
busy	busily
happy	happily
satisfactory	satisfactorily
temporary	temporarily

When the adjective ends in *able* or in *ible*, to form the adverb drop the final *e* and add *y*.

Adjective	Adverb
noticeable	noticeably
considerable	considerably
forcible	forcibly
horrible	horribly

Note the change in spelling when we transform these adjectives into adverbs.

Adjective	Adverb
due	duly
true	truly
whole	wholly

Turn to Programed Reinforcement S1 through S13

2. CHOOSING between adverbs and adjectives

On the job you will have to choose between using an adjective or an adverb in many sentences. Will you know which to use? For example: **The situation looks (bad) (badly).** Which is correct? By the time you finish this lesson, you will know how to solve such problems easily.

You learned in the chapter on verbs that there are two types of verbs — *action* verbs and *linking* verbs. If you don't know the distinction between them right now — and

know it well — do not read further in this lesson. The whole problem of when to use adverbs and when to use adjectives hinges on the distinction between action and linking verbs. STOP! Review Lesson 4 right now if this distinction is not crystal clear in your mind.

The rule is very simple:

Use an *adverb* to modify an *action* verb.
Use an *adjective* after a *linking* verb.

The fire burned fiercely. *Burned* is an *action* verb; therefore, we used the *adverb* *fiercely*.

The material was sent promptly. *Sent* is an *action* verb; therefore, we use the *adverb* *promptly*.

The tiger attacked fiercely. *Attacked* is an *action* verb; therefore, we use the *adverb* *fiercely*.

The fierce tiger attacked. Here *fierce* describes the noun *tiger;* it is an adjective. What about this sentence: **The tiger is fierce.** In the lesson on adjectives you learned that *fierce* is still an adjective even though it is separated from its noun by a linking verb. **The tiger is fierce** is the same as saying **the fierce tiger.**

The same is true in this sentence: **The tiger looks fierce.** You know that *looks* in this sentence is a *linking* verb. *Looks* could be replaced by *is*: **The tiger looks (is) fierce.** So again we use the adjective *fierce* because it follows a linking verb and really describes the subject-noun *tiger* and not the verb *looks*.

What about this sentence: **He looked (fierce, fiercely) for the missing wallet.** Is *looked*, as used here, an action or a linking verb? Could it be replaced by *was*? No. Therefore, *looked* is an action verb (meaning *searched*) and requires the adverb *fiercely*: **He looked fiercely for the missing wallet.**

Linking verbs take adjectives.
Action verbs take adverbs.

Good – adjective
well – adverb

Earlier in this lesson, we gave as an example the problem-sentence: **The situation looks (bad) (badly).** You should be able to solve this easily now. *Looks,* as used here, is a *linking* verb; therefore, we use the adjective *bad*: **The situation looks bad.**

Here is a similar sentence: **The boy feels (bad) (badly).** It is conceivable that either word may be used if you stretch your imagination. How? If the boy has burned his fingers and they have become insensitive, you could say *The boy feels badly (with his fingers).* The adverb *badly* is then used to describe the *action* verb *feels.* Hardly likely, but possible!

For our purposes, however, *feels* in this sentence is a linking verb that really means *is.* **The boy feels** (*is*) **bad** (*unhappy*). Remember, therefore, to say **I feel bad** if you want to describe your emotional or physical condition – NOT: **I feel badly.**

Turn to Programed Reinforcement S14 through S19

adjective meaning *healthy.* In such a case, since *well* is an *adjective,* it can be used after a *linking* verb. **He is well** (*healthy*). **He feels well** (*healthy*). **He looks well** (*healthy*).

BUT remember: **The flower smells good. He works well.**

B. Most and Almost *nearly.*

(Most, Almost) all the orders were sent. A simple test to determine whether to use *most* or *almost* is to substitute the word *nearly.* If *nearly* fits, then you know that *almost* is proper. **Nearly all the orders were sent.** Therefore: **Almost all the orders were sent.**

In the following sentence it is obvious that *nearly* would not fit, so *most* is proper: **Who had the most errors?**

BUT: **It was almost too late to catch the train.** The same as: **It was nearly too late . . . .**

---

3. USING adverbs

A. Good and Well *adjective adverb*

Dinner tasted (good) (well). Good is an adjective. *Well* is usually an adverb. Since *tasted* is a *linking* verb, we use the adjective *good.* **Dinner tasted good.** Note again that *tasted* really means *was*: **Dinner was good** or **a good dinner.** Simple, isn't it?

He performed (good) (well). *Performed* is an *action* verb; therefore, we use the adverb *well.* **He performed well.** The only exception to this rule occurs when *well* is used as an

---

C. Double Negatives

Time and again you have heard people say that two negatives make a positive. For our purposes, two negatives generally make poor English; so you must avoid double negatives. What is a double negative? Here is a common example:

Wrong: **They don't know nothing.**

This sentence contains two negative words, *don't* and *nothing.* Each of these negatives destroys the other. By eliminating either one of them we get a correct sentence:

Right: **They know nothing.**

Right: **They don't know anything.**

except when well means healthy.

131

Real - adjective
very - adverb

Remember: Avoid double negatives.

1. Right: **He didn't say anything.**

Right: **He said nothing.**

Wrong: He didn't say nothing.

2. Right: **It was nothing.**

Right: **It wasn't anything.**

Wrong: It wasn't nothing.

You may have a little more difficulty with words that don't look negative but really are—words such as *scarcely, hardly, never, neither, but.* They will cause you no trouble if you remember that these words are *negative* in themselves. Never add the word *not* to them.

1. We can scarcely see you in this fog. NOT: We *can't* scarcely see you . . . .

2. We could hardly have decided otherwise. NOT: We *couldn't* hardly . . . .

3. It could never happen here. NOT: It *couldn't* never happen here.

4. It was neither of them. NOT: It *wasn't* neither of them.

5. I understand all but one of them. NOT: I *don't* understand all but one . . . . If you really mean what is said in the latter sentence, you'd be clearer to say **I understand only one of them.** Do you see why this means the same thing?

adjective
quite
adverb
extremely
genuine

D. Real and Very

I am (real) (very) pleased. *Real* is an adjective that means *genuine. Very* is an adverb that means *extremely.* When faced with a choice of *real* or *very*, substitute *genuine* or *extremely.* If *genuine* fits, *real* is correct. If *extremely* fits, *very* is *correct.*

Our problem-sentence reads properly if we insert *extremely*: **I am extremely pleased.** Therefore, use *very*: **I am very pleased.** (NOT: *I am real pleased.*)

One further point about the use of the adverb *very.* It is considered less-than-perfect English to have *very* modify a verb *directly. Very* is a peculiar adverb that should modify only another adverb or an adjective. So for our problem-sentence to be perfectly correct, it should read: **I am very much pleased.** Similarly: **I am very much interested** is better than **I am very interested; I am very well satisfied** is better than **I am very satisfied.**

Returning to the use of *real* or *very*, let's substitute *genuine* or *extremely* to check a few other sentences:

Right: **It gives me real (genuine) pleasure to introduce the next speaker.**

Right: **We are very (extremely) well pleased with the outcome.**

Right: **It was a real (genuine) diamond.**

Right: **It was a very (extremely) wonderful movie.**

E. Comparison of Adverbs

Adverbs may be compared, just like adjectives. One- or two-syllable words add *er* and *est*: *soon, sooner, soonest; early, earlier, earliest.* Adverbs that are longer are usually formed by using the words *more* and *most*: *happily, more happily, most happily; sincerely, more sincerely, most sincerely.* Remember to use the *comparative* form when comparing *two;* use the *superlative* only when comparing *three or more.* **I will arrive earlier than he. Of them all, I arrived earliest.** How about this sentence: **I arrived earlier than any of them.** Why do we use the comparative when *them* tells us that there are at least two others? You are right (we hope). We use *earlier* because it compares you with *any* of *them*, and you know from Lesson 1 that *any* is always singular — it means *any one.*

F. Unnecessary Adverbs

Sometimes the adverbial meaning of *how, when, where,* or *how much* is expressed in other words in the sentence. In that case do not use the adverb unnecessarily. In the following sentences, why is each word in parentheses redundant and therefore unnecessary?

Recopy this page *(over)*.
I shall repeat the question *(again)*.
He has returned *(back)* **from Europe.**
They must co-operate *(together)* **to be a perfect pair.**
Erase this *(out)*.

G. Compound Words Confused With Adverbs

Sometimes you may be confused between compound expressions, usually beginning with **all**, that resemble adverbs, and the adverbs themselves. If you examine these expressions, however, you will see that the meanings are quite different.

all together (meaning *many combined*)
altogether (meaning *completely*)
They worked all together until they were altogether satisfied with the results.

all ways (meaning *every manner*)
always (meaning *forever*)
Always remember that there are all ways of reaching happiness.

all ready (meaning *completely prepared*)
already (meaning *previously*)
The employees were all ready at five o'clock, though some had already punched out.

Note: **All right** is always written as two words, never as one word. There is no such word as *alright* just as there is no such word as *alwrong*.
Correct: **all right all wrong**

H. Sure and Surely *certainly*

Don't use the *adjective* **sure,** which means *confident* or *certain,* when you want to say *certainly* or *undoubtedly.* In that case you must use the *adverb* **surely.**

He (sure, surely) did an unusually effective job! We must use **surely** since we mean *certainly.*

(Sure, Surely) I'll go with you. (**Surely,** meaning *certainly.*)

BUT: **He is quite sure of himself.** (Confident)

Turn to Programed Reinforcement S20 through S44

S1

Adjectives modify (describe) nouns; adverbs modify not only v _ _ _ _ but also adj _ _ _ _ _ _ _ and other ad _ _ _ _ .

R1 verbs; adjectives; adverbs

S2

The girl typed slowly. The adverb **slowly** modifies the word _____ which is a _____ .

R2 **typed;** verb

S3

This is a very efficient operation. The adverb **very** modifies the word _____ which is an _____ .

R3 **efficient;** adjective

S4

He filed the paper quite carelessly. Quite is an adverb that modifies the word _____ which is a(n) _____ .

R4 **carelessly;** adverb

S5

An adverb usually answers the questions **how, when, where, how much.**

True ☐   False ☐

R5 True

S6

Most adverbs are formed by adding _ _ to the adjective.

R6 ly

S7

Swiftly is an ad _ _ _ _ derived from the ad _ _ _ _ _ _ _ **swift.**

R7 adverb; adjective

S8

Circle the two misspelled adverbs: **separately, accidentally, minutly, purposly.** Write them correctly: _____ _____

R8 **minutely; purposely**

S9

When an adjective ends in **y,** to form the adverb you change the **y** to _ as in **busy-busily, happy-happily.**

R9 i

S10

Change the following adjectives into adverbs: **easy, satisfactory, lazy —**

_____ _____ _____ .

R10 **easily; satisfactorily; lazily**

S11

To form the adverb from an adjective ending in **able** or **ible,** as in **noticeable,** drop the _____ and add _____ .

R11 **e; y**

S12

Change the following adjectives into adverbs: **forcible, peaceable, changeable —**

_____ _____ _____ .

R12 **forcibly; peaceably; changeably**

R13
truly;
wholly;
duly
● TURN TO Exercise 27

R14
action; linking

R15
is (or **to be**)

R16
well; action

R17
bad; linking

R18
adjective; linking;
adverb; action

R19
a) **sweet;**
b) **bitter;**
c) **healthy**

● TURN TO
Exercise 28 and 29

R20
adjective; healthy

R21
Almost

R22
Almost

S13
Some adjectives become adverbs by other spelling changes. Write the adverbs for **true, whole, due** —

_____ _____ _____.

S14
In deciding whether to use an adjective or an adverb after a verb, you should remember that an adverb modifies an a __ __ __ __ __ verb while an adjective comes after a l __ __ __ __ __ g verb.

S15
A linking verb shows a state of being, not an action. It may be substituted by the verb _____.

S16
He writes (good, well). We use the adverb _____ because **writes** is a(n) (action, linking) verb.

S17
He feels (bad, badly). We use the adjective _____ because **feels** is a(n) (action, linking) verb.

S18
This machine is slow. We use the ad _____ **slow** because **is** is a(n) _____ verb. **This machine runs slowly.** We use the ad _____ **slowly** because **runs** is a(n) _____ verb.

S19
Choose the correct form:
a) **The flowers smell (sweet, sweetly).**
b) **The cake tastes (bitter, bitterly).**
c) **He feels (healthy, healthily).**

S20
Well is usually an adverb, as in **He runs well.** In the sentence **He feels well,** the word **well** is an ad _____ that means h __ __ __ __ __ y.

S21
Which is correct? **(Almost, most) all of the merchandise was returned.**

S22
(Almost, most) everyone was present. The correct word is _____, meaning **nearly.**

S23

A double negative in a sentence should generally be avoided because: A) it is always incorrect; B) one negative cancels out the other, making a positive. Check one: ☐ Only **A** is true ☐ Only **B** is true ☐ Both **A** and **B** are true.

R23

Only **B** is true.
(A double negative may be correct if you intended to state the positive.)

S24

Circle the two negative words in the sentence **He didn't file nothing right in the file cabinet.** This sentence illustrates the sentence error called the d ＿ ＿ ＿ ＿ ＿ n ＿ ＿ ＿ ＿ ＿ ＿ ＿ .

R24

didn't; nothing
double negative

S25

Rewrite this double-negative sentence correctly: **The salesman wasn't able to see none of the buyers.**

＿＿＿＿＿＿＿＿＿＿＿＿＿＿＿＿＿＿＿＿＿＿＿＿

＿＿＿＿＿＿＿＿＿＿＿＿＿＿＿＿＿＿＿＿＿＿＿＿

R25

The salesman wasn't able to see any of the buyers. Or, The salesman was able to see none of the buyers.

S26

We aren't never going to go. The double negative in this sentence can be corrected by changing the word ＿＿＿＿＿＿ to ＿＿＿＿＿.

R26

never to ever
or aren't to are

S27

I can't hardly wait until vacation comes. To correct this sentence change the word ＿＿＿＿ to ＿＿＿＿.

R27

can't to can

S28

It wasn't neither of them who made the error. To correct the d ＿ ＿ ＿ ＿ ＿ n ＿ ＿ ＿ ＿ ＿ ＿ ＿ error in this sentence, change the word ＿＿＿＿＿ to ＿＿＿＿＿ or change the word ＿＿＿＿＿ to ＿＿＿＿＿.

R28

double negative
wasn't; was;
neither; either

S29

Real and **very** are sometimes confused. ＿＿＿＿ is an adjective meaning **genuine**; ＿＿＿＿ is an adverb meaning **extremely**.

R29

Real; very

S30

I am (real, very) happy to work here. The correct word ＿＿＿＿ is an ad ＿ ＿ ＿ ＿ modifying **happy** which is a(n) ＿＿＿＿＿＿＿.

R30

very;
adverb;
adjective

S31

Very should not be used to modify a verb directly. Use **very** to modify an adjective or another adverb.
I am (very, very much) interested in these plans.

R31

very much

S32
Adverbs may be compared just like adjectives. Write the comparative and superlative for these adverbs:

soon _____er _____est
quietly _____ _____
well _____ _____

R32
soon; sooner; soonest;
quietly; more quietly;
most quietly;
well, better; best

S33
Write the correct form: **Ethel drives the** (superlative of **badly**) **of all three.** Answer:_____.

R33
worst

S34
Unnecessary adverbs should be eliminated. Circle the words that should be omitted: a) **He returned the bills back to me.** b) **Please repeat the dictation again.**

R34
a) **back;** b) **again**

S35
Circle the words that should be omitted:
a) **Recopy the page over.** b) **Will you erase this mistake out?**

R35
a) **over;** b) **out**

S36
Altogether and **all together** are sometimes confused.
_____ means **many combined;**
_____ means **completely.**

R36
all together; altogether

S37
The members of the staff worked (altogether, all together) until they were (altogether, all together) satisfied.

R37
all together; altogether

S38
A secretary should (all ways, always) try to excell in (all ways, always).

R38
always; all ways

S39
The workers were (all ready, already) finished by noon, and they were (all ready, already) for lunch.

R39
already; all ready

S40
Cross out the incorrect form: **(all right, alright). All right** is the opposite of _____ **wrong.**

R40
alright; all wrong

S41
Cross out the wrong words and write the correct words above them. **The union members are working altogether to make the contract come out alright.**

R41
all together; all right

S42
Sure means **certain; surely** means **certainly. I am (sure, surely) happy that prices have leveled off.** The correct word is _____ which is an ad___ ___ ___ that modifies **happy** which is an ad___ ___ ___ ___ ___ ___.

R42
surely; adverb; adjective

S43

(Sure, Surely) I'll lend you the money.

R43
Surely

S44

Review time! a) An adverb modifies a v _ _ _ , an ad _ _ _ _ _ _ _ , or another a _ _ _ _ _ , b) It usually answers the question w _ _ _ _ , w _ _ _ , h _ _ , and h _ _ m _ _ _ . c) It often ends in the letters _ _ .

R44

a) verb, adjective, adverb

b) where, when, how, how much

c) ly

● **TURN TO**
Exercise 30 and Review

EXERCISE 27 — Recognizing Adverbs

A. This problem deals with recognizing adverbs. Underline the adverb in each of the following sentences with one line. Then, underline the word it modifies with two lines.

SCORING: DEDUCT 7 POINTS FOR EACH ERROR.

1. The plane traveled swiftly.
2. We are very much pleased to hear from you.
3. We walked quietly to the side.
4. Quickly he leaped into his car.
5. The matter is entirely finished.
6. No two men are completely alike.
7. This occurrence is most unfortunate.
8. We strongly urge you to accept this offer.
9. Recheck thoroughly all outgoing mail.
10. They came here much later than expected.
11. He was essentially interested in securing a patent.
12. We were unusually surprised by his work.
13. All our customers are comfortably dressed when they leave us.
14. Watch this maneuver intently.
15. Mr. Jones arrived at the meeting exactly at the appointed hour.

EXERCISE 27 — Changing Adjectives into Adverbs

B. This problem deals with changing adjectives into adverbs. Below is a list of adjectives. In the space next to each adjective, write the equivalent adverb.

SCORING: DEDUCT 7 POINTS FOR EACH ERROR.

1. careful — *carefully*
2. sole — *solely*
3. busy — *busily*
4. primary — *primarily*
5. noticeable — *noticeably*
6. principal — *principally*
7. whole — *wholly*
8. true — *truly*
9. considerable — *considerably*
10. substantial — *substantially*
11. real — *really*
12. extraordinary — *extraordinarily*
13. extreme — *extremely*
14. bad — *badly*
15. good — *well*

139

EXERCISE 28 | Review of Action and Linking Verbs

This is a review problem involving action and linking verbs. Underline the verb in each of the following sentences. Then, in the space provided, mark A if it is used as an action verb; mark L if it is used as a linking verb. Have you reviewed Lesson 4 on the distinction between action and linking verbs?

SCORING: DEDUCT 10 POINTS FOR EACH ERROR.

1. He looked at me with a piercing stare.   1. _A_
2. The office seems quite comfortable.   2. _L_
3. This bread smells very fresh.   3. _A_
4. John lay down on his bed after dinner.   4. _A_
5. This proposition is a once-in-a-lifetime opportunity.   5. _L_
6. Mr. Jones looks taller than his brother.   6. _L_
7. This situation seems positively uncanny.   7. _L_
8. John rests.   8. _A_
9. By tomorrow I shall have been there and back.   9. _L_
10. He knows the answer to our problems.   10. _A_

EXERCISE 29 | Choosing Between Adverbs and Adjectives

This problem deals with choosing between an adjective and an adverb. Below is a series of sentences. In the space provided write the proper form of the word in parentheses in each sentence. Remember, use an adverb to modify an action verb; use an adjective after a linking verb.

SCORING: DEDUCT 3 POINTS FOR EACH ERROR.

1. Candy tastes (sweet).   1. _sweet_
2. He tasted the mixture (careful).   2. _carefully_
3. Return the merchandise as (quick) as possible.   3. _quickly_
4. He is very (content).   4. _content_
5. The situation seems (bad).   5. _bad_
6. I am (extreme) tired from my long journey.   6. _extremely_
7. The plant grew more and more (quick).   7. _quickly_

(continued)

EXERCISE 29 (continued)

8. The whole garden smells (sweet).   8. _sweet_

9. We (certain) hope you are comfortable.   9. _certainly_

10. We feel he has been (extraordinary) competent at his task.   10. _extraordinary_

11. Ordinarily the bell tolls (soft), but today it sounds (loud).   11. _softly_ _loudly_

12. Our situation has grown (bad).   12. _bad_

13. She looks (beautiful).   13. _beautiful_

14. We can accomplish our goals (easy).   14. _easily_

15. He has done (good, well) in his new post.   15. _well_

16. Our product is becoming more and more (desirable) in its line.   16. _desirable_

17. Mr. Jones became (angry) and threatened his employee (loud).   17. _angry_ _loudly_

18. He feels (indignant) because he cannot attend.   18. _indignant_

19. The whole story sounds (strange).   19. _strange_

20. You are paying an (extreme) large amount.   20. _extremely_

21. We will (glad) repay your losses.   21. _gladly_

22. This is a very (poor) constructed problem.   22. _poorly_

23. The river flowed (rapid).   23. _rapidly_

24. Do business conditions look (bad) to you?   24. _bad_

25. Rewrite the entire page (correct).   25. _correctly_

26. Please have a clerk file these papers (quick).   26. _quickly_

27. Mr. Roberts certainly is a (quick) thinker.   27. _quick_

28. When faced with an emergency, Mr. Roberts thought (quick).   28. _quickly_

29. There is no doubt about Mr. Roberts' being (quick).   29. _quick_

30. Mr. Smith tasted his soup (hungry).   30. _hungrily_

31. To Mr. Smith, the soup tasted (delicious) and (inviting).   31. _deliciously_ _inviting_

32. The table was set (inviting).   32. _invitingly_

33. I feel (bad) about your leaving.   33. _bad_

141

SCORE

A_____

EXERCISE 30   Good and Well

A. This problem deals with the proper use of good and well. In the space provided, write the proper word — either good or well.

SCORING: DEDUCT 10 POINTS FOR EACH ERROR.

1. You did the job very (good, well).
2. You did a very (good, well) job.
3. It sounds (good, well) to me.
4. You look (good, well) in your new suit.
5. He performs (good, well) on the piano.
6. The job was done quite (good, well).
7. The proposition sounds (good, well).
8. We feel confident you shall do (good, well) in your new position.
9. Though he was sick, he is now completely (good, well).
10. He was extremely (good, well) in the part of Hamlet.

1. _well good_
2. _good_
3. _good_
4. _well good_
5. _well_
6. _well_
7. _good_
8. _well_
9. _well_
10. _good_

SCORE

B_____

EXERCISE 30   Most and Almost

B. This problem deals with the proper use of most and almost. In the space provided, write the proper word. Remember, use almost only where the word nearly could be used as well.

SCORING: DEDUCT 10 POINTS FOR EACH ERROR.

1. These are (most, almost) all of the supplies that are left.
2. We found that (most, almost) people did not answer.
3. He is (most, almost) as good as his competitor.
4. (Most, Almost) everything was finished by noon.
5. (Most, Almost) of the time we work quite hard.
6. It was (most, almost) too good to be true.
7. We feel that (most, almost) of our staff is doing a top-notch job.
8. It seems that (most, almost) all of the men answered our plea.
9. He can sell (most, almost) as (good, well) as any of our other salesmen.
10. (Most, Almost) anyone who dresses (well, good) can look (well, good).

1. _almost_
2. _most_
3. _almost_
4. _almost_
5. _most_
6. _almost_
7. _most_
8. _almost_
9. _almost well_
10. _almost well good_

SCORE

C_____

EXERCISE 30 — Double Negatives

C. This problem deals with double negatives. Rewrite the following letter, correcting all double-negative expressions.

SCORING: DEDUCT 10 POINTS FOR EACH ERROR.

Dear Mr. Bronson:

Mr. Marshall from your office hasn't scarcely visited us more than a few times in the past few months. We certainly hope that we haven't done nothing to offend him. After all, we haven't hardly started in our association with your firm, and we certainly wouldn't want to do nothing that would jeopardize our fine relationship.

Sincerely,

Mr. Marshall, from your office hasn't ever visited us more than a few times in the past months. We certainly hope we haven't done anything to offend him. after all we haven't started in our association with your firm, & we certainly wouldn't want to do anything that would jeopardize our fine relationship.

SCORE

D_____

EXERCISE 30 — Real and Really

D. This problem deals with the proper use of real and really. In the space provided, write the proper word.

SCORING: DEDUCT 10 POINTS FOR EACH ERROR.

1. These diamonds are (real, really). 1. *real*
2. He was (real, really) pleased to meet them. 2. *really*
3. It gives us (real, really) satisfaction. 3. *real*
4. We are (real, really) sorry we cannot comply. 4. *really*
5. After a day's work he was (real, really) tired. 5. *really*
6. Were the (real, really) situation known, there might be a scandal. 6. *real*
7. The teachers were (real, really) concerned about her grades. 7. *really*
8. This matter is (real, really) important. 8. *really*
9. We have (real, really) valid reasons for our stand. 9. *really*
10. Are you (real, really) sure of your facts? 10. *really*

SCORE

E _____

EXERCISE 30   Unnecessary Adverbs

E. This problem deals with the use of unnecessary adverbs. If an adverb is used unnecessarily, write it in the space; if there is no unnecessary adverb, write the letter C for correct.

SCORING: DEDUCT 10 POINTS FOR EACH ERROR.

1. Please repaint this wall again.   1. _again_
2. Exit out this way.   2. _out_
3. Return those papers back to me.   3. _back_
4. Cooperate together with your associates.   4. _together_
5. Please repeat the letter again.   5. _again_
6. Let us reconvene again on Monday morning.   6. _again_
7. In re-examining the ledger, they discovered the error.   7. _C_
8. We want nations to coexist together in harmony.   8. _together_
9. The new fan has conquered over all competition.   9. _over_
10. Try to cooperate as fully as you can.   10. _C_

SCORE

F _____

EXERCISE 30   Compound Expressions

F. This problem deals with compound expressions that are confused with single adverbs. In the space provided, write the proper word or words.

SCORING: DEDUCT 10 POINTS FOR EACH ERROR.

1. He is (all together, altogether) wrong in his approach.   1. _altogether_
2. In (all ways, always) this edition seems superior.   2. _all ways_
3. Many students have (all ready, already) taken some college courses.   3. _already_
4. (All together, Altogether) I counted thirty-three people.   4. _All together_
5. It's (all right, alright) to leave before the bell.   5. _all right_
6. The new firm failed (all together, altogether).   6. _altogether_
7. He is in (all ways, always) a model employee.   7. _all ways_
8. I think the bank tellers are (all ready, already) to end their day's work.   8. _all ready_
9. Conditions are neither (all right, alright) nor (all wrong, alwrong.)   9. _all right_ _all wrong_
10. (All right, Alright), you may go when you are (all ready, already.)   10. _all right_ _all ready_

NAME   CLASS   DATE

REVIEW EXERCISE 6   Adverbs

The following letter contains many improper words. Cross out each improper word and write the correct word above it.
SCORING: DEDUCT 5 POINTS FOR EACH ERROR.

Dear Mr. Spears:

It was a ~~genuine~~ *real* pleasure to see you at the Acme Convention in Pittsburgh. I thought you looked ~~real good~~ *very well*, considering the seriousness of your recent illness. We sure hope you enjoyed your visit to Pittsburgh and that everything was ~~alright~~ *all right* there.

The Acme Company is growing very quickly. Last year's sales are a tiny fraction of our anticipated sales this year. Our situation is growing ~~more~~ better every day. I am certain that we can easily accomplish the goals we set for ourselves in Pittsburgh.

One situation I feel badly about is the growth of competition in the South. If one looks close at sales figures in the South, he will see that the rate of increase does not look as ~~well~~ *good* as we had first thought. I am ~~real~~ *very* concerned with this problem.

On the other hand, our Western office has done extremely ~~good~~ *well*. They are ~~real quick~~ *very quickly* rising to *the* Number One position in the nation. I wish that our other offices followed our advice as completely and thoroughly as they do.

By the way, John Raymond feels indignantly because he was not chosen as a speaker in Pittsburgh. Even though his speaking is ~~real~~ *very* poorly, he is an important person. While I am not positive that there will be time for him at the next convention, I am ~~most~~ *almost* surely that we can squeeze him in.

Please write and let us know if you are feeling ~~weller~~ *better*.

Sincerely,

Thursday

Test on Chapters
5 - 6.

adjectives & adverbs.

LESSON 7

PREPOSITIONS

1. using prepositions
2. the right preposition

Words such as the following are prepositions: **of, at, in, on, between.** Since most prepositions are very familiar words, they should give you little trouble.

A preposition is a word that connects a noun or pronoun with the body of the sentence. The noun or pronoun that the preposition connects to the body of the sentence is called the *object* of that preposition.

of John — John is the *object* of the preposition **of.**

at the time — time is the *object* of the preposition **at.**

in the room — room is the *object* of the preposition **in.**

on the way — way is the *object* of the preposition **on.**

between you and me — you and **me** are the *objects* of the preposition **between.**

The phrase that is introduced by a preposition is called simply a *prepositional* phrase. **I arrived on time.** In this sentence **on time** is a prepositional phrase. **On** is the preposition; **time** is the object of the preposition.

I went to his office. What is the prepositional phrase? That's right — **to his office. To** is the preposition; **office** is its object.

I went to his newly decorated office. The prepositional phrase is **to his newly decorated office.** The preposition is **to**; its object is still **office** despite the introduction of the descriptive words **newly decorated.**

In Lesson 8 you will be called upon to work with the *objects* of prepositions. For the moment let's just study the prepositions themselves. Here is a list of the most common prepositions. You undoubtedly recognize them all, but did you know they all are prepositions? Don't memorize this list, but learn to recognize these words as prepositions:

about, above, across, after, against, along, among, around, at, before, behind, below, beneath, between, beyond, but, by, concerning, down, during, except, for, from, in, into, of, off, on, over, regarding, respecting, since, through, throughout, till, to, toward, under, underneath, until, up, upon, with, within, without

In addition, there are a number of familiar word groups that are used as though the whole group were a preposition. Learn to recognize these word groups as prepositions.

as to, as for, as regards, apart from, by way of, contrary to, devoid of, from out, from beyond, instead of, in place of, in regard to, in reference to, on account of, to the extent of, with respect to

Turn to Programed Reinforcement S1 through S5

1. USING prepositions

A. From and Than

handwritten left margin: different from

Always use the word *from* after the word *different* when you mean that something is different *from* something else. It is *never* different *than* something else. (It may help you to remember that the *f* of *different* must be followed by the *f* of *from*.)

Right: This may differ from what you had thought.

Right: My theory is different from the one held by my boss.

Right: Sing the song differently from the way you sang it last night.

When *differ* is used as a verb meaning *disagree*, it calls for the preposition *with*.

We differ with your conclusion.

B. Among and Between

handwritten: (3 or more) (2)

There is a difference of opinion (among) (between) you and me.

Between is proper only when there are *two* people or things involved. *Among* is proper when there are *three or more*. Our sentence should read *between you and me* since there are only *two* people involved — *you* and *me*.

Right: Between you and me, we have nothing to fear.

handwritten: always me never I

Right: We shall place your display among the many others.

Right: We shall place your display between the other two.

C. In and Into

handwritten top margin: dread inside   were outside & are entering.

What is the difference between these two sentences?

1. The director is in the room.

2. The director went into the room.

In means *within*. *Into* means *from the outside to within*. In other words, *into* expresses an action of moving from one place (outside) to another place (inside). *In* expresses no action.

The carbon is in the drawer.

He put his hand into the drawer to get the carbon.

You will note that the words *in* or *into* in the same sentence may change the meaning completely.

He ran in the ring. (Was he afraid?)

He ran into the ring. (Was he eager?)

D. Off and Of

handwritten: never use "off of"

Do not use the word *of* after the word *off*.

Right: The radio fell off the table. NOT: The radio fell *off of* the table.

Right: The letter dropped off the file.

Right: He is coming off the gangplank.

Do not use *off of* when you mean *from*.

Right: He borrowed the money from me.

NOT: He borrowed money *off of* me.

Do not use *of* when you mean *have*. Remember, the word *of* never directly follows the word *might, must, could, should,* or *would*. It is true that when you speak quickly, the helping verb *have* sounds like the preposition *of*; that should not be mislead you, however.

Right: I might have gone. NOT: I *might of* gone.

Right: I would have been there by now.

Right: I should have known this would happen.

You should avoid unnecessary prepositions that merely clutter your sentence without adding thought content.

1. **Right: Where are you going?** NOT: Where are you going *to?*

2. **Right: Where is your home?** NOT: Where is your home *at?*

3. **Right: I cannot help expressing my gratitude.** NOT: I cannot help *from* expressing my gratitude.

4. **Right: I want you to see this.** NOT: I want *for* you to see this.

5. **Right: Until yesterday, I would have agreed.** NOT: *Up* until yesterday, I would have agreed.

6. **Right: In two weeks it will be over.** NOT: In two weeks it will be over *with.*

1. Do not use *over* for *to, at, during,* or *for. Over* means *on top of* or *in excess of.*

Right: Come to my house tonight. NOT: *over my house.*

Right: Let's have the meeting at my home. NOT: *over my home.*

Right: We held the meeting during the weekend. NOT: *over the weekend.*

2. In the lesson on verbs, you studied the word *to* as part of the *infinitive: to walk, to study,* etc. Now let's consider *to* as a preposition: *to the office, to next week,* etc. Do not use *to* for *at. At* indicates location whereas *to* indicates motion.

Right: I was at a meeting last night. NOT: *to a meeting.*

Right: I was at her graduation. NOT: *I was to her graduation.*
BUT: **I went to her graduation.**

3. Do not use the adverb *too* (meaning *also* or *excessively*) or the numeral *two* (meaning *2*) for the preposition *to.*

Right: There are too many people to give out only two prizes.

Right: Too much has been said to the public about the two world powers.

4. Do not use *around* (meaning *circular*) for *about* (meaning *approximately*).

Right: I'll be at the bank about an hour from now.

Wrong: I'll be at the bank around an hour from now.

at the side of   in addition to

To avoid confusing these two prepositions, remember that *beside* means *by the side of.*

He sat down beside her (*at her side*).

Besides with the *s* has a completely different meaning: *in addition to.*

The office will send a supervisor besides the typist and me.

No one will be there besides us two.

Wrong: He sat down besides her.

Do not omit prepositions that are necessary.

Right: What type of work do you do? NOT: What type work do you do?

Right: Tell him what style of cabinet we want. NOT: what style cabinet.

Do not omit the preposition *from* after the verb *graduate.*

Right: I was graduated from high school two years ago. NOT: I graduated high school.

2. the RIGHT preposition

Certain words call for one preposition and not another. You will be constantly using many such words in your work as a secretary. Below is a list of words and their proper prepositions. Study this list carefully. Repeat each expression over and over until it becomes familiar to you.

abide by (a decision)

absolve from (to free from)

abstain from (usual combination)

accede to (to express approval or give consent)

accompanied by (a person)
accompanied with (an object)

according to (done according to directions)

adapted to (adjusted to)

adhere to (to give support or to hold fast)

affiliate with (to associate oneself)

agree with (an opinion)
agree to (terms)
agree among (more than two people)
agree between (two people)

angry with (a person)
angry at (an occurence or object)

annoyed with (a person)
annoyed by (that which annoys)

appropriate to (suitable to)

argue with (a person)
argue for (something)

attend to (heed; listen; to direct one's care)

beneficial to (not "for")

blame for (not "on")

borrow from (not "of")

buy from (not "of")

capable of (having sufficient intelligence, resources, or strength)

careless about (appearance)
careless in (performance of actions)
careless of (others)

cause for (an action)
cause of (a result)

choose among (three or more)
choose between (two)

compare to (suggest a similarity)
compare with (specific similarities)

complementary to (not "with")

comply with (not "to")

coincide with (usual combination)

concur in (an opinion)
concur with (a person or thing)

confer with (compare views or take counsel)

confide in (to tell confidentially)
confide to (to entrust)

consist of (is made up of)
consist in (lies in)

contrast to (or "with" when **contrast** is a noun)
contrast with (when **contrast** is a verb)

convenient to (a location)
convenient for (a purpose)

conversant with (well-informed)

with – a person
by –

correspond with (writing letters)

correspond to (equivalent)

dates from (not "back to")

deal in (kind of business)

deal with (people)

depend upon (or "on"; to become
conditioned)

differ from (a thing)

differ with (an opinion)

disappointed at (or "in" a thing)

disappointed with (a person)

disgusted with (a person)

disgusted at (a thing)

disgusted by (behavior)

dispense with (not "of")

dissent from (not "with" or "of')

emerge from (to arise from)

enter into (inquire into or become a part of)

enter upon (a career)

entertained by (amused, diverted)

equivalent to (equal)

equivalent with (synonymous)

familiar with (conversant)

in accordance with (not "to")

in compliance with (usual combination)

identical with (uniform with)

identical to (equal to)

impose upon (or "on" meaning to infringe
or abuse)

independent of (not "from")

indifferent to (equal to)

inquire of (to ask a person)

inquire about (interrogate or question)

inquire after (one's health)

inseparable from (incapable of being disjoined)

insight into (power of seeing into)

interfere with (a person)

interfere in (something)

labor under (difficult conditions)

labor for (a person)

lend to (to add, furnish, or provide)

live in (a town)

live on (a street)

live at (a certain address)

live by (means of livelihood)

necessity for (urgent need)

necessity of (unavoidable obligation)

need for (urgent occasion for)

need of (lack or want)

object to (to oppose)

offended at (action)

offended with (a person)

participate in (to take part)

payment for (an article)

payment of (a fee or bill)

proceed with (to continue)

proceed from (to come forth)

profit by (not "from")

prohibit from (is usual form)

provide for (to supply what is needed)

take exception to (usual combination)

talk to (to speak to a person)

Turn to Programed Reinforcement S6 through S30

talk with –

	S1 A preposition connects a noun or pronoun with the body of the sentence. ☐ True; ☐ False
R1 True	**S2** The noun or pronoun that the preposition connects to the body of the sentence is called the o _ _ _ _ _ of that preposition.
R2 object	**S3** ...to the office .... In this group of words (called a **phrase**) **to** is a p_ _ _ _ _ _ _ _ _ _ _ and **office** is the o _ _ _ _ _ of **to**.
R3 preposition; object	**S4** Here is a list of prepositions with one adverb and one adjective inserted: **To, with, for, over, until, certainly, besides, during, smart, against.** The adverb is _____ and the adjective is _____.
R4 adverb — **certainly**; adjective — **smart**	**S5** Groups of two or three words sometimes act as though the whole group were a preposition. Circle two such phrases: **In regard to the order, the duplicate was used in place of the original.**
R5 **In regard to; in place of** ● **TURN TO Exercise 31**	**S6** The preposition that should follow the word **different** is (**from, than**).
R6 **from**	**S7** **Between** is a preposition that is used when (two, three or more) people are involved.
R7 two	**S8** Circle the correct words: **Since our profits are different (than, from) those of last year, we shall divide them (between, among) the ten supervisors.**
R8 from; among	**S9** He walked (in, into) the room. a) **In** is correct b) **Into** is **correct** c) Both may be correct
R9 c) Both may be correct	**S10** He got out of his car and went (in, into) the office.
R10 into	**S11** Circle the preposition that should be eliminated. **Please take that calendar off of the desk and put it into the basket.**
R11 of	

S12

In the sentence **He borrowed money off of the cashier,** the prepositions incorrectly used are _____ _____; the correct preposition is _____.

R12
off of; from

S13

I should of gone to the meeting. The preposition **of** is incorrectly substituted for the verb _____.

R13
have

S14

Unnecessary prepositions should be eliminated. Circle two you should eliminate in this sentence: **I want for you to tell me where you will be at this afternoon.**

R14
for; at

S15

Circle prepositions that are unnecessary in this sentence: **Where are you going to, and up until when will you stay?**

R15
to; up

S16

Which preposition, incorrectly used, is a physical impossibility except with an airplane? **Come (over, to) my house this evening.**

R16
over

S17

Circle the correct answer: **He worked on the accounts (over, during) the weekend.**

R17
during

S18

I was (to, at) a meeting this afternoon.

R18
at

S19

Too means **excessively** or **also**, as distinguished from **two** (one plus one) and **to** (direction). Circle the correct forms. **He is (to, two, too) busy (to, two, too) send the advertising copy to the (to, two, too) agencies.**

R19
too; to; two

S20

Besides and **beside** are prepositions that can be easily differentiated if you remember that _____ means **by the side of.**

R20
beside

S21

(Besides, Beside) all other considerations, the Treasurer should sit **(besides, beside)** the President.

R21
besides; beside
● TURN TO Exercise 32

S22

What necessary preposition is omitted in this sentence? **What type _____ addressing machine do you use?**

R22
of

S23

Certain words call for one preposition and not another. Circle the correct ones:
  a) **Abide (by, with) a decision**
  b) **Accompanied (by, with) a person**
  c) **Accompanied (by, with) a remittance**

R23
a) **by;** b) **by** c) **with**

S24
a) Agree (with, to) an opinion
b) Agree (with, to) terms
c) Angry (with, at) a person
d) Angry (with, at) an occurrence or object

R24 a) with; b) to; c) with; d) at

S25
a) Please comply (with, to) this request.
b) This store is convenient (with, to) all transportation.

R25 a) with; b) to

S26
a) Correspond to means (equivalent, writing letters); b) correspond with means (equivalent, writing letters).

R26 a) equivalent; b) writing letters

S27
As a review, circle the correct words in the following sentence: He should (have, of) divided the bonuses (between, among) the two men whose ideas were different (than, from) the others.

R27 have; between; from

S28
Circle the correct words: She cleaned the debris (off of, off) the table and threw it (in, into) the basket (beside, besides) the window.

R28 off; into; beside

S29
Come (over, to) the factory accompanied (with, by) an engineer (over, during) the weekend.

R29 to; by; during

S30
A phrase that is introduced by a preposition is called a _____ phrase. The noun or pronoun at the end of the phrase is called the _____ of the preposition.

R30 prepositional; object

● TURN TO
Exercise 33 and Review

EXERCISE 31   Recognizing Prepositions

This problem deals with recognizing prepositions. In each of the following sentences underline all prepositions with one line. Then circle the objects of those prepositions.

SCORING: DEDUCT 8 POINTS FOR EACH ERROR.

1. Did you hear of the trouble at the office?

2. Mr. Atwood was in his office when you called.

3. The reputation of Empire Fans has been built on high standards and fair dealings at all times.

4. Between you and me, I feel certain that one of the representatives will call at your office within a week.

5. In regard to any orders from your firm, we feel sure of our ability to fill them in time for your fall shipment.

6. With respect to your claim for damages, we are certain of a recovery to the extent of $3,000.

7. Contrary to our expectations, you will be refused a passport for the duration of the present emergency.

8. They have agreed among themselves to honor, without any question, all of the demands made by our client.

9. Against all odds, we have succeeded beyond expectation in our endeavor to enlist support for our cause.

10. Instead of being discouraged by his failure, he seemed to gain the strength of a lion in all his subsequent attempts.

11. Walking into the hall, the President of the United States and the members of his cabinet were greeted by the complete silence of the assembled guests.

12. In spite of his aversion to the tactics of high-pressure salesmen, Mr. Jones was so impressed by this young man that he agreed to buy his full line of goods.

NAME   CLASS   DATE

EXERCISE 32   Using Prepositions

A. This problem deals with the use of *from* after the word *different*. In the space provided, write the proper preposition.

SCORING: DEDUCT 10 POINTS FOR EACH ERROR.

1. My idea is different ___*from*___ yours.
2. Our course may differ ___*from*___ what you had expected.
3. Approach the topic differently ___*than*___ the way you did last time.
4. The Board differed ___*from*___ the advice of the Director.
5. His designs are no different ___*from*___ the designs he showed last time.
6. What we differ ___*from*___ is your desire for haste.
7. The course they chose was different ___*from*___ that outlined in the manual.
8. Our attorneys differ ___*from*___ this report's interpretation of the facts.
9. Have you nothing different ___*from*___ what you showed me last week?
10. The new car models are very different ___*from*___ the old ones.

EXERCISE 32   Among or Between

B. In the space provided, write either *among* or *between* whichever is correct.

SCORING: DEDUCT 10 POINTS FOR EACH ERROR.

1. There is a difference of opinion ___*between*___ the two men.
2. There is a difference of opinion ___*among*___ the jury.
3. The Big Three often differ ___*among*___ themselves.
4. Chicago is ___*between*___ New York and Seattle.
5. ___*Among*___ the people present were the President, the Vice-President, and the Secretary of State.
6. The jewelry was found ___*among*___ his belongings.
7. ___*Between*___ you and me, this plan will be a huge success.
8. ___*Among*___ the reasons for his success were his wisdom, honesty, and fairness.
9. Is there a great difference ___*between*___ the Ford and the Chevrolet?
10. There is little difference ___*among*___ these five jacket models.

EXERCISE 32   In or Into

C. In the space provided, write either in or into, whichever is correct.
SCORING: DEDUCT 10 POINTS FOR EACH ERROR.

1. He walked _____into_____ the room from the hall.
2. Behind a closed door, he paced back and forth _____in_____ his office all day.
3. There are some fascinating articles _____in_____ today's newspaper.
4. It doesn't take much to get _____into_____ a fight with him.
5. What sort of work would you like to get _____into_____?
6. Promotion is rapid, once you have established a name _____in_____ this field.
7. He opened the door and rushed _____into_____ his office.
8. I would tear this contract _____into_____ a thousand little pieces if I could.
9. Do you think you can get _____into_____ the public relations field?
10. You can work your way _____into_____ the confidence of your superior only by intense effort.

EXERCISE 32   Misusing of Prepositions

D. In the space provided, write the proper word or words.
SCORING: DEDUCT 7 POINTS FOR EACH ERROR.

1. Money was stolen (off of, from) the safe.
2. The child fell (off of, off) the chair.
3. I could (have, of) completed the job by noon.
4. They took the receipts (off of, from) me.
5. We all got (off of, off) the elevator at the same floor.
6. He borrowed money (off of, from) John.
7. They should (have, of) known he was lying.
8. The idol has toppled (off of, from) its pedestal.
9. The shirt was almost ripped (off of, off) the crooner's back.
10. With luck he might (have, of) pulled through.
11. I stepped (off of, from) the moving car.
12. They could (have, of) made many changes (among, between) the three of them.
13. He would (have, of) had very different opinions (from, than) mine.
14. When you went (in, into) this field, you should (have, of) been prepared for a life very different (from, than) college life.
15. Standing (between, among) his brothers, John and Bob, he would (have, of) looked very different (from, than) either of them.

1. _from_
2. _off_
3. _have_
4. _from_
5. _off_
6. _from_
7. _have_
8. _from_
9. _off_
10. _have_
11. _from_
12. _have among_
13. _have, from_
14. _into have from_
15. _between, have from,_

SCORE

E_____

EXERCISE 32   Unnecessary Prepositions

E. This problem deals with eliminating unnecessary prepositions. Twelve of the following sentences contain unnecessary prepositions. Three of the following sentences are correct. Cross out each incorrect preposition and list it in the box provided at the end of the sentence. If the sentence is correct, write C in the box.

SCORING: DEDUCT 7 POINTS FOR EACH ERROR.

1. This is the place where I am going.   1. _____C_____
2. Do you know where Mr. Smith is at?   2. _____at_____
3. Did the packages fall off of the shelves?   3. _____of_____
4. Here is a copy of the plans you ordered.   4. _____C_____
5. We wanted for him to receive the prize.   5. _____for_____
6. Up until last week we had not received any report.   6. _____up_____
7. Together we can seek out a solution.   7. _____out_____
8. It's a relief that summer is over with.   8. _____with_____
9. By the end of the summer your shipment will be ready.   9. _____C_____
10. Open up all the windows.   10. _____up_____
11. I didn't remember of having received the bill.   11. _____of_____
12. If I'd of known the answer, I would have won the contest.   12. _____of_____
13. In another few minutes it will be done with.   13. _____with_____
14. Of our many customers, you have been one our most pleasant.   14. _____one of_____
15. Get the books off of the desk.   15. _____of_____

SCORE

F_____

EXERCISE 32   Choosing Prepositions

F. This problem deals with prepositions that are incorrectly used. Write the correct word in the space provided.

SCORING: DEDUCT 8 POINTS FOR EACH ERROR.

1. I had a fine time (over, at) my friend's house.   1. _____at_____
2. Frank sat down (beside, besides) his friend.   2. _____beside_____
3. What (type, type of) suit are you going to buy?   3. _____type of_____
4. I'll be there (during, over) the holidays.   4. _____during_____
5. (Beside, Besides) my employer and me, who else is invited?   5. _____Besides_____
6. He ordered a new (style, style of) wall decoration for the office.   6. _____style_____
7. I was (to, at) the celebration last week.   7. _____at_____
8. What can we do (beside, besides) writing a letter of complaint?   8. _____besides_____
9. I want to go along (to, too, two).   9. _____besides_____
10. (Two, to, too) many times I hear the same complaints.   10. _____too_____
11. Did you (graduate, graduate from) high school?   11. _____grad. from_____
12. He (too, to, two) feels that (too, to, two) hours are enough.   12. _____two, two_____

NAME   CLASS   DATE

EXERCISE 33 — The Proper Preposition

This problem deals with recognizing the proper preposition for a given word. In the space provided, write the preposition that best completes the thought. This problem not only reviews material in the text but also introduces you to the correct use of other prepositions.

SCORING: DEDUCT 1 POINT FOR EACH ERROR.

1. Abide _by_ a referee's decision.

2. Accompanied _by_ his boss.

3. Accompanied _with_ a full payment.

4. Agree _to_ the terms of the contract.

5. Agree _with_ his views on politics.

6. Agree _with_ (or upon) this method of attack.

7. Angry _with_ the superintendent.

8. Angry _at_ the rainy weather.

9. Buy _from_ a salesman.

10. Borrow _from_ a friend.

11. Comply _with_ your request.

12. Convenient _to_ all trains.

13. Convenient _for_ all business needs.

14. Correspond _with_ his firm by mail.

15. Correspond _to_ my understanding.

16. Differ _from_ (with) his outlook on life.

17. Agree _among_ the three of us.

18. Disappointed _at_ (or with) the outcome.

19. Take advantage _of_ an offer.

20. Deal _with_ a problem.

21. Deal _in_ stocks and bonds.

22. In contrast _to_ (or with) other methods.

23. To contrast _with_ other methods.

24. Agree _between_ the two of us.

25. Provide _for_ future needs.

26. Equivalent _to_ a full gallon.

27. Emerge _from_ the depths of despair.

28. Labor _under_ pleasant conditions.

29. Labor _for_ a kind employer.

30. Labor _under_ (at) a difficult task.

31. A necessity _for_ promptness.

32. Inseparable _from_ one another.

33. In accordance _to_ (with) the vast majority.

34. Familiar _with_ the entire process.

35. An exception _to_ the rule.

36. Dates _from_ last June.

37. Lend _to_ a friend.

38. Accompanied _by_ (with) a cash payment.

39. Agree _to_ the terms.

40. Indifferent _to_ others.

(continued)

41. Inquire *about* one's neighbor.
42. In contrast *to* his former work.
43. Accede *to* his wishes.
44. Angry *at* the drop in sales.
45. Conversant *with* all details.
46. Agree *with* a plan of attack. *upon*
47. Adapted *to* your needs.
48. Talk *to* his audience.
49. Adhere *to* my previous decision.
50. Distinguish *between* the two methods.
51. Comply *with* orders from headquarters.
52. Different *from* other methods.
53. Consist *of* wood and metal.
54. Enter *into* an agreement.
55. Impose *upon* your neighbors.
56. Insight *into* complex matters.
57. Profit *by* former mistakes.
58. Coincide *with* the plans of others.
59. Approve *of* his behavior.
60. Dispense *with* all formality.
61. Correspond *with* air mail. *by*
62. Capable *of* doing a fine job.
63. Depend *upon* his parents.
64. Correspond *with* a friend overseas.
65. Accompanied *by* his mother.
66. Attend *to* business.
67. Conscious *of* the risks involved.
68. Appropriate *for* the occasion.
69. Participate *in* games.
70. Confide *in* his brother.

71. Correspond *to* his understanding.
72. Entertained *by* the comedian.
73. Identical *to* the original.
74. Confer *with* your doctor.
75. According *to* our contract.
76. In accordance *with* our contract.
77. Prohibited *by* doing an illegal act.
78. Concur *in* an opinion.
79. Abide *by* the court's ruling.
80. Depend *upon* your wits.
81. Angry *with* his employee.
82. Proceed *with* the current plan.
83. Accompanied *with* invoices.
84. Absolve *from* all guilt.
85. Abstain *from* voting.
86. Convenient *for* buses and trolleys. *to*
87. To object *to* certain conditions.
88. Different *from* his neighbor.
89. Agree *with* your opinion.
90. Participate *in* a contest.
91. Comply *with* your requests.
92. Correspond *to* our picture of events.
93. In contrast *with* other products.
94. Disagree *among* our opponents.
95. Differs *from* our old desk.
96. Disgusted *with* his boss.
97. In compliance *with* your order.
98. Differs *with* his boss.
99. Choose *among* the three.
100. Correspond *with* telegram.

REVIEW EXERCISE 7   Prepositions

In the following letter many prepositions are improperly used. Cross out each improper preposition and write the correct preposition above it.

SCORING: DEDUCT 5 POINTS FOR EACH ERROR.

Dear Mr. Smith:

    I am afraid that I cannot agree ~~upon~~ *with* your interpretation of our contract. Your interpretation is entirely different ~~than~~ *from* mine. Unfortunately, my attorney, accompanied ~~with~~ *by* his family, is ~~at~~ *on* a vacation so that I have been unable to obtain his advice. I am trying to correspond ~~to~~ *with* him by mail, but ~~up~~ until today have been unable to locate him.

    This difference of opinion ~~among~~ *between* you and me must be reconciled at once. You realize that I am not angry ~~at~~ *with* you. I am angry ~~at~~ *with* the conditions that brought about this situation.

    I am quite willing to comply ~~to~~ *with* all the provisions in Paragraph X, but I cannot agree to your interpretation of Paragraph XI. When I agreed to enter ~~in~~ *into* this contract, I interpreted Paragraph XI very differently ~~than your~~ *from* your present interpretation.

    Was it merely convenient ~~to~~ *for* you to change your mind once I was bound to the contract? You cannot be indifferent to standard business practice, and my understanding ~~to~~ *of* the contract is in complete accord ~~to~~ *with* standard business usage. Paragraph XI is identical ~~to~~ *with* Paragraph VII of the Standard Business Contract No. 109.

    I am forwarding a copy of this letter, accompanied ~~by~~ *with* a copy of Paragraph XI, ~~up~~ to the National Business Board.

    I will abide ~~with~~ *by* their decision if you will agree to abide ~~with~~ *by* it too.

            Respectfully,

nominative Case	objective Case
(subject of a verb)	(object of a verb)
(after a linking verb)	(object of a preposition)

singular {
I
you
he
she
it
}

me
you
him
her
it

plural {
we
~~us~~
you
they
}

us
you
them

nominative after linking verb.

It is I.
It is we.
It was they.

object of prep. into

The car ran into (they, them)

MORE ABOUT PRONOUNS

1. types of pronouns   2. using pronouns   3. who and whom

4. whoever and whomever   5. whose and who's

6. any one, anyone   7. like as a preposition

8. but, meaning except

"Me Tarzan. Me king of jungle." A movie script may sound like that, but your daily conversation had better not. Undoubtedly, you use the pronouns **I** and **me** properly most of the time, which is more than we can say for Tarzan. You automatically say:

> **I** want it. NOT: **Me** want it.
> Give it to **me**. NOT: Give it to **I**.

But in complicated sentences, your choice may become more difficult. Try this sentence, for example:

He thought it was (I) (me) who had ordered the circulars.

Do you know whether **I** or **me** is correct? Do you know how to distinguish between the use of **he** and **him, she** and **her, we** and **us,** or **they** and **them**? Do you know when to use **who** and when to use **whom**? If you use these words properly at all times, you are a rare and fortunate person. In fact, you are probably a genius and we would advise you not to read further in this lesson. If, however, you are an ordinary mortal like the rest of us, you will occasionally have difficulty choosing the proper pronoun and this lesson is designed for you. We're going to show you how to make the choice of pronouns easy.

1. TYPES of pronouns

Look at these sentences. They show you when to use **me** rather than **I**.

1. **Give it to me.** (**Me** is the *object* of the preposition **to.**)

2. **He thanked me.** (**Me** is the *object* of the verb **thanked.**)

Learn this simple rule: Always use **me**, not **I**, when the pronoun is the *object* of a preposition or the *object* of a verb. In fact, **me** is called the objective case of the pronoun **I**. Similarly, **him** is the objective case of **he**; **her** is the objective case of **she**; **us** is the objective case of **we**; and **them** is the objective case of **they**.

Give it to him . . . . to her . . . . to us . . . . to them.
He thanked him . . . . thanked her . . . . thanked us . . . . thanked them.

Quickie Review: What should you know about *objective* pronouns? Only these two simple points:

1. The *objective* pronouns are: *me, him, her, us, them.*

2. You use *objective* pronouns as *objects* of verbs or *objects* of prepositions. That's all.

When do you use the pronoun *I, he, she, we,* and *they*? Do these examples answer your question?

1. **I want to go.** (**I** is the *subject* of the sentence.)

2. **It is I.** (**I** follows the *linking verb* **is.**) That's all there is to it. Use *I, he, she, we,* or *they*:

1. as the *subject* of a sentence or of a clause;

2. after a *linking* verb.

I want to go. He . . . . She . . . . We . . . . They want to go.

It is I. It is he. It is she. It is we. It is they.

NEVER: *It's me.*

I, he, she, we, or *they* is called the *nominative* case of the pronoun because it *names* the subject of a sentence (or its equivalent after a linking verb).

Do you recognize the subject of a sentence when you see it? Do you remember what a clause is? If not, review Lesson 1 on the parts of a sentence. Do you recognize a linking verb when you see one? You should by now. You studied linking verbs in Lessons 4, 5, and 6. Review Lesson 4 right now if you are at all uncertain of linking verbs.

Quickie Review: What should you know about the *nominative* pronouns *I, he, she, we, they*? Remember these two points:

1. Use **I, he, she, we,** or **they** as the *subject* of a sentence or of a clause.

2. Use **I, he, she, we** or **they** after a *linking* verb.

Now look again at the problem sentence you had at the beginning of this lesson: **He thought it was (I) (me) who had ordered the circulars.** Isn't this sentence easy now? The pronoun (*I* or *me*) comes after the *linking* verb *was*. After a linking verb what do we use? That's right! *I.* Therefore: **He thought it was I who had ordered the circulars.** Simple, isn't it? (It it isn't, you had better reread this lesson.)

Let's take a few more difficult sentences. We'll show you a technique to make them easy. How would you complete this sentence:

1. The invoice was sent by John and (I) (me).

You would have no trouble if the sentence read:

2. The invoice was sent by (I) (me).

By just reading Sentence 2 aloud, you would hear that *me* is correct.

The invoice was sent by me.

Me is the object of the preposition *by*.

In Sentence 1, ignore the word *John* and use the same pronoun you would use if the pronoun were alone.

The invoice was sent by (John and) me.

Learn this simple rule: Use the same form of a pronoun when it is joined with another pronoun or a noun that you would use if the pronoun were alone.

Look at these examples:

1. *I* will move. (Subject of a sentence.)
   (Bob and) *I* will move.

2. *He* is an expert. *I* am an expert.
   He and *I* are experts.

3. Did you know it was *he*? (After linking verb.)
   Did you know it was (Bob and) *he*?

4. The order was sent to *me*. (Object of preposition.)
   The order was sent to (John and) *me*.

5. The report interests *me*. The report interests *him*. (Object of verb.)
   The report interests *him* and *me*.

6. Send *me* the folder. Send (Lou and John and) *me* the folder.
   Send *them* and *me* the folder.

7. Submit the report to either (*him or her*) (*he or she*).
   Submit the report to *him*. Submit the report to *her*.
   Submit the report to either *him or her*.

Turn to Programed Reinforcement, S1 through S

2. USING pronouns

A. Us and We

Here's a tricky sentence: **(We) (Us) secretaries have interesting work.**

To solve this problem-sentence, merely leave out the word **secretaries.**

(We) (Us) have interesting work.

Answer: **We have interesting work.**

Therefore: **We secretaries have interesting work.**

Here are some similar examples:

1. The prize was given to (*we*) (*us*) girls.
   Omit *girls*. The prize was given to *us*. (NOT: ... to *we*.)
   Therefore: The prize was given to *us* girls.

2. The director asked (*us*) (*we*) boys to be present.
   The director asked *us*.... (NOT: asked *we*.)
   Therefore: The director asked *us* boys to be present.

3. (*We*) (*Us*) students should be cheerful and efficient.
   We should be.... (NOT: *Us* should be.)
   Therefore: *We* students should be cheerful and efficient.

B. Than and As

1. She is a better stenographer than (I, me.)

2. She was not so good as (he, him).

Here's a technique that will make it easy for you to choose the proper pronoun after *than* or *as*. Add a little word that completes

165

the meaning of the sentence — a <u>word</u> such as *am, do,* or *was.*

For example:

1. **She is a better stenographer than (I, me).** This means:

She is a better stenographer than (I, me) *am.*

Answer: . . . . *I am.* NOT: *me* am.

Therefore: She is a better stenographer than *I.*

2. **She was not so good as (he, him).** This means:

She was not so good as (he, him) *was.*

Answer: . . . . *He was.* NOT: *him* was.

Therefore: She was not so good as *he.*

3. **She does a better job than (I, me).** This means:

She does a better job than *I (do).*

4. **He would rather eat with John than (me, I.)** This means:

He would rather eat with John than *(with) me.*

C. Between You and Me

preposition always take an object.

Between you and (I, me), there's nothing to worry about.

If you remember from Chapter 6 that *between* is a *preposition,* you know that *me* must be correct because *me* is the *object* of the preposition *between.* Always say <u>be-tween you and me</u>—never, *between you and I.*

Between you and me, I think this will work.

Between you and me, who do you think will win?

The profits were divided between Mrs. Smith and him.

Turn to Programed Reinforcement S15 through S20

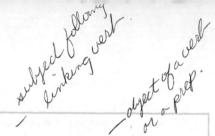

subject following linking verb

object of a verb or a prep.

3. Who and Whom

Whom is the *objective* case of the pronoun *w̄ho.* From this fact, you immediately know that you use *whom* as:

1. The *object* of a verb
2. The *object* of a preposition.

Who is in the *nominative* case, so you know that you use *who*:

1. As the *subject* of a sentence or a clause
2. After a *linking* verb.

Many people find the choice of *who* or *whom* difficult, but here's a technique that will make this choice easy for you. Whenever you choose between *who* and *whom,* merely substitute <u>*he* or *him.*</u> If *he* fits, *who* is correct. If *him* fits, *whom* is correct.

Remember: **He = Who . . . . Him = Whom.** Note the *m* in both hi**m** and who**m.**

Let's try some examples:

1. **(Who, Whom) is it?**
Substitute *he* or *him.*
He is it. NOT: *Him* is it.
Therefore: **Who is it?**

2. **It is (who, whom)?**
Substitute: **It is he.** NOT: It is *him.*
Therefore: **It is who?**

3. **(Who, Whom) do you want?**
Substitute and place *he* or *him* at the end of the question for the sake of clarity: **Do you want him?** NOT: Do you want *he*?
Therefore: **Whom do you want?**

4. **You were referring to (who, whom)?**
Substitute: **You were referring to him.** NOT: You were referring to *he.*
Therefore: **You were referring to whom?**

5. **(Who, Whom) threw the overalls into Mrs. Murphy's chowder?**

You should know the answer to this one. Test it by substituting *he* or *him*.

6. He is a man (who, whom) is loved by all.

This sentence can be broken into two parts that you know we call *clauses* because each part has a subject and a predicate:

a. **He is a man...**

b. **... (who, whom) is loved by all.**

In such a sentence test *who* or *whom* in its own clause. Whichever form is correct in its own clause is correct in the entire sentence.

Substitute: b. **... he is loved by all.** NOT: *him* is loved by all.

Therefore: **He is a man who is loved by all.**

7. He is a man (who, whom) we all love.

This sentence also divides into two clauses:

a. **He is a man...**

b. **... (who, whom) we all love.**

Again we test *who* or *whom* in its own clause.

Substitute: b. **... we all love him.** NOT: we all love *he*.

Therefore: **He is a man whom we all love.**

8. There is an urgent need for men (who, whom) we can trust.

Substitute: **... we can trust him.** NOT: *he*.

9. He is a man (who, whom) I am positive can be trusted. Do not let *I am positive* fool you. This sentence can be rearranged to read: **I am positive he is a man (who, whom) can be trusted.**

The rearranged sentence can be broken into:

a. **I am positive he is a man...**

b. **... (who, whom) can be trusted.**

Substitute: **He can be trusted.** NOT: *Him* can be trusted.

Therefore: **He is a man who I am positive can be trusted.**

10. (Who, Whom) did you say was at the door?

Rearrange this sentence to read: **Did you say (who, whom) was at the door?**

Substitute: **He was at the door.** NOT: *Him* was at the door.

Therefore: **Who did you say was at the door?**

11. The man (who, whom) I think will be our next president will be here soon.

Break this sentence down as follows:

a. **The man... will be here soon.**

b. **... (who, whom) I think will be our next president.**

Substitute in its own clause: **I think he will be our next president.**

NOT: I think *him* will be....

Therefore: **The man who I think will be our next president will be here soon.**

12. The man (who, whom) I believe we all love is standing next to me.

a. **The man... is standing next to me.**

b. **... (who, whom) I believe we all love...**

Substitute in its own clause: **I believe we all love him.** NOT: we all love *he*.

Therefore: **The man whom I believe we all love is standing next to me.**

We pointed out earlier in this chapter that *whom* (like *him*) is in the objective case and should be used as the object of a verb or the object of a preposition. *Who* (like *he*) is in the nominative case and should be used as the subject of a sentence or after a linking verb. To double check your use of *who* and *whom* in the above sentences, re-examine them now to determine why your choice is correct. Why do we require the nominative case wherever we use *who?* Why the objective case wherever we use *whom?*

forget everything that comes before it.

— He — Him

4. Whoever and Whomever

Whomever is in the objective case. *Whoever* is in the nominative. Once again we can use a variation of our *he-him* trick and make the choice easy. Disregard ALL words in the sentence that come BEFORE *whoever* or *whomever*; then substitute:

he = whoever

him = whomever.

Let's study a few examples to see how this works.

1. (Whoever, Whomever) answers the phone should be pleasant.

Substitute: **He answers the phone.** NOT: *Him* answers the phone.

Therefore: **Whoever answers the phone should be pleasant.**

2. Give the prize to (whoever, whomever) you please.

Disregard all words in the sentence before *whoever* or *whomever*.

Disregard: **Give the prize to.**

Substitute: **You please him.** NOT: You please *he*.

Therefore: **Give the prize to whomever you please.**

3. Give the prize to (whoever, whomever) deserves it.

Disregard: **Give the prize to.**

Substitute: **He deserves it.** NOT: *Him* deserves it.

Therefore: **Give the prize to whoever deserves it.**

4. She always accepts help from (whoever, whomever) will give it.

Disregard: **She always accepts help from.**

Substitute: **He will give it.** NOT: *Him* will give it.

Therefore: **She always accepts help from whoever will give it.**

Turn to Programed Reinforcement S21 through S32

— who's
— who has

5. Whose and Who's

These two words are sometimes confused. Remember, however, that the apostrophe in *who's* indicates the *contraction* of two words, *who + is.*

Who's going to the luncheon?

Who is going to the luncheon?

Whose, without the apostrophe, is the *possessive pronoun.* We learned that possessive pronouns do not have apostrophes (*yours, his, hers, its, ours, theirs*).

Whose book is lost?

I don't know whose pen I have.

6. Any One, Anyone

No one is *always* written as two words. There is sometimes confusion about whether to write *anyone, someone,* or *everyone* as one word or two. A simple rule to follow is to write it as *two words* when it is followed by an *of* phrase and to write it as one word at other times.

Everyone was present.

Every one of the salesmen was present.

Can anyone enter the contest?

Let any one of the members enter.

168

"No one" always two words

7. LIKE as a preposition

Which is correct: **She swims like (I, me).** Since *like* is used here as a preposition, *me* is correct because it is the object of the preposition: **She swims like me.**

Why is it not correct to say: **She swims like I do.** It's wrong for the same reason that this famous cigarette slogan is grammatically incorrect: **Winston tastes good like a cigarette should.** *Like* is *never* a conjunction; it is a preposition. The slogan requires a conjunction to make it grammatically correct. *Winston tastes good* **as** *a cigarette should.* Our problem-sentence too requires a conjunction to make it grammatically correct. **She swims as I do.**

like me

as I do .

If you are not too clear on the proper use of conjunctions, don't worry; you'll learn all about them in the next lesson.

8. BUT meaning EXCEPT

conjunction

vs a preposition

Sometimes the word *but* is used as a preposition meaning *except:* **All but him are welcome.** You know that prepositions are followed by the objective case.

I want anybody but him for the position. NOT: I want anybody but *he* . . .

object

takes an object .

Turn to Programed Reinforcement S33 through

		S1	The pronouns **I, he, she, we,** and **they** are in the n _ _ _ _ _ _ _ _ _ case.
R1	nominative	**S2**	The pronouns **me, him, her, us,** and **them** are in the o _ _ _ _ _ _ _ _ case.
R2	objective	**S3**	**She** is in the _____ case. The objective case of **she** is _____.
R3	nominative; **her**	**S4**	Objective pronouns are used in two situations — as objects of v _ _ _ _ and as objects of p _ _ _ _ _ _ _ _ _ _ _.
R4	verbs; prepositions	**S5**	**Give the message to (he, him).** The correct pronoun is _____. It is in the o_____ case because it is object of the p_____ t___.
R5	**him;** objective; preposition; **to**	**S6**	**Give (she, her) the message.** The correct pronoun is _____. It is in the _____ case because it is object of the implied p_____ **t**_____.
R6	**her;** objective; preposition; **to**	**S7**	The nominative pronoun is used in two situations — as s_____ of a sentence or clause and after a l _ _ _ _ _ _ _ verb.
R7	subject; linking	**S8**	**(Me, I) want to apply for the job.** The correct pronoun is obviously _____. It is in the _____ case because it is the _____ of a sentence.
R8	**I;** nominative; subject	**S9**	**It was (they, them) who signed the petition.** The correct pronoun is _____. It is in the _____ case because it comes after the l _ _ _ _ _ _ _ v _ _ _ w _ _ _.
R9	**they;** nominative; linking verb; **was**	**S10**	You should never say **It is me** because **me** is in the _____ case. You say **It is I** because the nominative case is needed after the l _ _ _ _ _ _ _ v _ _ _ _ _ _.
R10	objective; linking verb; **is**		

170

R11

a) **she,** nominative

b) **me,** objective

S11

Circle the correct form in each sentence. In the space provided, write the case.

a) **He thought it was (she, her) who made the call.**_____

b) **The invoice was drawn up by (I, me).**_____

R12

Omit **Frank and;**

Correct pronoun: **me.**

S12

Underline the words that may be omitted in this sentence to determine more easily which pronoun to use: **The telegrams were accepted by Frank and (me, I).** Circle the correct pronoun.

R13

her; objective case;

object of preposition **by**

S13

Circle the correct pronoun. Give the case and reason. **The meeting was attended by John and (she, her).**

Case: _____

Reason: _____

R14

I; nominative case;

after linking verb **are**

● **TURN TO**
   Exercises 34 and 35

S14

Circle the correct pronoun. Give the case and reason. **The newest employees are Helen and (me, I).**

Case: _____

Reason: _____

R15

typists

S15

(We, us) typists should study some kind of shorthand. You quickly know the correct form is **we** if you omit the word

t __ __ __ __ __ __ __.

R16

us; omit **secretaries**

S16

Circle the correct pronoun. Underline the word you may omit to double check your choice. **Mr. Jones gave the production award to (we, us) secretaries.**

R17

do or **type**

S17

To determine which case of pronoun should follow the conjunction **as** or **than,** it is wise to add a simple verb after the pronoun in question. What test verb would you use here? **He types as well as (me, I).** Answer: _____

R18

she; nominative;

subject; **is (than she is)**

S18

Circle the correct pronoun: **Frank is more ambitious than (her, she).** The _____ case is correct because the pronoun is the s __ __ __ __ __ __ __ of the understood verb __ __.

R19

me; objective;

object; **for (than for me)**

S19

Circle the correct pronoun: **He would rather work for Mr. Clark than (me, I).** The _____ case is correct because the pronoun is the o __ __ __ __ __ __ of the understood preposition __ __ __.

S20

Between is a preposition. Circle the correct pronouns: **The boss divided the work between (him, he) and (me, I).** The _____ case is correct because the pronouns are the o _ _ _ _ _s of the p _ _ _ _ _ _ _ _ _ _ **between.**

R20

him; me; objective; objects; preposition

● **TURN TO**
Exercises 36 and 37

S21

The pronouns **who** and **whom** sometimes cause trouble. It must be remembered that **who** is in the n _ _ _ _ _ _ _ _ _ _ case while **whom** is in the o _ _ _ _ _ _ _ _ case.

R21

nominative; objective

S22

Since **who** is in the nominative case, it may be used in only two situations: as _____ of a sentence or clause and after a _____ verb.

R22

subject; linking

S23

To make it easy to know whether to choose **who** or **whom**, you can substitute _____ for **who** and _____ for **whom**.

R23

he; him

S24

The ending letter _____ is the same for the objective pronoun **whom** and the objective pronoun _____ which we can substitute for **whom**.

R24

m; him

S25

Circle the correct pronoun. Give the case and reason. **(Who, whom) in your opinion will win the game?**
Case: _____
Reason: _____

R25

Who; nominative; subject of the sentence.

S26

I wonder (whom, who) we should give the prize to. You know that the correct form is **whom** because you may substitute the pronoun _ _ m and say: **We should give the prize to _____.**

R26

him; **him**

S27

Circle the correct pronoun: **He is the man (who, whom) I believe erased the signature.** By substituting _ _ for _ _ _, you could rearrange the clause to read: **I believe _ _ erased the signature.**

R27

Who; he; who; **he**

S28

Circle the correct pronoun. Remember to substitute **he** for **who, him** for **whom. Tell me (who, whom) you think is the mechanic to (who, whom) we should give the bonus.**

R28

who (**he** is the mechanic); **whom** (to **him**)

S29 Circle the correct pronouns in this sentence: **He is the writer (whom, who) I am positive is the one (whom, who) we should select as editor.**

R29
who
   (**he** is the one);

whom
   (we should select **him**)

S30 **Whoever** and **whomever** are used exactly like **who** and **whom**. That means that **whoever** is in the _____ case; you may substitute _____ for **whoever. Whomever** is in the _____ case; for it you may substitute _____.

R30
nominative; he;
objective; him

S31 When choosing between **whoever** and **whomever**, disregard all words that come (before, after) it. **I will choose (whoever, whomever) I wish.** Underline the words you should disregard and circle the correct pronoun.

R31
before;
Disregard **I will choose;**
whomever (I wish **him**)

S32 Underline the words you should disregard and circle the correct pronoun. **I will choose (whoever, whomever) is better.**

R32
Disregard **I will choose;**
whoever (he is better)
● TURN TO Exercise 38A

S33 **Whose** and **who's** are words that should never be confused if one remembers that **who's** is a contraction of the words _____ _____.

R33
who is

S34 Circle the correct words: **Tell me (whose, who's) dictation this is, and I'll tell you (whose, who's) responsible for the confusion.**

R34
whose; who's

S35 Circle the correct words. **I wonder (whose, who's) pen this is and (whose, who's) going to claim it.**

R35
whose; who's

S36 Pronouns like **anyone, someone,** and **everyone** may be written as one word or two words. They are written as (one, two) word(s) when a phrase beginning with **of** follows: **(Everyone, Every one) of the crates was returned.**

R36
two; **Every one**

S37 Circle the correct words: **(Everyone, Every one) of the girls may go, but (noone, no one) has gone yet.**

R37
Every one; no one

S38 When **but** means **except,** it is used as a preposition and takes the o_____ case after it. **Everyone but (he, him) went along.**

R38
objective; **him**

S39 Circle the correct pronouns: **No one but (she, her) may have the key, but (she, her) must report early.** The first answer is **her** because **her** is the _____ of the preposition _____. The second answer is _____ because that pronoun is the ___ ___ ___ ___ ___ ___ of its clause.

R39
her; she;
object; **but;**
she; subject

S40 When **like** is used as a preposition (meaning **similar to**), it takes the objective case after it. Circle the correct answers. a) **He writes like (I, me).** b) **Mary looks like (she, her).**

R40
a) **me;** b) **her**

S41 Let's review pronouns by circling the correct words. **It is (we, us) stenographers (who, whom) are more deserving than (he, him).**

R41
we; who; he (is)

S42 Circle the correct pronouns: **Between you and (I, me) I don't care (who, whom) is promoted or (who, whom) they pick.**

R42
me; who; whom

S43 Choose the correct words: **(Whoever, Whomever) is the better executive is the one (who's, whose) getting the new insurance bonds of (theirs, they'res, their's).**

R43
Whoever; who's; theirs

S44 Circle the correct words: **(Anyone, Any one) of the secretaries but (she, her) works like (me, I) under pressure.**

R44
Any one; her; me

● TURN TO
Exercise 38B and Review

SCORE

A_____

EXERCISE 34   Action and Linking Verbs

A. This is a review problem dealing with action and linking verbs. In each of the following sentences is an italicized verb. In the space provided, mark A if it is an action verb; mark L if it is a linking verb.

SCORING: DEDUCT 10 POINTS FOR EACH ERROR.

1. It *would have been* easier had we been better prepared.   1. ___L___
2. Can we *expect* you before noon?   2. ___A___
3. It *became* difficult for him to work.   3. ___L___
4. He *tasted* the food with gusto.   4. ___A___
5. Things *look* bad for the moment.   5. ___A___
6. He *lay* down to rest.   6. ___A___
7. It *sounded* like a good idea.   7. ___A___
8. He *rose* at dawn.   8. ___A___
9. This *is* the truth.   9. ___L___
10. *Was* it he who met you?   10. ___L___

SCORE

B_____

EXERCISE 34   Objects of Verbs and Prepositions

B. This is a review problem that deals with the objects of verbs and the objects of prepositions. Underline each object of a verb or of a preposition in the following sentences. Write OV above the word if it is the object of a verb; write OP above the word if it is the object of a preposition.

SCORING: DEDUCT 10 POINTS FOR EACH ERROR.

1. John still loves Mary.
2. All of the men were dissatisfied with the wage offer.
3. It seemed to him that all was lost.
4. Send the books to us by fast mail.
5. Thank you for your cooperation.
6. We should like to place a definite order for holiday goods.
7. This is no time for him to leave the firm.
8. This is how we know when to start the machine.
9. We shall have our fall order ready for delivery as soon as we get word from our buyer.
10. We explained to your salesman that we did not want the shoes before August because we have our annual sale during July.

SCORE

A_____

EXERCISE 35 — Forms of Pronouns

A. This problem deals with the different forms a pronoun can take. In the space provided, write the objective case and the possessive cases of each pronoun.

SCORING: DEDUCT 5 POINTS FOR EACH ERROR.

Nominative Case	Objective Case	Possessive Cases	
1. I	*me*	*my*	*mine*
2. you	*you*	*yours*	*your*
3. he	*him*	*his*	*his*
4. she	*her*	*hers*	*her*
5. it	*it*	*its*	*its*
6. we	*us*	*ours*	*our*
7. they	*them*	*theirs*	*their*

SCORE

B_____

EXERCISE 35 — Nominative Case Pronouns

B. This problem deals with the use of the nominative case pronoun as the subject of a sentence. In the space provided, write the correct pronoun. These problems should be easy.

SCORING: DEDUCT 8 POINTS FOR EACH ERROR.

1. (I, me) am extremely pleased with his progress.
2. (He, Him) is an exceptionally gifted salesman.
3. Last night (us, we) went to the theater after dinner.
4. In the long run (her, she) will undoubtedly succeed.
5. Contrary to our advice (them, they) all agreed to the resolution.
6. During our last convention (we, us) presented the new idea.
7. To preserve our position as leader in our field, (I, me) propose a new concept.
8. In the beginning (she, her) was uncertain of her duties.
9. Until now (he, him) has the best selling record.
10. Despite their opposition (them, they) agreed to abide by our decision.
11. (Us, We) are certain (us, we) can stop their gains.
12. If it were my decision, (I, me) would tell them that either (them, they) work with us or (us, we) take drastic action.

1. _____ I
2. _____ He
3. _____ we
4. _____ she
5. _____ they
6. _____ we
7. _____ I
8. _____ she
9. _____ he
10. _____ they
11. _____ we, we
12. _____ I, they, we

EXERCISE 35 | Pronouns After Linking Verbs

C. This problem deals with the form of the pronoun after a linking verb. In the space provided, write the proper pronoun. Remember, use the nominative case after a linking verb.

SCORING: DEDUCT 4 POINTS FOR EACH ERROR.

1. It is (I, me).   1. _I_
2. It is (he, him).   2. _he_
3. It is (her, she).   3. _she_
4. It is (us, we).   4. _us we_
5. It is (them, they).   5. _they_
6. It was (I, me).   6. _I_
7. It was (he, him).   7. _he_
8. It was (her, she).   8. _she_
9. It was (us, we).   9. _~~they~~ we_
10. It was (them, they).   10. _they_
11. I thought it was (he, him).   11. _he_
12. I thought it was (her, she).   12. _she_
13. I thought it was (them, they)   13. _they_
14. It was (he, him) who sent the order.   14. _he_
15. If it was (he, him) who sent the order, (he, him) should be congrat-
    ulated.   15. _he_ , _he_
16. The last person to leave was (her, she). 16. _she_
17. The winners of the award were (them, they). 17. _they_
18. If I were (he, him) and he were (I, me), this would be a different
    world.   18. _he_ _I_
19. It must have been (her, she) who delivered the message. 19. _~~her~~ she_
20. That is (them, they) walking toward us. 20. _they_
21. That's (he, him) at the door now.   21. _~~him~~ he_
22. Could it have been (us, we) who swayed his opinion? 22. _we_
23. That might be (her, she) calling on the phone. 23. _~~her~~ she_
24. It was not (I, me) who made the error. 24. _I_
25. The man to get the promotion should have been (he, him). 25. _he_

EXERCISE 35 | Pronouns as Objects of Verbs

D. This problem deals with the use of the proper pronoun as the object of a verb. In the space provided, write the correct pronoun. Remember, use the objective case as object of a verb.

SCORING: DEDUCT 10 POINTS FOR EACH ERROR.

1. They hired (I, me) for the job.   1. *me,*
2. They hired (he, him) for the job.   2. *him*
3. The decision shocked (he, him.)   3. *him*
4. The explosion knocked (her, she) out of her chair.   4. *her*
5. In the end he lent (us, we) his support.   5. *us*
6. Send (them, they) the letters at once.   6. *them*
7. Permit (I, me) to voice my disapproval.   7. *me*
8. You have told (us, we) a most fascinating story.   8. *us*
9. They would not allow (he, him) to leave.   9. *him*
10. The director told (us, we) that his decision had been reached.   10. *us*

EXERCISE 35 | Pronouns as Objects of Prepositions

E. This problem deals with the use of the proper pronoun as the object of a preposition. In the space provided, write the correct pronoun. Remember, use the objective case as object of a preposition.

SCORING: DEDUCT 10 POINTS FOR EACH ERROR.

1. The message was sent to (I, me).   1. *me*
2. The message was sent by (he, him).   2. *him*
3. We had learned a great deal from (her, she).   3. *her*
4. The committee sent its congratulations to (us, we).   4. *us*
5. Mr. Smith walked right by (them, they) without even acknowledging their presence.   5. *them*
6. He came directly to (I, me) for the information.   6. *me*
7. They stared at (he, him) as he entered the room.   7. *him*
8. The idea came to (them, they) at the same instant.   8. *them*
9. The order was delivered directly to (us, we).   9. *us*
10. John stood between (I, me) and the door.   10. *me*

NAME   CLASS   DATE

EXERCISE 36   The Proper Pronoun – I

A. This problem deals with the use of the proper pronoun. In the space provided, write the correct pronoun.

SCORING: DEDUCT 10 POINTS FOR EACH ERROR.

1. The letter was sent directly to (he, him).   ✓1. _him_
2. We knew that (she, her) would accept the offer.   ✓2. _she_
3. It was (I, me) who ordered the books from (they, them). ✓3. _I them_
4. Did you see (us, we) at the theater?   ✓4. _us_
5. If I were (her, she), I would demand a raise.   ✓5. _she_
6. Are you certain that (they, them) will not accept your invitation? ✓6. _they_
7. Was it (he, him) who spoke to the representative? ✓7. _he_
8. Deliver this message to (they, them) at once.   ✓8. _them_
9. Permit (I, me) to differ with (he, him).   ✓9. _me, him_
10. Stop (I, me) if you've heard this.   ✓10. _me_

EXERCISE 36   Joining Proper Pronouns

B. This problem deals with the use of the proper pronoun when it is joined with another pronoun or a noun. Fill in the correct pronoun in the space provided. Remember, use the same pronoun you would use if it were alone.

SCORING: DEDUCT 10 POINTS FOR EACH ERROR.

1. Bob and (he, him) will go.   1. _he_ ✓
2. The men congratulated Mr. Robinson and (I, me).   2. _me_ ✓
3. Mr. Smith will introduce you and (he, him) to the staff. 3. _him_ ✓
4. Our office is certain that you and (her, she) will get the job. 4. _she_ ✓
5. (He, Him) and (I, me) will leave on the early train. 5. _He I_ ✓
6. They gave raises in salary to (he, him) and (I, me). 6. _he I him_ ✓
7. The winners of the prizes were (he, him) and (he, she). 7. _he, she_ ✓
8. Between you and (I, me), this is a dangerous proposition. 8. _me_ ✓
9. The salesmen in your territory are Mr. Johnson and (I, me). 9. _I_ ✓
10. The boys and (I, me) feel certain that the contract will be awarded to you and (they, them). 10. _I them_ ✓

SCORE

EXERCISE 37   The Proper Pronoun—II

This is an overall problem dealing with choosing the proper pronoun. In the space provided, write the correct pronoun.

SCORING: DEDUCT 4 POINTS FOR EACH ERROR.

1. Give it to (he, him).   1. _him_

2. (He, Him) likes this method of accounting.   2. _He_

3. This will shock (he, him).   3. _him_

4. It was (he, him) who started the trouble.   4. _he_

5. This message is for (she, her).   5. _her_

6. Here is a story that will astound (they, them).   6. _them_

7. Was it (I, me) you saw at the theater?   7. _I_

8. Are you sure you sent (I, me) the bill?   8. _me_

9. John and (he, him) are next on the list.   9. _he_

10. Give the order to Charles and (he, him).   10. _him_

11. (We, Us) salesmen must plan our campaign carefully.   11. _We_

12. (He and I) (Him and me) will leave at dawn.   12. _He + I_

13. Was it (he, him) you spoke to?   13. _him_

14. The order directed (us, we) secretaries to come to work fifteen minutes earlier.   14. _us_

15. He is not so clever as (I, me).   15. _I_

16. This man is a better salesman than (I, me).   16. _I_

17. He would rather work with John than (I, me).   17. _me_

18. Between you and (I, me), this work is easy.   18. _me_

19. Mr. Roberts is as good a manager as (he, him).   19. _him_

20. It was (she, her) who cut the endowment fund.   20. _She_

21. The trophy was presented to Smith and (I, me).   21. _Me_

22. He is pleased with (their, they're) success.   22. _their_

23. Is Judith taller than (she, her)?   23. _she_

24. They would rather choose Robert than (I, me).   24. _I_

25. It is up to (us, we) girls to show her the proper procedure.   25. _us_

NAME   CLASS   DATE

EXERCISE 38   Who and Whom

A. This problem deals with the choice of who or whom, whoever or whomever. In the space provided, write the proper word. Remember, substitute: He = who or whoever; Him = whom or whomever.

SCORING: DEDUCT 3 POINTS FOR EACH ERROR.

1. (Who, Whom) is at the door?   1. _who_
2. It is (who, whom) that you want to meet?   2. _whom_
3. (Who, Whom) did you say called?   3. _who_
4. Our choice is a man (who, whom) you all know.   4. _whom_
5. Our choice is a man (who, whom) is known by all.   5. _whoever_ who
6. He likes (whoever, whomever) is kind to him.   6. _whoever_
7. He is a man (who, whom) I think can be fully trusted in his
    position.   7. _whom_
8. (Who, Whom) were you speaking of?   8. _whom_
9. (Who, Whom) among you knows the answer?   9. _who_
10. (Whomever, Whoever) gets there first wins the prize.   10. _whoever_
11. He likes (whoever, whomever) he meets.   11. _whomever_
12. She is a woman (who, whom) I feel confident we can rely on.   12. _whom_
13. Upon (who, whom) will you bestow the award?   13. _whom_
14. She is a person (who, whom) is most talented.   14. _who_
15. She is a person (who, whom) we know to be talented.   15. _whom_
16. One man (who, whom) was chosen for accomplishment refused
    to take the job.   16. _who_
17. Choose (whoever, whomever) you think best.   17. _whomever_
18. It is the intelligent man (who, whom) succeeds.   18. _who_
19. Have you determined (who, whom) you want for the job?   19. _whom_
20. Please tell me (who, whom) you think will win.   20. _who_
21. The woman (who, whom) I expected did not show up.   21. _whom_
22. Show me the boy (who, whom) you suspect of having stolen the
    money.   22. _whom_
23. They want (whoever, whomever) comes to be on time.   23. _whoever_
24. (Who, Whom) will check the results in the files?   24. _who_
25. The story will be divulged to (whoever, whomever) you choose.   25. _whomever_
26. Their agent said that Mr. Smith, (who, whom) is one of his
    friends, is the man for the job.   26. _who_
27. They will select (whoever, whomever) they think best.   27. _whomever_
28. I know a man (who, whom) I am sure can do a perfect job.   28. _who_
29. Of all the people (who, whom) I know, he is the one (who, whom)   29. _who_
    can be counted on.   _who_
30. It was (he, him) to (who, whom) you spoke yesterday.   30. _he_
                                                                            whom

EXERCISE 38   Proper Use of Pronouns

B. This problem deals with the proper use of certain pronouns. Cross out any incorrect words in the following sentences and write the correct word above it. There may be more than one error in a sentence.

SCORING: DEDUCT 10 POINTS FOR EACH ERROR.

1. Tell me ~~whose~~ *who's* coming today so that no one but ~~he~~ *him* will be expected.

2. ~~Everyone~~ of the officials except ~~he~~ *him* has been assigned a post.

3. ~~Who's~~ *whose* typewriter needs repairing, his or ~~your's~~?

4. ~~There's~~ *Theirs* would be a most difficult task for any ~~one~~.

5. ~~There~~ *Their* roles would be exciting for any ~~one~~ with courage.

6. Every ~~one~~ wishes ~~they~~ *he* could sing like ~~he~~ *him*.

7. Between you and ~~I~~ *me*, no one is sure of his part.

8. The salesman ~~whose~~ *who's* coming looks like him.

9. ~~Our's~~ is a perfect relationship, and ~~every one~~ *everyone* knows it.

10. ~~Your's~~ is not so accurate as ~~our's~~.

REVIEW EXERCISE 8   More About Pronouns

A number of pronouns in the following letter are misused. Cross out each incorrectly written pronoun and write the proper pronoun above it.

SCORING: DEDUCT 5 POINTS FOR EACH ERROR.

Dear Mr. Backrack:

I would like to tell you more about Robert Gilbert, the man who I started to describe to you last week.

Mr. Gilbert is a man who has been constantly employed in top executive positions. Ten years ago it was ~~him~~ *he* and Bob

(continued)

Anthony whom raised the Eighth National Bank to its present position. It was him whom gave the Smith Company it's shot in the arm. It was him whom the Jones Corporation called upon when it needed help.

There are few such men left in the business world. If it were left to I, I would definitely choose Robert Gilbert for the Presidency of this firm. He is a man whom I believe can lead us out of our present difficulty. He is a man whom I believe we can accept as a leader and an inspiration. He is a man whom I believe will lead us to the top position in our field.

I am sure that whoever the Board chooses as President will do a fine job; however, I would choose Robert Gilbert. I cannot think of a man whom is better qualified, whom is more trustworthy, and whom will do a better job than him. If it were up to we salesmen, we would choose noone but he as a man whose reliable.

                Respectfully,

Lesson 9

Simple sentences - one thought, 1 indepent clause
John ran down the street.

compound sentence 2 or more indepent
clauses - may or not have
an independent clause.
John ran down the street and
played ball in the yard.
co-ordinate
conjunction

subordinate conj - join an independent
clause to a dependent.

complex sentence - one independent clause
& one or more dependent
clauses.

subordinate clause

depend clause.
Since Jack would not play
ball with Jim, Jim went home.
indep. clause

since, because, according to, otherwise,
nevertheless, if.

Independent precedes the dependent clause -
there is no comma between clauses.
The men shoveled the snow since
they had to go to work.
dependent first - unnatural order there is
a comma.
Since the men had to go to work
they shoveled snow.

subordinate — because, since,

CONJUNCTIONS

1. conjunctions and sentence structure

2. using conjunctions   3. interjections

A conjunction is the *glue* that we use to attach a word or thought to a related word or thought. **And, but, because, or, yet** — these are just a few of the hundreds of conjunctions in our language.

Conjunctions do more than just *connect* two or more ideas; they show the *relationship* between ideas. In your writing, use your conjunctions carefully so that they express the *precise* relationship you intend.

For example, in each of the following sentences which conjunction better shows the relationship between the ideas it connects:

1. **This book is heavy to carry, (and) (but) it is light reading.**
2. **This book is heavy, (and) (but) it is bulky too.**

Obviously, to convey the exact meaning intended in Sentence 1, **but** is proper. In Sentence 2 **and** is proper. There are hundreds of conjunctions in our language offering you a rich choice of words to show *precise* shades of relationship. Here are just a few that you use constantly: **accordingly, as soon as, besides, consequently, hence, inasmuch as, in order that, moreover, nothwithstanding, otherwise, therefore, though, thus, until, whereas**

join

1. Conjunctions and SENTENCE STRUCTURE

Let's review what we already know about how sentences are composed, and then let's add some new concepts involving the proper use of conjunctions.

You know that a simple sentence must contain two essential parts—a subject and a predicate—and that it must express a complete thought. In its simplest form you might have something like this: *Snow fell.* To add greater meaning to our simple sentence, you can add words and phrases that describe the subject or the predicate or both. For example: *Freezing snow fell on the highway.* This is still a simple sentence,

— and, but, or, nor
co-ordinate join co-equal parts.
I went and he stayed

but it provides added description. We have built up our simple thought by the addition of *modifiers* that describe our subject and predicate — an adjective, *freezing*, and a prepositional phrase, *on the highway*. We still have only a simple sentence consisting of a subject plus a predicate.

You have also learned that a simple sentence can have more than one subject or more than one predicate. For example: **Snow and sleet fell.** This is a simple sentence with a *compound* subject. Or we might have written: **Snow fell and froze.** This is a simple sentence with a *compound predicate*.

But now look at this example: **Snow fell and sleet froze.** Is this still a simple sentence? No. In effect, we have two complete sentences that are connected by the conjunction **and**: *Snow fell.* (AND) *Sleet froze.* The sentence **Snow fell and sleet froze** is called a *compound* sentence. A compound sentence is a sentence that is composed of two or more simple sentences that are joined together by a conjunction or a semicolon. We call each simple sentence that is part of a compound sentence by the name *independent clause.* In our example-sentence, **Snow fell** is an independent clause; **sleet froze** is an independent clause. They are *independent* because they can stand by themselves as complete sentences.

In a compound sentence, the conjunction that connects one clause with another is called a *coordinate conjunction.* **And, but, or, yet** — these are coordinate conjunctions. They are called *coordinate* because they connect two *coequal* parts. In a compound sentence they connect two coequal independent clauses.

Coordinate conjunctions can also be used as part of a compound subject — for example, **snow and sleet** — in which case they connect two coequal subjects; and coordinate conjunctions can be used as part of a compound predicate — for example, **fell and froze** — in which case they connect two coequal predicates. For the moment let us concentrate on the use of coordinate conjunctions in joining independent clauses to form compound sentences.

How many independent clauses can you weld together into one compound sentence? Theoretically, as many as you like. You have undoubtedly heard the tiresome talker who links all his thoughts together in one endless sentence that sounds something like this: **So snow fell and the wind blew, and I couldn't see enough to drive straight, so my car ran off the road, and I found myself in a ditch.** Of course, William Faulkner won the Nobel Prize for writing stories in which some sentences ran for pages without stopping. At the other extreme is another Nobel Prize winner, Ernest Hemingway, who wrote with a rat-a-tat style of short simple sentences: **Snow fell. The wind blew. I couldn't see to drive.**

How long should *your* sentences be? We would advise that you aim for a middle ground somewhere between the styles of these two great literary figures. In business correspondence your objective should be to say what you have to say as simply as possible. Thus you should tend toward the use of short simple sentences. By themselves, however, such sentences sound choppy and quickly become monotonous. Also, you will often find that simple sentences alone do not enable you to express certain *relationships* between ideas. So you will frequently want to use longer sentences composed of more than one clause. You have already learned about one such type of sentence — the compound sentence. Now, let's turn to another type of sentence — the *complex* sentence.

In Lesson 1 you learned about the *dependent* clause. This is a clause that contains a subject and predicate but does *not* express a complete thought by itself. For example, **since the snow fell** is a dependent clause. By itself, it leaves you up in the air without expressing a complete thought. It *depends* upon another thought to complete its meaning. Thus we might complete it like this: **We have received no shipments since the snow fell.** Now we have a complete sentence composed of an independent clause—**we have received no shipments**—and a dependent clause—**since the snow fell.** As you also learned in Lesson 1, this type of sentence composed of an independent clause plus a dependent clause is called a *complex* sentence. Observe in the following examples of complex sentences how two thoughts—an independent clause and a dependent clause—have been combined to show the relationship of one to the other.

> **We selected their product because it is best.**
> **We will ship the order unless we hear from you by Thursday.**
> **They will be on time if the weather is good.**

In each of the above examples, observe the conjunction that introduces the dependent clause — **because, unless, if.** Each of these conjunctions is called a *subordinate conjunction* because when it is added to an independent clause, it makes that clause incomplete by itself and dependent upon another clause for completion. In other words, it *subordinates* that clause to an independent clause.

Let's look at a few examples to see how this works. If we start with the independent clause **Snow falls** and add to it a subordinate conjunction like **if, when, although,** or **in case,** we end with a dependent clause:

If snow falls . . . .
When snow falls . . . .
Although snow falls . . . .
In case snow falls . . . .

There are hundreds of subordinate conjunctions. Here are just a few of the commonly used ones:

after	notwithstanding	though
although	on condition that	unless
as	otherwise	until
as soon as	provided	when
because	since	where
except	supposing	whereas
if	that	while

For practice, try to compose complex sentences using ten of these subordinate conjunctions. Note that in a complex sentence, the so-called *natural sequence* is for the independent clause to come first. For example:

Natural sequence —

We shall pay the bill unless we hear from you.

Independent Clause   *Dependent Clause*

You can reverse this sentence if you like.

Reverse sequence —

Unless we hear from you, we shall pay the bill.

Dependent Clause   *Independent Clause*

The most important point to notice is that you use a comma to separate the clauses *only* when you follow the *reverse* sequence. Observe these paired examples:

This plant will close when the patents expire.
When the patents expire, this plant will close.

The luncheon will be held even if it rains.
Even if it rains, the luncheon will be held.

An easy way to remember the natural sequence is to think of a dependent clause as being like the tail on a dog. The dog can get along without the tail, but the tail can't get along without the dog. Naturally, the tail ordinarily follows the dog; so if you put the tail in front of the dog, you've got an unnatural sequence. The comma is put into a reverse-order sentence to warn the reader: "Watch out! Don't expect this sentence to be in natural sequence. This tail comes *before* the dog."

Let's take a moment now to review what you have learned about the different types of sentences. You have met three types of sentences: the *simple* sentence; the *compound* sentence; and the *complex* sentence. The simple sentence is composed of a subject and predicate that express a complete thought. The compound sentence is composed of two or more independent clauses connected by a coordinate conjunction such as **and, or, but,** or by a semicolon. The complex sentence is composed of an independent clause connected to a dependent clause that contains a subordinate conjunction such as **since, if, because.**

At this stage you may wonder why people ever came to evolve so many different types of sentences. The first reason is to add variety to our language. With the different types of sentences available to you, you are able to add interest and change of pace to what otherwise might be dull and monotonous. In addition, by using complex and compound sentences, you are able to combine thoughts so as to pass along to your reader necessary shades of meaning and relationship.

In all your writing, therefore, strive for these twin objectives: 1) maintaining interest by employing variety in your sentence structure; and 2) expressing the relationships among your thoughts by intelligent use of conjunctions in compound and complex sentences.

Turn to Programed Reinforcement S1–S35

188

2. USING conjunctions

A. Pairs of Conjunctions

Certain conjunctions act together to connect ideas. They are called *correlative conjunctions* because they correlate one thought with another.

1. **Either ... or: Either** you work harder **or** you leave.
2. **Neither ... nor:** We want **neither** sympathy **nor** charity.
3. **Both ... and:** The true leader is **both** self-confident **and** humble.
4. **Not only ... but also:** We want you **not only** to visit our office **but also** to inspect our plant.
5. **Whether ... or: Whether** you act now **or** wait is a matter of great concern.

The major points to remember about these paired conjunctions are these:

1. With **neither** always use **nor** (NOT **or**).
   We want neither sympathy nor charity.

Remember that **neither** and **nor** go together; the positive equivalents are **either** and **or**.

2. With **not only** always use **but also** (NOT **but** alone).
   We want you not only to visit our office but also to inspect our plant.
3. Paired conjunctions should stand as near as possible to the words they connect.

Right: **My job has given me both pleasure and satisfaction.**

WRONG: **My job has both given me pleasure and satisfaction.**

Do you see why this is wrong?

Right: **The announcer has reported neither the time nor the place of the event.**

WRONG: **The announcer has neither reported the time nor the place of the event.**

B. LIKE and AS

In the lesson on prepositions, you learned that **like** can be used as a preposition but never as a conjunction. You learned why this cigarette slogan is incorrect:

"Winston tastes good like a cigarette should." Properly, it should read: "Winston tastes good *as* a cigarette should." In other words, it requires a conjunction (*as*) rather than a preposition (*like*). Don't make the error of confusing **like** with **as**.

Right: **He looks like me.**

Right: **It was done as you wanted.**

Right: **As I said, this is a great day.**

NOT: **Like I said, this is a great day.**

C. TRY AND ...

This sentence is wrong: **You must try and do it.**

You should say: **You must try to do it.**
Do you see why the logical relationship of thoughts dictates the use of *try to* rather than *try and?*

D. PROVIDED and PROVIDING

Provided is a conjunction. **Providing** is *not* a conjunction and should never be used to join two parts of a sentence.

Right: **We will arrive on time provided we have a tailwind.**

Right: **Provided there is time, you can give your speech.**

WRONG: **We will arrive on time, providing we have a tailwind.**

E. SO ... SO ... SO ... SO

Have you ever heard a poor speaker drag on his remarks by connecting them with interminable **so's**? **So** is a conjunction that should be used cautiously; do not use it too frequently.

WRONG: **I asked my boss for a raise. So he refused me. So I thought of another approach. So the next day, etc.**

It is better to use words like **therefore, consequently,** and **accordingly** to join ideas so that you have interest and variety in your speech and writing. Moreover, these words enable you to express sharply and exactly the precise relationship of ideas that you intend.

Better: **I asked my boss for a raise, but he refused me. Rather than despair, I thought of another approach, which I promptly tried the next day, etc.**

F. AS ... AS

When two *affirmative* statements are joined by paired conjunctions, use **as ... as**; when *negative* statements are joined, use **so ... as.**

Right: **He is as tall as a tree.**

Right: **He is not so tall as I had thought.**

G. WHERE for THAT

Don't use the conjunction **where** for **that**. Again, simple logic should show you why this is correct.

Right: **I read in the magazine that the price had been lowered.**

WRONG: **I read in the magazine where the price had been lowered.**

Note: Never say **the reason was because.** Say **the reason was that.** For example: **The reason was that I was tired.**

189

You may sometimes wonder whether to use the objective case (**me, him**) or the nominative case (**I, he**) after words like **before, after, but**. These words may be used either as conjunctions (followed by the nominative case) or prepositions (followed by the objective case), depending upon how you want to use them.

Right: I got to the office after him. (Preposition)

Right: I got to the office after he did. (Conjunction)

Right: She filed the letters before me. (Preposition)

Right: No one will go but him. (Preposition meaning *except*)

Right: She filed the letters before I did. (Conjunction)

Right: No one will go but he may come later. (Conjunction)

3. INTERJECTIONS

Just one word about interjections. That's all they deserve. An interjection is a word or group of words that expresses strong feeling. Always follow an interjection with an *exclamation point.*

Good! Surprise! Well done! Oh! Magnificent!

Turn to Programed Reinforcement S36-S50

R (Responses)	S (Frames)
	S1 A conjunction is a part of speech that (describes, joins, modifies) thoughts.
R1 joins	**S2** A simple sentence contains a s __ __ __ __ __ and a p __ __ __ __ __ __ __ and expresses a complete thought.
R2 subject; predicate	**S3** A clause is a group of words containing a subject and a predicate that may or may not express a complete thought. ☐ True ☐ False
R3 True	**S4** A clause that expresses a complete thought is called an _____ clause.
R4 independent	**S5** A clause that does not express a complete thought is called a _____ clause.
R5 dependent	**S6** A sentence that is composed of one independent clause is called a s __ __ ple sentence.
R6 simple	**S7** **We purchased stock** is a simple sentence because it is composed of one _____ clause.
R7 independent	**S8** **We purchased stock; then we sold it** is a sentence that contains (one, two) clause(s).
R8 two	**S9** **we purchased stock** **then we sold it** Each of the above is a(n) _____ clause.
R9 independent	**S10** **We purchased stock and then we sold it.** This is a c __ __ __ __ __ __ sentence because it consists of two independent clauses connected by a conjunction.
R10 compound	**S11** **We purchased stock; then we sold it.** This is a _____ sentence because it is composed of two _____ clauses connected by the mark of punctuation known as a _____ .
R11 compound; independent; semicolon	**S12** **We purchased stock and then we sold it.** The word **and** is a conjunction. It is called a co __ __ __ __ __ __ __ conjunction because it connects coequal parts. In a compound sentence it connects two _____ clauses.
R12 coordinate; independent	

	S13 A coordinate conjunction connects equal parts. It can connect two subjects, like **Jack and Jill,** in which case we have a _____ subject.
R13 compound	**S14** A coordinate conjunction can connect two predicates, like **sink or swim,** in which case we have a _____ predicate.
R14 compound	**S15** A coordinate conjunction can connect two independent clauses, in which case we have a _____ sentence.
R15 compound	**S16** A compound sentence is a sentence containing two or more _____ clauses connected by a _____ conjunction or a semicolon.
R16 independent; coordinate	**S17** A _____ sentence is a sentence containing two or more independent _____ connected by a _____ conjunction or a _____.
R17 compound; clauses; coordinate; semicolon	**S18** **We regret the delay.** This is a _____ sentence containing one _____ clause.
R18 simple; independent	**S19** **We regret the delay, but it was unavoidable.** This is a _____ sentence containing two _____ clauses connected by a c _ _ _ _ _ _ _ _ _ _ c _ _ _ _ _ _ _ _ _ _ _.
R19 compound; independent; coordinate conjunction.	**S20** **We regret the delay; it was unavoidable.** This is a _____ sentence consisting of two _____ clauses connected by a _____.
R20 compound; independent; semicolon	**S21** **We regret the delay, it was unavoidable.** This is an example of the error we call a run-on sentence. Here we have two _____ clauses connected by a comma. To create a correct compound sentence, you need a stronger "glue" than just a comma. You need either a _____ conjunction (with a comma) or a s _ _ _ _ c _ _ _ _ _.
R21 independent; coordinate; semicolon	**S22** **Although we regret the delay....** This is a clause because it contains a sub _ _ _ _ _ and a p _ _ _ _ _ _ _ _ _. It is a dependent clause because it does not express a _____ _____.
R22 subject; predicate; complete thought	

S23

If it was unavoidable.... This is a(n) _____ clause because, although it contains a subject and a predicate, it does _____ express a complete thought.

R23

dependent; not

S24

In S22 and S23, the words **although** and **if** are sub __ __ __ __ __ __ __ __ conjunctions because they render a clause incomplete and therefore dependent.

R24

subordinate

S25

Although we regret the delay, it was unavoidable.
This sentence contains (one, two) clause(s). The first is a _____ clause because it is not complete by itself. The second is an _____ clause because it expresses a complete thought.

R25

two;
dependent;
independent

S26

Although we regret the delay, it was unavoidable. This sentence contains a dependent clause and an independent clause. It is an example of a __ __ __ plex sentence.

R26

complex

S27

A complex sentence contains an _____ clause and a _____ clause.

R27

independent;
dependent

S28

There will be a delay if it is unavoidable. This is an example of a _____ sentence because it contains an _____ clause and a _____ clause. The word **if** is a _____ conjunction.

R28

complex; independent
dependent; subordinate

S29

There will be a delay if it is unavoidable. This sentence follows the natural sequence for a complex sentence; that is, the _____ clause comes first, followed by the _____ clause.

R29

independent;
dependent

S30

If it is unavoidable, there will be a delay. In this sentence the _____ clause comes first. This (is, is not) the natural sequence. We insert the comma after the _____ clause to indicate that this sentence is not in natural sequence.

R30

dependent;
is not;
dependent

S31

Let's review the three types of sentences. **He will arrive at nine.** This is a _____ sentence because it contains one _____ clause.

R31

simple;
independent

	S32	An independent clause is a group of words that contains a _____ and a _____ and expresses a _____ _____.
R32 subject; predicate; complete thought	**S33**	**He will arrive at nine, and he will stay till twelve.** This is a _____ sentence because it contains two _____ clauses connected by a _____ conjunction.
R33 compound; independent; coordinate	**S34**	**He will arrive at nine if he is not delayed.** This is a _____ sentence because it contains a(n) _____ clause followed by a(n) _____ clause. The word **if** is a _____ conjunction.
R34 complex; independent; dependent; subordinate	**S35**	**...if he is not delayed.** This is a _____ clause. It is a clause because it contains a _____ and a _____. It is a **dependent** clause because it does not express a _____ _____.
R35 dependent; subject; predicate; complete thought ● **TURN TO Exercise 39**	**S36**	Correlative conjunctions are found in pairs. Complete each of the following pairs: neither, _____; either, _____; not only, _____ _____.
R36 neither-**nor**; either-**or**; not only — but **also**	**S37**	Paired conjunctions should stand as close as possible to the words they connect. Which sentence is preferable: a) **My employer has studied neither in high school nor in college.** b) **My employer has neither studied in high school nor in college.**
R37 a)	**S38**	**Like** is never used as a conjunction. Correct this sentence. **He dictates like I do.** Answer: _____
R38 **He dictates as I do;** or **He dictates the way I do;** or **He dictates like me.**	**S39**	**Try and** is incorrect. Instead of the conjunction **and** you should use the word ____. For example: **Please try ____ finish by five o'clock.**
R39 to; to	**S40**	**Try (and, to) rectify the shortage in receipts.**
R40 to	**S41**	**Provided** and **providing** are sometimes confused. _____ is a conjunction; _____ is a verb.
R41 **Provided; providing**		

	S42 I will report early (provided; providing) that the boss is (provided; providing) for a longer lunch hour.
R42 provided; providing	**S43** So I told him about the campaign. So he agreed to join. So both of us met next day. The conjunction that is overused in these sentences is _____.
R43 so	**S44** To eliminate too many **so** words, it is wise to substitute words like **accordingly, therefore, consequently.** What part of speech are these words? Answer: _____.
R44 conjunctions	**S45** When an affirmative comparison is made, we say, for example: **He is as rich as Midas.** When a negative comparison is made, we say: **He is not _____ strong as Hercules.**
R45 so	**S46** Which word is better? **I read in the Wall Street Journal (that, where) stock prices are advancing.**
R46 that	**S47** As a review, choose the correct answers: The conjunctions **and, but, or,** and **yet** are called (coordinate, subordinate) conjunctions because they connect (equal, unequal) parts.
R47 coordinate; equal	**S48** Choose the correct forms: **Neither Sally (nor, or) Jane types like (I, me), so try (to, and) arrange a raise for me.**
R48 nor; me; to	**S49** Choose the proper words: **The tax penalty will not be (as, so) high as before (providing, provided) that forms are filed on time.**
R49 so; provided	**S50** A word or a group of words that expresses strong feeling, like **Ouch,** is called an _____. It is usually followed by an ex _ _ _ _ _ _ _ _ _ point.
R50 interjection; exclamation ● TURN TO **Exercise 40 and Review**	

English test
Thurs. Feb 16.
Prepositions & pronouns
Chapters 7 & 8

SCORE

A_____

EXERCISE 39   Independent Clauses

A. Underline each independent clause. Be sure to underline all words in the clause.

SCORING: DEDUCT 10 POINTS FOR EACH ERROR.

1. Since we went away, time has flown.
2. Forgetting his manners, he remained seated.
3. We won't forget this if we live to be a hundred.
4. They came; they saw; they conquered.
5. I feel satisfied.
6. Mail a check for the balance as soon as possible.
7. They tried to resist, but they could not.
8. Either they go or we do.
9. Although he is on in years, he is sprightly.
10. Won't you come in without further delay?

SCORE

B_____

EXERCISE 39   Dependent Clauses

B. Underline each dependent clause, if any. If there is no dependent clause in a sentence, leave it blank.

SCORING: DEDUCT 10 POINTS FOR EACH ERROR.

1. Since we went away, time has flown.
2. Forgetting his manners, he remained seated. *phrase*
3. We won't forget this if we live to be a hundred.
4. They came; they saw; they conquered. *None*
5. Although I am tired, I feel satisfied.
6. Mail a check for the balance as soon as possible. *None*
7. They tried to resist, but they could not. *None*
8. We will go if we must.
9. Although he is on in years, he is sprightly.
10. We will come in if we are invited.

EXERCISE 39 | Types of Sentences

C. In the space to the right of each sentence, indicate what type of sentence it is — simple, compound, or complex.

SCORING: DEDUCT 10 POINTS FOR EACH ERROR.

1. Since we went away, time has flown. — 1. *complex*
2. Forgetting his manners, he remained seated. — *simple* 2. *complex*
3. We won't forget this if we live to be a hundred. — 3. *complex*
4. They came; they saw; they conquered. — 4. *compound*
5. I feel satisfied. — 5. *simple*
6. Mail a check for the balance as soon as possible. — *simple* 6. *complex*
7. They tried to resist, but they could not. — 7. *compound*
8. Either they go or we do. — 8. *compound*
9. Although he is on in years, he is sprightly. — 9. *complex*
10. Won't you come in without further delay? — *simple* 10. *complex*

EXERCISE 39 | Complex Sentences

D. In the space to the right of each of these complex sentences, mark N if the sentence follows the natural sequence; mark U if the sequence is in unnatural order. Insert a comma in any sentence from which it is omitted.

SCORING: DEDUCT 10 POINTS FOR EACH ERROR.

1. As soon as we arrived, the festivities began. — 1. U
2. Assuming that he was right, he proceeded without further instructions. — 2. U
3. We will order now, although we are overstocked. — 3. N
4. Until I hear from you, I shall say no more. — 4. U
5. We won't despair while there is still hope. — 5. N
6. Although he is still a minor, he is old enough to be responsible. — 6. U
7. Because he was modest, he refused adulation. — 7. U
8. We will fight back until they retreat. — 8. N
9. Don't underestimate the opposition if you hope to conquer them. — 9. N
10. Before I leave, let me congratulate you. — 10. U

SCORE

A_____

EXERCISE 40   Correlative Conjunctions

A. This problem deals with choosing the proper conjunction. In the space provided, write the correct word.

SCORING: DEDUCT 10 POINTS FOR EACH ERROR.

1. Either you ship the goods (or, and) I will sue.
2. Neither the chair (or, nor) the desk is in perfect condition.
3. Both the fan (and, or) the motor were defective.
4. He not only refused to accept the goods (but, but also) refused to pay.
5. Neither the dictionary (or, nor) the glossary included the term.
6. He not only gave us dinner (but, but also) invited us to stay for the evening.
7. They are willing to offer you not only a discount (but, but also) a bonus gift.
8. They offered either a straight salary (and, or) a commission.
9. Our latest model is not only functional (but, but also) artistic.
10. Either the ledger (or, nor) the receipt (is, are) incorrect.

1. _or_
2. _nor_
3. _and_
4. _but also_
5. _nor_
6. _but also_
7. _but also_
8. _or_
9. _but also_
10. _or_ _is_

SCORE

B_____

EXERCISE 40   Proper Conjunctions

B. This problem deals with choosing the proper conjunction. In the space provided, write the proper word.

SCORING: DEDUCT 10 POINTS FOR EACH ERROR.

1. I acted (as, like) you advised.
2. Would you try (and, to) correct the error.
3. We will accept (provided, providing) you lower your price.
4. We would appreciate it if you would try (and, to) locate the lost files.
5. The computer was fully (as, so) large as a room.
6. We will go not only to Paris (but, but also) to London.
7. This contract is valid (provided, providing) the shipment arrives on schedule.
8. (Like, As) I said yesterday, this must stop.
9. Neither time (or, nor) effort is to be spared (provided, providing) they cooperate.
10. It looks very much (like, as) your automatic washer.

1. _as_
2. _to_
3. _provided_
4. _to_
5. _as_
6. _but also_
7. _provided_
8. _As_
9. _nor, provided_
10. _like_

SCORE

C_____

EXERCISE 40 | Correcting Conjunctions

C. Wherever necessary, cross out incorrect words or insert correct words. Two sentences are correct.

SCORING: DEDUCT 10 POINTS FOR EACH ERROR.

1. He is not ~~as~~ *so* smart as I thought he was.

C 2. I read in a book that censorship is on the increase.

3. The reason I left was ~~because~~ *that* I was tired.

4. The reason he was discharged was ~~because~~ *that* he had been late too often.

5. Acme Products is not ~~as~~ *so* large as General Electric.

C 6. The gain is not so great as I had anticipated.

7. I notice in the newspapers ~~where~~ *that* employment figures are increasing.

8. I read ~~where~~ *that* China and Russia are feuding.

9. I heard ~~where~~ *that* Frank was promoted in his firm.

10. This looks excellent ~~like~~ *as* I expected.

SCORE

_____

REVIEW EXERCISE 9 | Conjunctions

In the following copy, cross out all errors and write your corrections in the space above each. Insert any omitted punctuation.

SCORING: DEDUCT 5 POINTS FOR EACH ERROR.

~~Like~~ *As* I said in my last letter, sales have not only fallen but *also* we have lost some salesmen too. This is not ~~as~~ *so* bad as you might think since we were going to try ~~and~~ *to* hire some new salesmen anyway. You probably have read in the papers ~~where~~ *that* the reason sales are down is ~~because~~ *that* demand has fallen. ~~Providing~~ *Provided* this downward trend in demand is reversed I feel confident our sales will soon be back to record levels.

C O M M O N   E R R O R S

In this lesson, twenty-six common mistakes are discussed from A to Z. Since each of these mistakes is easily corrected, we have not included any Programmed Reinforcement in this unit. Note that some of the mistakes discussed here are also covered elsewhere in this course. We have repeated them for extra emphasis.

A. DOUBLE SUBJECT

Mr. Smith, our President, will attend the dinner.

This sentence is correct, but look at the following sentence:

WRONG: Mr. Smith, our President, *he* will attend the meeting.

Obviously, the word *he* is just excess baggage. It tells us absolutely nothing new about our subject. Since it adds nothing, throw it out.

Right: **Mr. Smith, our President, will attend the dinner.**

Right: **Our firm, The Acme Company, is the finest in its field.**

WRONG: Our firm, The Acme Company, *it* is the finest in its field.

Right: **Mr. Roberts and Mr. Smith will arrive soon.**

WRONG: Mr. Roberts and Mr. Smith *they* will arrive soon.

B. DOUBLE COMPARISON

This sentence is correct:

I am happier than a lark.

Happier than a lark, however, is not happy enough for some people. To show how ecstatic with joy they are (and how bad their English is) these people say:

WRONG: I am *more* happier than a lark.

More **happier** is an unhappy combination of words. **Happier** by itself is all right. **More happy** is permissible. But NOT *more happier*. As we pointed out in Lesson 5, such *double comparisons* are wrong.

Right: **This is the best job I've ever had.**

WRONG: This is the *bestest* job I've ever had. (If you speak this way, you won't have the job very long. There is no such word as *bestest*. You can't be better than **best**.)

Right: **This is the best job I've ever had.**

201

WRONG: This is the *most* best job I've ever had. (Once again, **best** is as good as you can get. Drop *most*.)

Note that *unique* is already a superlative, meaning *one of a kind*. Accordingly, avoid the phrase *most unique* which is a double comparison.

C. THIS HERE

Do you ever make these errors:
WRONG: This *here* book is interesting.
WRONG: That *there* desk is beautiful.
WRONG: These *here* books are heavy.
WRONG: Those *there* desks are light.

If you ever say these things, STOP doing so at once. It is a sure sign of a poor education to say *this here, that there, these here,* or *those there*. The word *here* or *there* is unnecessary in each of the sentences above.
SAY:

Right: **This book is interesting.**
Right: **That desk is beautiful.**
Right: **These books are heavy.**
Right: **Those desks are light.**

D. KIND OF

It is bad usage to say the following:
WRONG: He is a fine kind of *a* man.
The *a* before *man* is unnecessary.
Right: **He is a fine kind of man.**
Never use *a* after *kind of, sort of,* or *type of.*
Right: **This is the type of job I like to see.**
(NOT: type of *a* job ....)
Right: **What sort of problem have you encountered?**
(NOT: sort of *a* problem ....)

E. HAS GOT

Do not use *has got* to indicate possession.
Right: **He has a fine idea.**
(NOT: He has *got* a fine idea.)

Right: **What have you in your file?**
(NOT: What have you *got* in your file?)
Right: **They have a few things to say.**
(NOT: have *got* a few ....)
Right: **This boy has to go.**
(NOT: has *got* to go.)

● TURN TO Exercise 41

F. TEACH — LEARN

Do not confuse the words *teach* and *learn*.

To **teach** means to *give* knowledge *to* someone else.

To **learn** means to *receive* knowledge *from* someone or something.

The teacher teaches her class.

The class learns from the teacher.

G. LEND — BORROW

A frequent mistake is this:
WRONG: Can I *lend* your pencil?
What you mean to say is:
Right: **May I borrow your pencil?**

Lend means to *give* someone else your property temporarily.

Borrow means to *accept* someone else's property temporarily.

I borrowed John's typewriter last week and returned it to him yesterday.

John lent me his typewriter.

Another error is this: WRONG: *Loan* me your pencil. **Loan** is a noun. A **loan** is the *thing* that is lent. Remember, it is a *thing*, not an action. **Lend** is a verb. It is the *act* of giving a loan.

Right: **I need a loan of $500.**
Right: **I will lend it to you.**
Right: **The company asked for a thousand-dollar loan.**
Right: **The bank agreed to lend the thousand dollars to the company.**

H. STAYED — STOOD

There is a famous story of the fight promoter who, upon seeing his prize boy being decisively beaten, tore at his hair and moaned those classic words of despair: **I shoulda stood in bed.**

This language may be all right if you are a prize-fight promoter; but if you are planning to go into any other line of business, you had better learn the difference between **stayed** and **stood.**

Stayed is the past tense of **stay.**

Stayed means the same as **remained.**

I should've stayed in bed.

We stayed to watch the fight to the very end.

Stood is the past tense of **stand.**

The soldier stood at attention throughout the ceremony.

I don't know how he stood the strain.

Of course, there is no such word as *shoulda.* You should say **should have** or use the contraction **should've.**

So our unhappy fight promoter should have said: **I should've stayed in bed.** If he had, his sentence would have been grammatical, but his cry of despair would probably have been forgotten long ago.

I. CAN — MAY

Can means *is capable of. In other words,* **can** refers to physical *ability.*

May means *has permission to.* In other words, **may** refers to *consent.*

May I leave work an hour early? (Means: Will you give me *permission* to leave early?)

Can you spare me? (Means: are you *capable* of getting along without me?)

May we have the car tonight?

I understand the car is being repaired. Can we have it by tonight?

J. TWO — TOO — TO

Two is a number — **2.**

Send me two pairs of shoes.

They ordered two dozen shirts.

To is a *preposition.*

I am going to another department.

He rose to his feet.

To is also part of the *infinitive.*

I want to go at once.

To err is human.

Too is a word that *intensifies* the meaning of something. It means *more than* or *also.*

I want to go too.

There is too much work.

Our inventory is too large.

To help you choose between **to** and **too,** remember that the double **o** in **too** *intensifies* the word. So use **too** when you want to *intensify* your meaning.

● TURN TO Exercises 42 and 43

K. BEING THAT

There is no such conjunction as *being that.* It just does not exist, so erase it from your vocabulary.

Right: **Since you don't want to go, I'll go alone.**

WRONG: *Being that* you don't want to go, I'll go alone.

Right: **Because he is ill, I'll stay late.**

WRONG: *Being that . . . .*

L. AIN'T

The word *ain't* is not good English usage. To use it is to advertise your poor English. SAY:

I am not going. (NOT: I *ain't* going.)

He isn't going. (NOT: He *ain't* going.)

I'm doing rather well, am I not? (NOT: . . . *ain't* I?)

203

M. NOWHERES — SOMEWHERES — ANYWHERES

There are no such words. The correct words are:

nowhere, somewhere, and anywhere.

Remember: Omit the **s** at the end.

Right: He could find it nowhere.

Right: Somewhere over the rainbow, skies are blue.

Right: Put the machine anywhere that's convenient.

N. REGARDLESS

There is no such word as *irregardless*. **Regardless** is all that you need.

Regardless of the weather, we shall leave on time.

These stocks will maintain their value regardless of the market.

O. OVER YOUR HOUSE

A common error in some parts of the country is to say something like this:

WRONG: Let's play bridge *over* my house.

Can you just picture what this means? Can't you see the bridge table suspended in mid air about thirty feet above the chimney? We doubt if you would accept an invitation to play bridge in such a precarious position.

What your host should say is:

Right: Let's play bridge at my house.

So avoid the *over my house* habit.

Right: Come on to my house.

WRONG: Come on over my house.

Right: Let's go to Jane's house.

WRONG: Let's go over Jane's house.

● TURN TO Exercise 44

P. GERUNDS

In the chapter on verbs you learned that by adding **ing** to a verb you form the progressive tense.

I sing. I am singing.

I write. I am writing.

You also learned that it is possible to use the word **singing** or **writing** not as a *verb*, but as a type of *noun* called a *gerund*.

My singing has improved.

His writing is too uneven.

As used in each of the above sentences, **singing** and **writing** are *gerunds* and are the equivalent of nouns. Do you see why they are acting like nouns? That's right; because each of them *names* an activity. You remember that a *noun* is a word that *names*.

Here are a few other examples of *gerunds*:

What did you think of his acting?

Filing is a mechanical skill.

His thinking is very logical.

We felt his playing had improved.

Now that you have learned to recognize *gerunds*, try a sentence like this:

We thought that (him) (his) writing had improved.

Obviously **his** is correct.

We thought that his writing had improved.

Next, try this sentence:

What do you think of (him) (his) winning the bonus?

Do you know which is correct? Let's reason it out. **Winning** is a *gerund* (noun). You modify a noun with the *possessive* pronoun (**his**) rather than the objective pronoun (**him**). For example, you would say:

Look at his coat. (NOT: Look at *him* coat.)

So, since **winning** as used here is a *noun*, you should say:

What do you think of his winning the bonus?

Learn this rule: When modifying a *gerund*, use a *possessive* noun or pronoun.

We were pleased with John's receiving the award.

His losing the account was unforgivable.

The Board's deciding not to vote came as a shock to us all.

Of course, don't confuse *gerunds* with the *progressive verbs* you studied in Lesson 4.

We could see him running in the distance. (**Running** as used here is a *verb*.)

The jury, obeying the judge, arrived at a verdict.

The manager, going over the problem, found no solution.

But:

We watched his running with keen interest.

The jury's obeying the judge can lead to no other verdict.

The manager's studying of the problem brought no solution.

● TURN TO Exercise 45

Q. LET-LEAVE

Leave (**left**) means *to go away*. It should not be confused with **let** meaning *to allow or permit*.

Right: **Let me work alone.**

WRONG: *Leave* me work alone.

Right: **You should have let him go.**

WRONG: You should have *left* him go.

Note: **Leave me alone** and **Let me alone** are both correct, but each has a different meaning. **Leave me alone** suggests politely that you go away. **Let me alone** suggests more brusquely that you should stop irritating me.

R. LEAD (verb), LEAD (noun), LED (verb)

Don't incorrectly substitute the present tense of the verb **to lead** (rhymes with *need*) for the past tense **led** (rhymes with *red*).

Right: **He led the company in sales last week.**

WRONG: He *lead* the company in sales last week.

Just remember that **lead** as a verb is pronounced like *need*. Do not confuse **led,** the past tense, with the noun **lead** (also pronounced like *red*) meaning the metal used for plumbing.

Right: **The general led the army yesterday.**

Right: **He has led a virtuous life.**

Right: **He may lead his class in marks.**

Right: **The lead was mined as an ore.**

S. RESPECTFULLY – RESPECTABLY – RESPECTIVELY

Some writers make the error of substituting **Respectably** (in a decent fashion) for the proper letter closing — **Respectfully** (full of respect). **Respectively** is also quite unrelated; it means in *proper sequence* or *in order*.

Right: **Please answer soon. Respectfully yours,**

Right: **He spoke respectfully** (full of respect) **to the minister.**

Right: **He was dressed respectably** (in a decent fashion) **for the occasion.**

Right: **I want Charles and James respectively to address the group.** (In the named sequence or order.)

Right: **Roosevelt, Truman, and Eisenhower respectively had their impacts on the American people.**

T. LOSE-LOOSE

The verb **lose** is always pronounced *looz*. It means *to suffer loss*. This is quite different from **loose**, pronounced like *moose*, which means *free, not close together*, or as a verb, *to untie, to make free*. Just remember that **lose** means a *loss*, with one *o* in each word; **loose** means *free*, with a double vowel in each word.

Right: Did you lose your books?

Right: I shall lose my temper soon.

Right: The animals broke loose.

Right: Let's pull the loose ends together.

WRONG: You will *loose* your wallet if it sticks out of your pocket.

U. ANXIOUS for EAGER

Anxious is an adjective that is derived from the noun **anxiety**, meaning *worry*. An anxious person is therefore someone who is perplexed, concerned, or disturbed. **Eager** comes from **eagerness**, meaning *enthusiasm, interest, desire*. An eager person, therefore, is enthusiastic.

Right: I am eager to go on vacation.

Right: I am anxious about my father's health.

WRONG: I am *anxious* to see my girl friend tomorrow. (If you were worried, not eager, you would say: I am **anxious** about my girl friend's reaction to me tomorrow!)

● TURN TO Exercise 46

V. ANGRY and MAD

Years ago we were told that dogs go mad and froth at the mouth while people simply get angry. Do not use *mad* to imply anger or peevishness. *Mad* means insane.

Right: I am angry at his impertinence.

Right: A mad person may be confined to an asylum.

WRONG: She is *mad* at him because he snubbed her.

W. DISINTERESTED for UNINTERESTED

The prefix **dis** means *away from* or *apart*. A **disinterested** person is interested, but his interest is away from or apart from the issue. In other words, a *disinterested* person is *impartial, fair, interested but aloof*. A judge should always be disinterested, but never uninterested. The prefix **un** means *not*. *Uninterested* means *not interested*. Would we want an umpire to be uninterested or disinterested?

Right: I want a disinterested arbiter to make the decision.

Right: I am uninterested in impressing people.

WRONG: He yawned at his desk showing he was *disinterested* in the work.

X. MYSELF for ME

Pronouns ending in **self** are reflexive; that is, like a knee reflex, the action *comes back* to the doer.

Right: I hurt myself.

Right: The boy cut himself.

Do not use this **self** or reflexive form when a simple pronoun is required.

Right: Frank and I went to the movies.

WRONG: Frank and *myself* went there.

Y. AND or BUT as Sentence Openers

In the lesson on conjunctions you learned that **and** and **but** are coordinate conjunctions — words that join equal words, phrases, or clauses. Remember that you should *not* begin a sentence with **and** or **but**.

This is a common error and it generally reveals poor writing ability. If **and** and **but** are connecting words, they must have something to connect. Otherwise you have a sentence fragment.

Right: I saw Frank, but he didn't see me.

WRONG: I saw Frank. *But* he didn't see me.

Great authors have privileges that good letter writers may not have. Some authors occasionally begin sentences with *and* or *but* to avoid a long compound sentence. Since in business you will not be aiming for a Pulitzer Prize, avoid **and** or **but** as an opening word.

Z. THAN and THEN

Do not use **then** meaning *at that time* or *later* (an adverb) when you want to use the conjunction **than** which indicates a comparison.

Right: He is bigger than I.

Right: John is taller than Jack.

Right: If you ask, then I will answer.

WRONG: He is older *then* I.

● TURN TO Exercise 47 and Review

EXERCISE 41   Common Errors—A-E

A. Each of the following sentences contains an unnecessary word or words. Cross out all unnecessary words and all improper punctuation.

SCORING: DEDUCT 7 POINTS FOR EACH ERROR.

1. The Ajax Company, ~~it~~ will open its fall season campaign soon.
2. Our sales this year have been the ~~most~~ highest in our history.
3. This ~~here~~ gentleman is interested in your offer.
4. This sort of ~~an~~ investment should pay big dividends.
5. Mr. Smith has ~~got~~ a slight cold.
6. Bob, walking down the street, ~~he~~ fell.
7. This sample of lace is ~~more~~ finer than the last one you sent.
8. That ~~there~~ desk would fit perfectly.
9. What type of ~~a~~ man is he?
10. What has he ~~got~~ in mind?
11. Miss Jones, our representative, ~~she~~ will call on you soon.
12. Undoubtedly, this is the ~~most~~ best model we have ever put on the market.
13. Those ~~there~~ machines will be the answer to your needs.
14. This kind of ~~a~~ job will be fine.
15. He has not ~~got~~ a good reason for his absence.

EXERCISE 41   A-E Review

B. Cross out the improper words in the following sentences. Note that there may be more than one mistake in a sentence.

SCORING: DEDUCT 10 POINTS FOR EACH ERROR.

1. Our experience shows that the Acme Company is the ~~most~~ best producer of farm machinery.
2. Mr. Jones ~~he~~ is the sort of ~~a~~ man you can trust.
3. This ~~here~~ office ~~it~~ is located on a residential type of ~~a~~ street.
4. These ~~here~~ salesmen, Mr. Robertson and Mr. Johnson, ~~they~~ have done an excellent job.
5. Did you forget to send that ~~there~~ message to Mr. Woodburn?
6. Mr. Roberts is a ~~more~~ finer man than any other man I know.
7. He is the type of ~~a~~ man that you are proud to know.
8. According to our latest reports, Jones and Company ~~it~~ is not the type of ~~a~~ firm that you would like to do business with.
9. These ~~here~~ invoices ~~they~~ should have been filed long ago.
10. What's this ~~here~~ I hear about your resigning?

EXERCISE 42   Common Errors — F-J

In the space provided, write the correct word.
SCORING: DEDUCT 7 POINTS FOR EACH ERROR.

1. When students do not like a teacher, she will find it difficult to (teach, learn) them.
2. I had to (borrow, lend) money from my employer to get home.
3. I (stood, stayed) at the office until well after dark.
4. (Can, May) you reach the shelf if you stretch?
5. There are (to, too, two) many people in the office force.
6. A student who studies hard has no difficulty (learning, teaching) his lessons.
7. I am sure you will repay this (lend, loan) as soon as you have the money.
8. They (shoulda, should've) asked us before they (lent, borrowed) the money from the bank.
9. (Can, May) we be excused from the exercises?
10. Send the (to, too, two) packages (to, too, two) the Acme Agency.
11. Our bitter experience has (learned, taught) us to avoid risky deals.
12. The bank was very willing to (lend, loan) us the money despite the size of the (lend, loan) we were seeking.
13. The men (stayed, stood) at attention until the ceremony was over.
14. (Can, May) he attain the goals he set for himself?
15. (To, Too, Two) many cooks spoil the broth.

1. *teach*
2. *borrow*
3. *stayed*
4. *Can*
5. *too*
6. *learning*
7. *loan*
8. *should've borrowed*
9. *May*
10. *two to*
11. *taught*
12. *lend loan*
13. *stood*
14. *Can*
15. *Too*

EXERCISE 43   Review of Common Errors A-J

Proofread this paragraph, crossing out all errors and writing corrections in the space above each error.
SCORING: DEDUCT 10 POINTS FOR EACH ERROR.

May
Can I offer you some good advice? My opinion is that one should not lend money from a *borrow* bank unless he is certain he will be able to repay the lend *loan* when it is due. I was learned *taught* my lesson by sad experiences when I was to young to know any better. Experience learned *taught* me that I should have stood *stayed* away from borrowing.

NAME   CLASS   DATE

EXERCISE 44   Common Errors—K-O

A. Cross out any errors and write your corrections in the space above each error.
SCORING: DEDUCT 7 POINTS FOR EACH ERROR.

1. ~~Being~~ *Since* that it is a cold winter, our heaters will sell exceptionally well.
2. I ~~ain't~~ *has'nt* seen no one around here for weeks.
3. Our reports could be found nowheres.
4. ~~Irregardless~~ *Regardless* of your feelings in the matter, we must go on.
5. Would you study ~~over~~ *at* my house?
6. We feel that he will do a good job ~~being~~ *because* that he is so intelligent.
7. There ~~ain't no~~ *is'nt any* reason for this delay.
8. Somewheres you will locate the man who can handle the job.
9. They will go ahead irregardless of all obstacles.
10. Let's have dinner ~~over~~ *at* my house.
11. They will complete the job on time ~~being~~ *since* that they are working so hard.
12. ~~Ain't~~ *Are'nt* we going to leave before noon?
13. You will find it nowheres.
14. I would buy that necklace irregardless of its price.
15. They are having a meeting ~~over~~ *at* the plant.

EXERCISE 44   Review K-O

B. Cross out all errors, writing your corrections in the space above each error.
SCORING: DEDUCT 10 POINTS FOR EACH ERROR.

~~Being~~ *Since* that the proper handling of incoming mail is a matter of great importance in any

office, irregardless of ~~it's~~ *its* size, it should be handled with the greatest care. The morning

mail, which is usually the most heaviest, should not be opened just anywheres. ~~Over~~ *At* our of-

fice our clerks use a large vacant table to make sure that the letters ~~ain't~~ *are'nt* mixed with other

papers that might be ~~laying~~ *lying* around. The first thing they do is to separate the first-class

matter from all other's — catalogues, circulars, packages, and even unsolicited letters ~~to~~ *too*.

NAME   CLASS   DATE

EXERCISE 45   Gerunds

A. Underline any gerunds in the following sentences. Don't confuse gerunds with progressive verbs.
SCORING: DEDUCT 10 POINTS FOR EACH ERROR.

1. We went <u>hunting</u> last winter.
2. Realizing his mistake, he retreated.
3. I am thrilled by his <u>winning</u> of the race.
4. <u>Filing</u> is a routine skill.
5. It was a thrilling victory.
6. They will keep <u>fighting</u> until it is too late.
7. Our <u>entering</u> the contest was a wise move.
8. Have you heard of his <u>forgetting</u> his speech?
9. We are <u>forging</u> ahead into a lead.
10. Don't forget their <u>signing</u> of the agreement.

EXERCISE 45   Possessives with Gerunds

B. In the space provided, write the proper word.
SCORING: DEDUCT 10 POINTS FOR EACH ERROR.

1. We heard about (him, his) winning the contest. — 1. *his*
2. Despite the fog, they could see (him, his) swimming in the distance. — 2. *him*
3. How good is Miss (Smith, Smith's) typing? — 3. *Smith's*
4. (Our, We) working together has brought substantial results. — 4. *Our*
5. They say that (me, my) writing shows definite possibilities. — 5. *my*
6. What did you think of Senator (Jones, Jones') voting against the tariff? — 6. *Jones'*
7. There is no reason for (him, his) working late tonight. — 7. *his*
8. (We, Our) checking of all receipts did not disclose the error. — 8. *Our*
9. The (bookkeeper, bookkeeper's), seeing the error, made all necessary corrections. — 9. *bookkeeper*
10. We tried to prevent (him, his) seeing the results until they were published. — 10. *his*

EXERCISE 46   Common Errors Q-U

A. In the space provided, write the correct word.

SCORING: DEDUCT 7 POINTS FOR EACH ERROR.

1. He won't (let, leave) me finish my work.
2. John (lead, led) all the students in his class.
3. He closed the letter, "(Respectfully, Respectably, Respectively) yours."
4. The dentist worked on the (lose, loose) tooth.
5. I am (anxious, eager) to get a fresh start in my job.
6. He (let, left) the room angrily.
7. He has (lead, led) an athletic existence for years.
8. He gave a (respectful, respectable, respective) salute to the officer.
9. Whatever you do, do not (lose, loose) your head in an emergency.
10. He was (anxious, eager) about the hospital report.
11. If you will (let, leave) him be, he will not be so irritable.
12. The (lead, led) in the pencil is too soft.
13. James Wilson was second in sales in his firm, a highly (respectful, respectable, respective) position.
14. That rattle seems to come from a (lose, loose) bolt in the chassis.
15. One should be (anxious, eager) about the effects of smoking.

1. _let_
2. _led_
3. _Respectfully_
4. _loose_
5. _eager_
6. _left_
7. _respectful led_
8. _respectful_
9. _lose_
10. _anxious_
11. _let_
12. _lead_
13. _respectable_
14. _loose_
15. _anxious_

SCORE

B_____

EXERCISE 46   Review Q-U

B. Cross out all errors, writing your corrections in the space above each error.

SCORING: DEDUCT 10 POINTS FOR EACH ERROR.

~~Leave~~ *Let* us point to a few factors that may save you from ~~loosing~~ *losing* a fine job opportunity the next time you apply. Let us assume that a classified ad has ~~lead~~ *led* you to an interview. Of course, you are ~~anxious~~ *eager* to make a good appearance; so dress appropriately. After the receptionist has ~~lead~~ *led* you into the interviewer's office, don't sit until asked to do so. Act ~~respectably~~ *respectfully* toward your interviewer, but don't be so timid that you ~~loose~~ *lose* the opportunity to explain all your qualifications. Let the interviewer lead the discussion, and don't be so ~~anxious~~ *eager* to reply that you interrupt. When he indicates that the interview is over, thank him ~~respectively~~ *respectfully*; then take your leave without losing another moment.

213

NAME CLASS DATE

EXERCISE 47 Common Errors V-Z

In the space provided, write the correct word.

SCORING: DEDUCT 4 POINTS FOR EACH ERROR.

1. Don't be (mad, angry) with me.
2. A good judge must be (disinterested, uninterested) in the case before him.
3. This secret is between Frank and (me, myself).
4. Are these sentences punctuated correctly? I know that every office worker must do his part. And I will do mine too. (Answer: *Yes* or *No*)
5. He studies harder (than, then) she.
6. The designer liked the new colors so much, he seemed to be (mad, angry) about them.
7. His failure shows he was (disinterested, uninterested) in the school work.
8. The ball hurt (me, myself) as it hit my face.
9. Are these sentences punctuated correctly? A sales manager has problems. But he must overcome them. (Answer: *Yes* or *No*)
10. Go to the office and (than, then) look for the document.
11. Never show that you are (mad, angry) if you are kept waiting for an appointment.
12. A clerk who is (disinterested, uninterested) in his firm will probably not succeed.
13. I cut (me, myself) as I opened the file.
14. Is this sentence punctuated correctly? The director tried to give the report to his colleague, but he refused it. (Answer: *Yes* or *No*)
15. She takes dictation faster (than, then) any other employee.
16. He appeared to be (mad, angry), so a psychiatric examination was requested.
17. The referee was selected because he was (disinterested, uninterested) in the two sides presented.
18. It isn't right for me to praise (me, myself) for my excellence.
19. Are these sentences punctuated correctly? Nothing succeeds like success. And all of us secretly want it. (Answer: *Yes* or *No*)
20. He cashed the check and (than, then) went home.
21. The good salesman never gets (mad, angry) with the customer.
22. (Disinterested, Uninterested) United Nations observers were sent to the scene.
23. The prank boomeranged and the boys hurt (them, themselves).
24. Are these sentences punctuated correctly? The transcript seemed correct. But the letter was not folded properly. (Answer: *Yes* or *No*)
25. A faster tennis player (than, then) Pancho Gonzales at his prime would be hard to find.

1. *angry*
2. *disinterested*
3. *me*
4. *No*
5. *than*
6. *mad*
7. *uninterested*
8. *me*
9. *No*
10. *then*
11. *angry*
12. *disinterested*
13. *myself*
14. *Yes*
15. *than*
16. *mad*
17. *disinterested*
18. *myself*
19. *No*
20. *then*
21. *angry*
22. *Disinterested*
23. *themselves*
24. *No.*
25. *than*

NAME   CLASS   DATE

REVIEW EXERCISE 10 | Common Errors from A-Z

The following paragraph contains many errors. Cross out all incorrect words and phrases, and
write the correct forms above them.
SCORING: DEDUCT 5 POINTS FOR EACH ERROR.

Dear Mr. Abrams:

Regardless of your business, you will find at the
Exposition all the equipment that your office should have
got. Here is your opportunity to test, to compare, and ~~for~~ *to*
~~choosing~~ the office machinery that will fit your particular
office needs.

This
~~These~~ kind of ~~an~~ exhibit is ~~most~~ unique among business shows. It is the result of the combined efforts of the
exhibitors, local civic figures, the police department, and
~~with~~ the local business organizations.

Unless your office has ~~got~~ all the equipment it will
ever need, you and your staff should attend this important
meeting. We are certain that you visiting and seeing this
exposition will be an important turning point in your business career. Plan to make your ticket reservations in the
very near future.

let *lose*
Do not ~~leave~~ this opportunity pass, for if you ~~loose~~
angry with
this chance, you undoubtedly will be ~~mad at~~ yourself later. *latter*
ego
~~on.~~ We are ~~anxious~~ to see you at the Exposition, and we
know you will not be disinterested in the equipment. We,
respectfully
therefore, ~~respectively~~ urge that you be more alert ~~then~~
some of your competitors. And make your reservation now.

Respectfully yours,
Respectably yours,

ACME EQUIPMENT

PUNCTUATION

1. the period   2. the question mark

3. the exclamation point   4. the comma   5. the colon

6. the semicolon   7. quotation marks

8. the apostrophe   9. the hyphen   10. parentheses

11. the dash   12. ellipses   13. capitalization

Can you read this:

marksofpunctuationtellthereaderwhentopause

Now, try it this way:

Marks of punctuation tell the reader when to pause.

Easier, isn't it? What a difference a few little spaces make. These spaces make a sentence easier to read because they break a long mumble-jumble of letters into easy-to-understand words. In the same manner, marks of punctuation make sentences easier to read because they break a mumble-jumble of thoughts into easy-to-understand ideas.

If you want your writing to say exactly what you mean, you must learn to punctuate correctly and carefully. Improper punctuation will not only confuse the reader but also may completely mislead him. For example, see how a comma completely changes the meaning of this sentence:

No price is too high.
No, price is too high.

In business you must be able to punctuate perfectly, so study this section thoroughly and carefully. Your mastery of the rules of punctuation will pave your way to a higher-paying position.

1. THE PERIOD (.)

The use of this mark of punctuation is very easy. You have probably used it properly throughout your life, so the five rules below should be a review for you.

RULE 1.

Place a period at the end of a sentence that makes a statement.

The shipment will be delivered by Friday.

Note 1: Review what you learned in Lesson 1 concerning the proper use of the period at the end of a *complete* sentence and the avoidance of sentence fragments and run-on sentences.

Note 2: When typing a sentence, *space twice* after the period before starting the next sentence.

```
    Please pay the bill.   It is long
overdue.
```

RULE 2.

Place a period at the end of a sentence that states a command.

Bring it here.
Don't leave.
Order the goods immediately.

Note 1: When the command is phrased in the form of a question for the sake of politeness, use a period rather than a question mark.

Will you put it here, please.

Note 2: Use the period after a condensed expression that stands for a full statement or command.

Yes.   Go.   Next.   Sit.

RULE 3.

Place a period after an abbreviation.

Mr.   Dr.   N. Y. C.
e.g.   J. Gordon Jones, Jr.

Note 1: When a sentence ends with an abbreviation, use only *one period*.

Address the letter to Fulton Boyd, Esq.

The shipment goes to Morris Van Lines, Inc.
BUT: **The plant is open for inspection all day (9 a.m. to 5:30 p.m.).**

Note 2: Miss is *not* an abbreviation. **Mr., Mrs., Messrs.,** and **Mmes.** are abbreviations.

Dear Miss Smith: Dear Mrs. Smith:

Note 3: Abbreviations composed of a series of lower case letters should be typed with no space after each period. Space only after the final period; then use a single space unless you are starting a new sentence, in which case you use a double space.

```
    The price quoted is f.o.b.
Detroit.
    We received a c.o.d. shipment
from the Denver warehouse.
```

Note 4: Abbreviations composed of *capital* letters should be typed with a single space after each period. Pay particular attention to this spacing in typing the abbreviations in a person's name.

```
    The C. P. A. examination is
scheduled for early June.
    Our new Chairman is J. P.
Roberts.
```

Note 5: Certain abbreviations are written in solid capital letters, without either periods or spaces. Consult a dictionary for the correct form when you are unsure of the correct abbreviation.

YMCA   VA   NOMA   FHA

Note 6: At the end of this book appears a listing of the official United States Post Office abbreviations for the names of the fifty states. In business correspondence avoid abbreviating the names of states except in tabulations. Also avoid abbreviating the names of cities.

Note 7: Recognize the difference between a contraction and an abbreviation. A contraction that is written with an apostrophe does not require a period.

Gen'l   Gov't   Rec't   Sec't   Sup't

Note 8: The following numbers are considered contractions and do not require periods: **1st, 2nd (2d), 3rd (3d), 4th, 5th . . . 10th . . . 23rd . . . 100th . . . etc.**

RULE 4.

Use a period to separate cents from dollars in a money amount.

$2.58 $10.10 $4,372.27

Note 1: Do not put a period after a dollar amount if no cents are indicated.

	$2	**$10**	**$4,372**
BUT:	**$2.00**	**$10.00**	**$4,372.46**

Note 2: Use the period as a decimal point.

.0   .06   .006   3.1416

Note 3: Do not space after the period used in a dollar amount or in a decimal.

$2.58   3.1416

RULE 5.

A period may be used in tabulations. When a list is numbered or lettered, put a period after each number or letter. Do not put a period or other mark of punctuation after the items in the tabulation unless each item is a full sentence.

Basic to our way of life are these fundamental rights:
1. **Freedom of speech**
2. **Freedom of assembly**
3. **Freedom of religion**
4. **Freedom of the press**

Note 1: When a list is numbered or lettered, you may enclose the numbers or letters in parentheses. In this case, do not use a period.

Basic to our way of life are these fundamental rights:
(a) **Freedom of speech**
(b) **Freedom of assembly**
(c) **Freedom of religion**
(d) **Freedom of the press**

Turn to Programed Reinforcement S1 through S4

2. THE QUESTION MARK (?)

The use of this mark, too, should be easy. You use the question mark in only one place — after a *direct* question. In typing skip two spaces after the question mark at the end of a sentence.

Can they deliver by May 15?   I doubt it.

Note 1: Do *not* use a question mark after a command that is phrased in the form of a question for the sake of politeness. As you have just learned, such a command ends with a period.

Will you please let us hear from you in the very near future.

Won't you come in, please.

If you are uncertain as to whether a particular sentence is a question or a command, ask yourself, "Does the sentence really require an answer or is it merely a courteous command?" If the sentence requires an answer, use a question mark. If the sentence does not require an answer, use a period.

Note 2: Be wary of run-on sentences in your use of the question mark.

Right: **Will you be at the banquet? We certainly hope so.**

Comma to seperate words, phrases, clauses.
I like apples, pears, oranges.
list of adjectives — don't use the comma if you wouldn't
use it alone with the last adjective.
He lives in a tall building
He lives in a new, air conditioned
tall building

NOT: Will you be at the banquet, we certainly hope so.

Note 3: The question mark punctuates a *direct* question. Do not use a question mark at the end of a sentence that refers indirectly to a question; use a period.

Direct Question: **Do you know when the new models will be available?**

Indirect Question: **He wonders if you know when the new models will be available.**

Note 4: No matter how long a direct question may be, end it with a question mark. Don't let the length of a question deceive you.

Are you certain that we can expect delivery of the merchandise by January 14 despite the newspaper's report that a strike may be called by the union at midnight on December 31?

Note 5: The question mark usually *ends* a sentence. On infrequent occasions, however, the question mark may be used in the *middle* of a sentence that contains a series of closely related questions. After each such question mark, skip two spaces and start the next word with a lower-case letter.

    Can you name four Presidents?
    four Vice-Presidents? four Chief
    Justices?

    What would be our unit price if
    we purchase six gross? twelve
    gross? twenty gross?

after strong emotion

3. THE EXCLAMATION POINT (!)

Here's the mark of punctation that's simplest to use. *Use the exclamation point after an exclamation*—that is, after a word or words of strong feeling or emotion:

Hurrah!

No!

Wait until you test drive the new Ford!

That's life!

What a wonderful day!

The exclamation point is effective in creating emphasis provided it is not overused. Too often the inexperienced writer peppers the page with so many exclamation points that it loses all value as a mark of emphasis. Try to "hoard" your exclamation points and use them only for that infrequent thought that *really* commands special emphasis. Use your exclamation points sparingly!

Space twice after an exclamation point before starting the next sentence.

    Alas! Our time is up.

Turn to Programed Reinforcement S5 through S9

4. THE COMMA (,)

Do you use commas correctly at all times? About a hundred years ago the use of the comma was a great problem. You see, at that time there was almost a competition between authors to see who could write the most obscure sentences. The literary style of the day favored long, complicated, tedious sentences, besplattered with commas and semicolons. It was left to the poor reader to unravel this cobweb of confusion as best he could.

Thank heavens, times have changed. Today the tendency is toward short, simple sentences and easy-to-follow punctuation. Nowadays you commit a serious error if you use too many commas. You must have a *definite reason* for every comma you insert. If you don't have a reason, leave it out.

There really aren't many rules governing the use of the commas. In fact, we can break the use of the comma into only six easy-to-master rules.

He purchased a good used car.

math, science and history — these are my favorite subjects.

RULE 1.

Use commas to separate words or phrases listed in a series. Each of the following sentences illustrates this use of the comma in a different instance.

1. Our new offices are located in a towering, ultra-modern, air-conditioned skyscraper.

2. The Electrex Meter has been carefully, precisely, and painstakingly assembled for maximum sensitivity.

3. Wool, cotton, linen, or silk will be used in the manufacture of this dress.

4. The newly installed bookkeeping machine automatically bills, posts, and maintains an inventory control.

5. The Armed Forces are ever-alert on land, in the air, and on the sea.

6. In this course your objectives are to write, to speak, and to think clearly.

7. That our opponent is aggressive, that he is clever, and that he is ruthless must be recognized.

8. Turn the ignition key, gently press the gas pedal, and push the starter button.

Note 1: Examine all of the sentences above. Notice that a comma has been placed *before* the conjunction when it precedes the last item in the series. This is the modern rule of punctuation.

Note 2: Often you may be undecided about whether or not to place a comma *after* the last item in a series. You can solve this problem by testing the last item as though it were alone in the sentence and not part of a series. For example:

1. Our offices are located in a towering, ultra-modern, air-conditioned (, ?) skyscraper.

TEST: *Our offices are located in an air-conditioned skyscraper.* (Needs no comma.)

THEREFORE: .... a towering, ultra-modern, air-conditioned skyscraper.

In technical terms, what this shows you is that when a series of adjectives modifies a noun, you should not put a comma after the last adjective. If you forget this technical explanation, no matter; the important thing is that you remember how to *test* your answer. Then you can never go wrong.

2. The Electrex Meter has been carefully, precisely, and painstakingly (, ?) assembled.

TEST: *The Electrex Meter has been painstakingly assembled.* (No comma)

THEREFORE: .... carefully, precisely, and painstakingly assembled. Technically: When a series of adverbs modifies a verb (or other part of speech), do not put a comma after the last adverb.

3. Wool, cotton, linen, or silk (, ?) will be used in the manufacture of this dress.

TEST: *Silk will be used* ... (No comma)

THEREFORE: Wool, cotton, linen, or silk will be used ... Technically: When you have a compound subject, do not use a comma to separate the last item in the subject from the predicate.

4. Courage, fortitude, and wisdom (, ?) these are the strength of the nation.

TEST: ... *wisdom, (this) is the strength of the nation.* (Needs a comma.)

THEREFORE: Courage, fortitude, and wisdom, these are the strength of the nation. Technically: Use a comma after the last word in a series if the series is followed by a *complete* sentence.

BUT: Courage, fortitude, and wisdom are the strength of the nation. (No comma)

Note 3: Occasionally a series will be written with correlative conjunctions between *all* items in the series. In this type of series omit the commas.

The Electrex Meter has been carefully and precisely and painstakingly assembled.

Wool or cotton or linen or silk will be used.

Note 4: Do you see why no comma is placed after *new* in the following sentence?

Try our new scouring powder.

New is an adjective and **scouring** is an adjective, but they are not in series. **New** modifies the word-group **scouring powder,** not just the noun **powder.** Here are other examples of the same situation:

We are looking for an intelligent, pleasant, enthusiastic young man. (*Young man* is treated as a word-group.)

The government's objectives are secure national defenses and rapid national growth. (*National defense* and *national growth* are treated as word-groups.)

Note 5: Sometimes *pairs* of words or phrases will be listed in series. In these instances, use commas to separate the *pairs* from one another.

To write and speak well, to think and act rigorously, and to live and fight courageously are your ideals.

Note 6: Many firm names are composed of a series of names of individuals. Be sure to separate the names with commas in precisely the format used on the firm's official letterhead. For example:

Merrill Lynch, Pierce, Fenner & Smith
Batten, Barton, Durstine & Osborne

As a general rule a comma is not placed before the ampersand (&) that often precedes the last name in a series.

Note 7: Frequently a long list will be ended with the abbreviation *etc.,* meaning *and others.* A comma should be placed before the *etc.* and should also be placed after the period unless it ends the sentence.

Never write *and etc.* since this would mean *and and others,* which is obviously redundant.

Generally, do not use the abbreviation *etc.* when you can find a more explicit, less

vague ending for the series. Do not use the abbreviation *etc.* when the series has been begun with *for example* or a similar phrase setting forth the incomplete nature of the lists. Do you see why this too is redundant?

Permissible: **The candidate expressed his views on farm policy, foreign relations, fiscal management, labor relations, etc.**

Improved: **The candidate expressed his views on farm policy, foreign relations, fiscal management, labor relations, and other vital national issues.**

NEVER: **The candidate expressed his views on vital national issues such as farm policy, foreign relations, fiscal management, labor relations, etc.** (Omit the *etc.* and the sentence becomes correct; or omit the phrase *such as.* You can't have both.)

Note 8: When typing, allow a single space after the comma.

Turn to Programed Reinforcement S10 through S17

RULE. 2.

Use commas to set off expressions that if omitted would not destroy the sentence nor change its meaning. This rule covers a great variety of situations. To make it easier for you to apply Rule 2, we shall break it down into individual parts. But don't forget, they are all part of the *one* overall rule.

PART A.

Use commas to set off the name of a person directly addressed.

Mr. Smith, we know that you will cooperate.

We can omit **Mr. Smith** and still have a complete sentence:

Omit: **Mr. Smith**

Remainder: **We know that you will cooperate.**

Therefore, we set off **Mr. Smith** with a comma.

Observe that the name of the person addressed is set off with commas no matter where it appears in the sentences

Mr. Smith, we know that you will cooperate.
We know, Mr. Smith, that you will cooperate.
We know that you will cooperate, Mr. Smith.

Note 1: When the name of the person addressed occurs in the middle of the sentence, place a comma *before and after* the name.

On your honor, John, did you do it?
With your help, Mr. Jones, we cannot fail.

Note 2: This rule applies only to the name of a person who is *directly* addressed. If you are talking *about* someone, you don't set off his name with commas.

Smith is a good man.
Smith, you are a good man.

Note 3: Use commas when you *directly* address someone with a term other than his name.

You, my friend, are in for a surprise.
Let me tell you, fellow alumni, what the committee has done.

Here's a little test of what you learned thus far. See how omitting a comma changes the meaning of these two sentences:

1. **Mr. Jones, our salesman, will see you.**

2. **Mr. Jones, our salesman will see you.**

Do you see the difference in meaning? In Sentence 1 the salesman, whose name is **Jones,** will see you. In Sentence 2 *your* name is **Jones** and you will be seen by a salesman whose name we don't know. Let this be an object lesson that you must place your commas carefully.

Turn to Programed Reinforcement S18 through S21

Use commas to set off an expression that explains a preceding word.

1. **Mr. Jones, President of Acme Steel, is here.**
President of Acme Steel merely explains who **Mr. Jones** is. We could omit it and still have a full sentence unchanged in meaning.

Omit: **President of Acme Steel**
Remainder: **Mr. Jones is here.**

2. **The Pacific Ocean, the largest body of water on earth, must be protected by a vast naval system.**

Omit: **the largest body of water on earth.**
Remainder: **The Pacific Ocean must be protected by a vast naval system.**

3. **We will send Mr. Smith, our representative, to visit your office.**

Omit: **our representative**
Remainder: **We will send Mr. Smith to visit your office.**

4. **The company, having been dormant for years, is finally reawakening.**

Omit: **having been dormant for years**
Remainder: **The company is finally reawakening.**

5. **Our firm will show you how, merely by changing your circulars, you can double your business.**

Omit: **merely by changing your circulars**
Remainder: **Our firm will show you how you can double your business.**

6. **Butter that is rancid is sickening.**

Omit: **that is rancid**
Remainder: **Butter is sickening.**

Do we actually mean that **butter is sickening?** NO! Only certain butter—rancid butter—is sickening. Go back and look at Rule 2 again. It says that we use commas to set off expressions that if omitted would not destroy the sentence *nor change its meaning.* **That is rancid** is *essential* to the meaning of our sentence. Therefore, it should *not* be set off by commas.

Butter that is rancid is sickening.

7. **Butter, which is in great demand, is selling well.**

Omit: **which is in great demand**

Remainder: **Butter is selling well.**

Do we mean to say that **butter is selling well?** Yes. Therefore, the use of commas is proper since the expression **which is in great demand** is *not* necessary to the meaning of the sentence.

8. **Air that is polluted is bad for you.**

Omit: **that is polluted**

Remainder: **Air is bad for you.**

Do we mean that **air is bad for you?** NO! Only **polluted air** is bad for you. Therefore, **that is polluted** should not be set off with commas since it is essential to the meaning of the sentence.

9. **The men in our office, who won the prize, will get a bonus.**

Omit: **who won the prize**

Remainder: **The men in our office will get a bonus.**

The use of commas here is correct if *all* the men in the office won the prize. The Remainder tells us that *all* the men in the office will get bonuses. Suppose that the men in our office won a bowling contest against the men in another office. Then the use of commas in this sentence is correct.

Suppose, however, there was a bowling contest in which each man was on his own. Some men in the office won and others did not. In such a case we would not use commas.

The men in our office who won the prize will get a bonus.

In this case, **who won the prize** is essential to the meaning of the sentence since it tells us exactly which men get bonuses.

Now, let's get technical for a moment to analyze what you have been doing in the last few example-sentences:

Butter that is rancid is sickening.

Butter, which is in great demand, is selling well.

The men in our office who won the prize will get a bonus.

Do you notice that each of these sentences contains a clause that begins with a relative pronoun — *that, which,* or *who?* These clauses are known as *relative clauses.* It is around these clauses that we sometimes put commas and sometimes do not, depending upon our meaning.

When a relative clause is essential to our meaning, it is called a *restrictive clause.* For example, in the sentence **Butter that is rancid is sickening,** the clause **that is rancid** is a restrictive clause because it restricts the type of butter we are talking about to one type: **butter that is rancid.**

When a relative clause is not essential to our meaning, it is called a *nonrestrictive clause.* For example, in the sentence **Butter, which is in great demand, is selling well,** the clause **which is in great demand** is a nonrestrictive clause. It does not restrict our meaning to any one type of butter — *all* butter is selling well.

So what you have really learned in Sentences 6-9 is that *restrictive clauses* are not set off with commas because they are essential to the meaning of a sentence; *nonrestrictive clauses* are set off with commas because they are not essential to the meaning of a sentence.

Where does this information leave you? Right back with the necessity to *test* whether a clause is essential or not. Even if you forget the technical names for these clauses, the important point is that you remember how to test to see if a clause or phrase is essential to a sentence.

One fine point that you may want to remember is this: In choosing between *which* or *that* at the beginning of a relative clause, use *that* if the clause is restrictive; use *which* if the clause is nonrestrictive. Go back to Sentences 6-9 to see how this has been applied.

Now, on to a few more examples of using commas to set off explanatory matter.

10.   My son, Alan, is attending college.

The commas around **Alan** lead to the inference that Alan is an only son. *Test it.*

Omit: **Alan**

Remainder: **My son is attending college.** (Correct if he is an only son.)

If Alan has any brothers, the commas should be omitted since we are restricting our meaning to this one son. His brothers may still be in kindergarten.

My son Alan is attending college.

11.   Jackson Polk, of Harvard, will address the meeting.

If there is also a Jackson Polk at Yale, you would omit the commas to restrict your meaning to the Polk at Harvard. Do you see why? Similarly, do you see why commas are omitted from the following sentences?

My friend George has written of you often.

The philosopher Locke expressed the rights of man.

The year 1933 ushered in the New Deal.

The word togetherness is overused nowadays.

The candidate expressing his honest ideals despite wide-spread public disapproval of them will often win out.

Test each of the following sentences to see why various elements have been considered explanatory and have, therefore, been set off with commas. Can you omit each of these elements that have been set

off with commas and still have a complete thought that is unchanged in meaning?

Automation, or the use of automatic controls, is a new science.

The new playwrights, such as Arthur Kopet and Edward Albee, have brought renewed vitality to the American theater.

Our organization, like any young business, is eager to explore new markets.

These figures, all of which have been carefully checked, point to a disastrous conclusion.

We discussed a number of possibilities, none of which proved workable.

The candidate, realizing that the election was lost, conceded defeat.

This last sentence could be written: **Realizing that the election was lost, the candidate conceded defeat.** It should never be written: **Realizing that the election was lost, defeat was conceded by the candidate.**

The latter sentence would imply that *defeat* realized the election was lost. Always place the subject of a sentence directly after the introductory phrase or clause that modifies it.

You have already met the participial phrase in the unit on *Dangling Participles*. For example, in the sentence **Walking down the street, I slipped,** the phrase **walking down the street** is a participial phrase. **Walking** is the present participle of the verb **to walk**; hence, the name *participial phrase*. Pick out the participial phrases in these sentences:

Fighting for his life, he lashed out viciously.

The architect, seeing the finished building, was elated.

We ordered rather late, counting on immediate service.

Do you notice how each of the participial phrases in these sentences could be omitted without changing the basic meaning of each sentence? Following our general rule, therefore, you know that you should set them off with commas because they are merely explanatory phrases.

Observe this sentence, however:

Prices rising at a rapid pace are a sure sign of inflation.

Here we have the participial phrase **rising at a rapid pace.** Can it be omitted from our sentence? No. This phrase is essential to the meaning of our sentence. It is acting like a restrictive clause and, therefore, should not be set off with commas. In fact, it really is a restrictive clause "in disguise." What this sentence really says is this:

Prices **that are rising at a rapid pace** are a sure sign of inflation.

So, remember, when you start a sentence with a participial phrase, be sure to follow it *immediately* with the subject to which it refers. Otherwise you will have a dangling participle.

Right: **Checking our inventory, we noted a shortage.**

Wrong: **Checking our inventory, a shortage was noted.**

At this point your mind may well be reeling from exposure to complex sentences, dependent clauses, restrictive clauses, nonrestrictive clauses, participial phrases (restrictive and nonrestrictive)—and so forth. We can't blame you if you're beginning to get confused, so let's simplify all this down to the key point of RULE 2: *Use commas to set off expressions that if omitted would not destroy the sentence nor change its meaning.* If you just learn to use this rule, the rest will fall in place even if you forget all the technical terminology after this course. It's *usage,* not terminology, that counts.

Turn to Programed Reinforcement S22 through S34

PART C.

Use commas to set off a word, phrase, or clause that interrupts the natural flow of a sentence. By *interrupt* we mean that it forces you to pause. Here is a list of commonly used words, phrases, and clauses that should be set off with commas when they interrupt the natural flow of a sentence.

accordingly	namely
again	naturally
also	next
besides	nevertheless
consequently	notwithstanding
finally	otherwise
furthermore	personally
hence	respectively
however	still
indeed	then
meantime	therefore
moreover	too

as a rule	in brief
as you know	in the first place
at any rate	in other words
by the way	of course
I believe	on the other hand
for example	on the contrary
if any	that is
in fact	to be sure

Note 1: The expressions listed above are not *always* set off with commas. When such an expression is used in a sentence in a manner that does not interrupt the natural flow of the sentence, you do not set it off with commas. Notice how these expressions do not force you to pause as you read the following sentences aloud.

However expensive the remodeling, we will go through with it.

If he is otherwise occupied, we will return later.

We therefore feel that you must act with caution.

BUT: **We feel, therefore, that you must act with caution.** (Here the placement of **therefore** makes you pause.)

Note 2: Exclamations such as **oh, yes, no,** and **well** should be set off with commas when they are used in a conversational manner to start a sentence.

Oh, you don't say.

Yes, we will attend.

No, I cannot accept your offer.

Well, you are probably right.

Use a comma to set off a question that is added to a statement.

1. **You sent the letter, did you not?**
Omit: **did you not?**
Remainder: **You sent the letter.**
2. **Lovely day, isn't it?**
Omit: **isn't it?**
Remainder: **Lovely day.**
3. **You will do as we ask, won't you?**
Omit: **won't you?**
Remainder: **You will do as we ask.**

Use a comma to set off a contrasting expression within a sentence — an expression that usually starts with **not, seldom,** or **never.**

1. **Mr. Smith has gone to Chicago, not to St. Louis.**
Omit: **not to St. Louis.**
Remainder: **Mr. Smith has gone to Chicago.**
2. **Our Board meets often in private, seldom in public.**
Omit: **seldom in public.**
Remainder: **Our Board meets often in private.**
3. **We have always enjoyed high attendance, never low, during Easter.**

Omit: **never low.**

Remainder: **We have always enjoyed high attendance during Easter.**

The abbreviation **Jr., Sr.,** *or* **Esq.** *(Esquire) at the end of a man's name is considered explanatory in nature. So too is* **Inc.** *and* **Ltd.** *at the end of a company name.* Always place a comma *before* each of these abbreviations. Always place a comma *after* each of these abbreviations unless it ends the sentence in which case one period is all you need.

George Henry Smathers, Jr., is our newly elected President.

Enclosed is a letter from Robert G. Cyrus, Esq., our attorney.

Johnson and Johnson, Inc., recently published its latest profit figures.

If you use the title *Esq.* after an attorney's name, do not write *Mr.* before the name. **Robert G. Cyrus, Esq., or Mr. Robert G. Cyrus** is correct.

Never: Mr. Robert G. Cyrus, Esq.

College degrees or honorary awards listed after a person's name are similarly set off with commas.

Elizabeth C. Ramsey, LL.D., Ph.D., has joined our faculty.

Kent Smith, D.F.C., is your Flight Commander.

RULE 1.

The year written after a month and a date should be set off with commas since it is in the nature of an explanation of which month and day. Frequently, the careless writer omits the second comma that should follow the year in the middle of a sentence.

The Declaration of July 4, 1776, is still our guiding beacon.

If the name of the day as well as the date is used, use commas to set off the explanatory material.

The meeting on Tuesday, August 18, is scheduled for noon.

The meeting on August 18, Tuesday, is scheduled for noon.

RULE 2.

The name of a state or country after a city should be set off with commas since it identifies the particular city. Again, don't forget the comma *after* the name of the state or country in the middle of a sentence.

When in Rome do as the Romans do — and this means Rome, Italy, and Rome, Georgia, too.

When a street address is written out in a sentence, use commas to separate the various elements. Note that a comma is placed *after* the Postal Zone number but not before it. If you use a Zip Code number, place it immediately after the name of the state without a comma and omit the zone number.

Mrs. Porter has lived at 2234 Peachtree Street, Atlanta 13, Georgia, for seven years. OR: **2234 Peachtree Street, Atlanta, Georgia 30013, for seven years.**

RULE 3.

Use a comma to set off a short quotation from the rest of the sentence.

He said, "I will not budge an inch."

"Do unto others as you would have others do unto you," is the Golden Rule.

"Send the bills at once," he threatened, "or there will be trouble around here."

Note 1: When the quotation is not direct and not in quotation marks, no comma is necessary.

He said that he would not budge.

The Golden Rule says that we should do unto others as we would have them do unto us.

Note 2: When the quotation is not a complete thought in itself but is a necessary part of the entire sentence, you omit the comma even though you use quotation marks.

He said he was "extremely humiliated."

The summer days are "dog days."

Note 3: When a comma ends a direct quotation, *always* place the final comma *inside* the final quotation marks.

Right: **"Send your payment or suffer the consequences," he threatened.**

NOT: "Send your payment or suffer the consequences", he threatened.

If the quoted material ends with a question mark or exclamation point, you use this mark inside the quotation marks and omit the comma.

"Who will help me?" he asked.

"Wow!" he exclaimed.

If the quoted material ends with a period, you substitute a comma for the period, as follows:

"We are pleased to submit our payment," the letter stated.

BUT: **The letter stated, "We are pleased to submit our payment."**

Turn to Programed Reinforcement S35 through S40

RULE 4.

Use a comma to separate two complete thoughts that are connected by a coordinate conjunction such as **but, and, or, nor, yet.** *In other words, in a compound sentence place commas between all independent clauses.*

Our offer was made in good faith, and we trust that you will give it full consideration.

We are not prepared to act now, nor will we be prepared for many months.

He went, but I stayed.

long sentence with and.

228

Note 1: Note that in each of the foregoing examples the comma comes *before* the conjunction. There is no comma after the conjunction. The reason for this is obvious if you realize that the conjunction is part of the final clause.

Note 2: In a short sentence composed of two independent clauses connected by *and* or *or*, you may omit the comma if the meaning of the sentence is clear. As a rule of thumb, you may omit the comma if either part of the sentence is composed of five words or fewer.

Your order arrived and we shipped it immediately.

Pay the bill or return the merchandise.

If the two thoughts are connected by **but** or **yet**, include the comma no matter how short the parts of the sentence.

We are ready to deal with you now, but we won't be forever.

They were not expected, yet they came.

Note 3: You should know what's wrong with the use of the comma in this sentence:

Wrong: **We must change our advertising appeal, we may lose a large part of our market.**

You should remember from your study of run-on sentences that a comma by itself is not a strong enough "glue" to weld two independent clauses into a compound sentence. To correct this error either use a semicolon or a comma plus a coordinate conjunction or make two separate sentences.

Right: **We must change our advertising appeal; we may lose a large part of our market.**

Right: **We must change our advertising appeal, or we may lose a large part of our market.**

Right: **We must change our advertising appeal. We may lose a large part of our market.**

Note 4: Three or more complete thoughts (independent clauses) may be joined in a series in a single compound sentence. Separate all independent clauses with commas. Don't forget the comma before the final coordinate conjunction.

He came, he saw, and he conquered.

Plan your campaign, put it into operation, and guide it to a successful conclusion.

Note 5: Don't confuse a compound sentence composed of *two or more complete thoughts* with a sentence that contains a compound predicate composed of two or more predicates. In this latter type of sentence, do not use commas to separate the parts of the compound predicate. Examine the following two sentences:

We carefully set up our booth at the fair and arranged the displays attractively. (One subject: *We*. Compound predicate: **set up ... and arranged.**)

We carefully set up our booth at the fair, but the public did not attend in large numbers. (Two complete thoughts — **We set up.... The public did not attend.**)

Turn to Programed Reinforcement S41 through S46

RULE 5.

You have already learned about the dependent clause. This is the type of clause that contains a subject and a predicate but does not express a complete thought. For example: **Since the order arrived** .... Subject: **the order.** Predicate: **arrived.** Complete thought? No.

To complete the meaning of a dependent clause, you must attach it to an independent clause. Thus: **We have worked hard since the order arrived.** You have learned that this is called a *complex* sentence. You have also learned that the natural sequence of a complex sentence is for the independent clause

229

to come first, followed by the dependent clause. To help you remember this, we described the analogy of the independent clause being like a dog, and the dependent clause being like its tail. The tail should follow the dog—that's the natural sequence. Here are examples of complex sentences in the natural sequence:

We have started retooling since the order arrived.

They ran to congratulate him as soon as they heard the news.

She left the theater because she failed to get the part.

Frequently, however, the sentence may be inverted and the dependent clause placed at the beginning to give it greater emphasis. *When a sentence begins with a dependent clause, you use a comma to separate the dependent clause from the independent clause.* This comma indicates the inverted nature of the sentence. This comma warns the reader that the tail is coming before the dog.

Since the order arrived, we have started retooling.

As soon as they heard the news, they ran to congratulate him.

Because she failed to get the part, she left the theater.

Here are other examples of dependent clauses in inverted sentences. In studying these sentences, first examine the dependent clause and ask yourself, "Why does this clause not qualify as a complete thought?" Then examine the independent clause and check to see why it *does* express a complete thought.

Although you agree, we cannot accept.
After hearing your reply, he reconsidered.
As I arrived, they left.
As long as you try, you are bound to succeed.
As soon as I hear from you, I will decide.

Before you leave, drop in.
However unhappy you may feel, don't despair.
If you have an extra catalog, please send it to me.

Note 1: Remember that a dependent clause always contains a verb. (Check each of the above examples.) Don't confuse a dependent clause with a prepositional phrase. If a sentence begins with a phrase that does *not* contain a verb, do not use a comma to separate the phrase from the sentence unless the phrase is very long. For example:

On June 27 we received your offer.
In our previous correspondence we thoroughly discussed the various proposals.
At the last meeting a new President was elected.
BUT: **At the last meeting that you attended, a new President was elected.**
To gain access to the hall, try the back door.

Note 2: When you invert the normal order of a person's name and put the last name first, separate the names with a comma.

Jones, John Paul   BUT: **John Paul Jones**

Turn to Programed Reinforcement S47 through S54

RULE 6.

Use commas in special instances to avoid confusion within a sentence.

a. *Use a comma to separate words that otherwise might be misread.* Note how the comma helps the reader in the following sentences: *complete sentence*

Ever since, we have been increasing sales.
On second thought, of all our employees he is the most ambitious.
Only three days before, he came to New York.

b. *Use a comma to separate a word that is repeated twice in succession or any two sets of figures in succession.*

It has been a long, long time.

Whatever happened, happened fast.

I bowled 123, 158, and 185 on successive evenings.

BUT NOTE: I need two 5-cent stamps.

c. *Use a comma to indicate the omission of a word or phrase.*

This election we polled 14,372 votes; last election, 12,991. (The words *we polled* are omitted from the second clause.)

America gained twelve gold medals; Sweden, six; Britain, four; France, two. (What word is omitted?)

d. *Use commas to separate a large number into units of three digits.*

The national debt is greater than $300,000,-000,000.

e. Letters: *Use a comma after the complimentary close of a letter except when using open punctuation.*

Sincerely,

Very truly yours,

Respectfully,

Sincerely yours,

Cordially yours,

Note that you capitalize *only* the first word in the complimentary close.

REVIEW OF COMMON COMMA ERRORS TO AVOID

1. Do not separate a subject from its predicate-verb by a comma if the predicate comes immediately after the subject.

Wrong: An inefficient, unreliable worker, should be discharged.

Right: An inefficient, unreliable worker should be discharged.

2. Do not separate a predicate from its object by a comma if the object comes directly after the predicate.

Wrong: Dale Carnegie wrote, *How to Win Friends and Influence People.*

Right: Dale Carnegie wrote How to Win Friends and Influence People.

3. Do not write the comma *after* the conjunction **but, and,** or **or** when it joins clauses in a sentence. Always place the comma before the conjunction.

Wrong: He applied for the position but, he did not get it.

Right: He applied for the position, but he did not get it.

4. Do not use a comma to separate the two parts of a compound subject, a compound predicate, or a compound object when they are connected by **and, or,** or **but.**

Wrong: The men, and the women proved equally capable. (Compound subject)

Right: The men and the women proved equally capable.

Wrong: She typed, or filed from nine to five. (Compound predicate)

Right: She typed or filed from nine to five.

Wrong: They shipped autos, and tractors from the warehouse. (Compound object)

Right: They shipped autos and tractors from the warehouse.

5. Do not use a comma to set off a *reflexive* pronoun (a pronoun ending in *self*) used for emphasis.

Wrong: Mr. Jones, himself, will give the report.

Right: Mr. Jones himself will give the report.

6. Do not use a comma before **than** in a comparison.

Wrong: It is wiser to fail, than not to try at all.

Right: It is wiser to fail than not to try at all.

7. Do not use a comma after a prepositional phrase at the beginning of a sentence unless the phrase is very long.

Wrong: On June 15, our vacations will begin.

Right: **On June 15 our vacations will begin.**

Wrong: In the winter, business shows an improvement.

Right: **In the winter business shows an improvement.**

Turn to Programed Reinforcement S55 through S60

5. THE COLON (:)

The colon is an easy mark of punctuation. You use it in only four simple ways.

RULE 1.

Use the colon after the salutation of a business letter except when using open punctuation.

Dear Madam:
Gentlemen:

RULE 2.

Use the colon to introduce a quotation of one long sentence or of two or more sentences regardless of length. Use a comma to introduce a quotation of one short sentence or part of a sentence.

Senator Jones replied as follows: "I know the importance of this investigation, but I would be ill-advised to become party to such a circus."

He said simply, "I accept."

RULE 3.

Use the colon to formally introduce a list or idea. Generally, a formal introduction includes a word or phrase such as **as follows, the following, these, this, thus.**

Erect the desk as follows: Attach the legs to the side panels; then nail the side panels to the top.

The following invoices are unpaid: No. 3721, No. 3723, and No. 3746.

The real problems are these: the price in Britain, the shipping cost, and the tariff.

Note 1: Observe the examples above to see when the word following the colon is capitalized and when it is not. It is capitalized when a *complete* sentence follows the colon. It is not capitalized when less than a complete sentence follows the colon.

Note 2: Compare the following sentences. Do you see why a colon is used in the first sentence but not in the second? What word makes the first introduction "formal"?

These are the reasons he succeeded: his great initiative, his perseverance, and his cleverness.

The reasons he succeeded are his great initiative, perseverance, and cleverness.

Note 3: In some sentences the formal introductory expression (**as follows, namely,** etc.) is omitted, but clearly understood. In such a sentence use a colon or a dash.

We missed three trains: the 5:15, the 6:07, and the 7:03.

OR:

We missed three trains — the 5:15, the 6:07, and the 7:03.

Note 4: Space *twice* after a colon before starting the next word.

RULE 4.

Use the colon to separate hours from minutes when expressed in figures.

6:43 a.m.   5:06 p.m.

Note 1: On a timetable the colon is often replaced with a period.

6.43 a.m.   5.06 p.m.

Note 2: Do not space after the colon in numbers of this type.

Turn to Programed Reinforcement S61 through S65

232

① Dear Sir :

② 3:45 pm

③ long or formal quotation, The prime minister stated :

④ He ordered the following :

6. THE SEMICOLON (;)

The semicolon is a useful mark of punctuation provided that you use it sparingly. Its function in a sentence is to indicate a major pause or break. It indicates a greater pause than a comma, though not quite so great a pause as a period. Some writers have a bad tendency to write long, complicated, tedious sentences, using semicolons to string separate thoughts together like linked frankfurters. No more than you can easily digest a long string of frankfurters, can the average reader digest such a long string of thoughts. A complicated sentence is far more easily read and understood if it is broken into two or more smaller sentences by the use of the period rather than the semicolon. The semicolon, however, has a very definite and useful function when properly employed. So learn these three basic rules for the *proper* use of the semicolon.

RULE 1.

Use the semicolon to separate two closely related complete thoughts that are not separated by a conjunction such as **and, but, for, or, nor.** In other words, as you have already learned, semicolons can be used to connect two or more independent clauses to create a compound sentence.

Prices rose; wages fell. (The semicolon implies a relationship between the two events.)

OR: **Prices rose, but wages fell.** (The conjunction *but* expresses the relationship.)

OR: **Prices rose. Wages fell.** (The period does not necessarily imply any relationship.)

NEVER: **Prices rose, wages fell.** (This is a run-on sentence.)

Right: **To err is human; to forgive, divine.**

Right: **Mail the enclosed card now; you will receive your gift by return mail.**

Note 1: How do you connect the two independent clauses in a compound sentence? You have already studied three ways that should be familiar by now:

1. Use a coordinate conjunction (*and, but, or, nor, yet*) preceded by a comma.

2. If one of the clauses is very short (five or fewer words), you may omit the comma and use a coordinate conjunction by itself.

3. You may omit the coordinate conjunction and use a semicolon by itself.

There is one more way to connect the clauses in a compound sentence:

4. If each clause is very long, and if one or more of the clauses contains commas within itself, then you may use a coordinate conjunction preceded by a *semicolon* instead of a comma. The semicolon used in this manner helps the reader follow a complicated sentence without confusion. For example:

Naturally, having heard of the offer, he rushed to the employment office; but, despite his haste, he found that the job had already been filled.

Employing every means at his disposal, the U.S. Ambassador, Gregory C. Wright, attempted to befriend the inhabitants of that small, underdeveloped nation; and his efforts were ultimately rewarded by success, which was justly earned.

The American is noted for friendliness and innocence; the Englishman, for formality and reserve; and the Frenchman, for explosiveness and warmth.

Note 2: You have already learned about the use of the comma to separate items

233

listed in series. Observe how a semicolon should be used to separate items in series where commas would be confusing.

Our new Board of Directors is composed of Rodney G. Jones, President; Augustus E. Smythe, Vice-President; and Ormand Cole, Jr., Secretary-Treasurer.

The totals are 3,728; 2,142,607; and 42,429.

Note 3: When using the semicolon in a sentence, skip only one space before the next word.

RULE 2.

Use the semicolon to separate two complete thoughts (independent clauses) that are connected by a conjunctive such as **accordingly, also, consequently, further, hence, however, indeed, in fact, moreover, nevertheless, then, therefore, thus, whereas.**

The deadline has passed; accordingly we are canceling our order.

The odds were insurmountable; nevertheless he fought on.

Please give us your exact measurements; then we can tailor-fit the suit to your dimensions.

The doors open at seven; however, you will be admitted at six.

Note 1: Do you see why commas would have been incorrect where semicolons are used in the four sentences above? Only the coordinate conjunctions *and, but, or, nor,* and *yet* are strong enough "glue" to hold independent clauses together when used with a comma. For "weaker" conjunctions like those listed above, you need the strength of a semicolon, not a comma.

Note 2: Observe that a comma has been placed after the conjunction *however* in the fourth sentence but has not been placed after the conjunctions in the other three sentences. The word *however* in Sentence 4

is independent of the thought expressed by its clause; it almost *requires* a pause. This is not true of the other conjunctions as used here; hence they do not require commas.

RULE 3.

Use a semicolon to precede an expression such as **for example, e.g., namely, viz., that is, i.e., to wit,** *when this expression introduces a list or explanation.* A comma is *always* used immediately following each of the above expressions.

He had one credo; namely, do unto others as you would have them do unto you.

We can choose from among many fine potential locations for the convention; for example, New York, Chicago, Los Angeles, or Honolulu.

If the list or explanation occurs in the middle of the sentence rather than at the end, use dashes rather than semicolons.

Many fine potential locations — for example, New York, Chicago, Los Angeles, or Honolulu — are available for us to select for the convention.

Turn to Programed Reinforcement S66 through S75

7. QUOTATION MARKS (")

RULE 1.

Use quotation marks to enclose a direct quotation. A direct quotation repeats the *exact* words of what was originally said or written.

In your letter of July 9 you state: "Our records indicate that shipment was made on June 15 via Universal Shippers, Inc."

Do not use quotation marks around an indirect quotation. An indirect quotation is a *rewording* of the original statement. It is frequently introduced by the word **that.**

In your letter of July 9 you write that the shipment was sent via Universal Shippers on June 15.

Note 1: Use a colon to introduce a direct quotation of one *long* sentence or of two or more sentences regardless of length. Use a comma to introduce a direct quotation of one short sentence or of part of a sentence.

The President declared: "In a time of peril such as this we must jealously guard our liberties and defend our national integrity against all encroachments."

The President said, "I am confident of victory."

Note 2: When a complete statement is quoted and ends the sentence, the period is placed *inside* the final quotation marks.

Patrick Henry shouted, "Give me liberty or give me death."

When a complete statement is quoted but does not end the sentence, a *comma* is placed inside the final quotation mark.

"Give me liberty or give me death," shouted Patrick Henry.

When a complete statement being quoted is broken into more than one part, enclose each part in quotation marks. Do not start the second part with a capital letter. Note the use of commas.

"Send us the bill," he wrote, "and we will mail you a check by return mail."

Note 3: When recording the direct conversation of two or more persons, place the statements of each person in separate quotation marks and in separate paragraphs.

The chairman shouted, "Order! Order in the house!"

"I will not be silenced," answered Jones, jumping from his seat with arms waving wildly.

"Gentlemen," interrupted Brown, "let us look at this matter in a calmer frame of mind."

Note 4: If a quotation consists of more than one sentence, the quotation marks go at the beginning and at the end of the entire statement. If the single quotation consists of more than one paragraph, the quotation marks go at the *beginning* of *each* paragraph, but at the *end* of *only* the *last* paragraph.

The letter read: "We are making this offer just this week. Note that it is being made together with our sale of daytime dresses. We are sure you will like our selection.

"Any time during the morning that is best for you will be best for us. Will you come?"

Note 5: Use single quotation marks to indicate a quotation within a quotation.

He said, "I believe in the old saying, 'Haste makes waste.'"

Note 6: When typing quotation marks, do not skip a space after the beginning quotation mark or before the closing quotation mark.

RULE 2.

Use quotation marks around the title of an article or chapter in a magazine, newspaper, or book. The name of a magazine, newspaper, or book is usually written either in italics or in all capital letters rather than in quotation marks. To indicate italics, you underline the name.

This month's Scientific American includes Professor Anderson's fascinating article on "Solar Particles and Cosmic Rays."

LIFE is doing a series on "The Universe."

Note 1: If the article *A, An,* or *The* is a part of the title of an article, it should be capitalized and included within the quotation marks. If it is part of the name of a magazine, it should be included as part of the material that is italicized (or underlined) or written in all capital letters.

RULE 3.

Use the quotation marks around unusual words, coined phrases, or colloquial expressions.

Our sales staff must be "on-the-ball."

We feel that Mr. Jones is a "square-shooter."

The way to understand this problem is to "conceptualize" it in your mind.

RULE 4.

Quotation Marks and Other Punctuation — Here's where a great deal of trouble can arise unless you are careful. Study these simple rules and you'll easily master this trouble spot.

1. *Always place a final period or comma inside the quotation marks.*

He said, "Let the chips fall."

"Give me the statistics," Jones retorted, "and I'll have the answers in a minute."

2. *Always write a final colon or semi-colon outside the quotation marks.*

Here is a partial list of causes cited in "The Rising Cost of Living": higher wages, increased tariffs, lower rates of productivity growth.

The encircled troops were told, "Surrender or die"; they chose to fight on.

3. *The question mark, exclamation point, and dash are placed inside the quotation marks when they relate specifically to the quoted material.*

"Will you join me?" he asked.

"Wow!" was all he could say.

"Our flight position is —" were the pilot's last recorded words.

4. *The question mark, exclamation point, and dash are placed outside the quotation marks if they relate to the entire sentence.*

Did you read our article, "The Higher Light"?

Congratulations on your latest article, "How To Invest"!

"To be or not to be . . ." — Shakespeare.

Turn to Programed Reinforcement S76 through S86

8. THE APOSTROPHE (')

RULE 1.

Use the apostrophe to indicate the omission of a letter or letters in a contraction. Do not place a period after a contraction as you would after an abbreviation. Note where the apostrophe goes and what letters it replaces in the following contractions:

aren't	I'll	he's	Gen'l
can't	he'll	I'm	Gov't
couldn't	she'll	it's	Nat'l
isn't	they'll	they're	Rec't
weren't	we'll	we're	Sec'y

RULE 2.

Use the apostrophe to form the possessive case of a noun. If the noun does not end in *s*, add apostrophe *s* ('s). If the noun ends in *s*, add an apostrophe only.

A teacher's success depends upon a student's efforts.

John's office called, but Charles' line was busy.

Stenographers' skills will determine their success.

Remember, the possessive form of a *pronoun* does not take an apostrophe: **hers, its, ours, yours, theirs.**

Is this book hers?

Yours truly,

The firm sent its representative.

It's is a contraction of **it is. Its** is a possessive pronoun.

It's a fine day.
We think it's not going to last.
The stock was put on its shelf.

RULE 3.

Use the apostrophe to form the plural of letters and numbers.

Mississippi has four i's, four s's, and two p's.
This month we ordered a new shipment of No. 105's.

The plural of words being used simply as words is usually formed by just adding *s*. If, however, a particular plural formed this way might appear confusing, apostrophe s (*'s*) is added.

We want no ifs, ands, or buts.
He uses six I's in his very first sentence.

9. THE HYPHEN (-)

RULE 1.

Use the hyphen to divide a word that cannot be completed at the end of a line.

He thought that it would be too dif-ficult.

The trend in letter writing today is to avoid the use of word divisions whenever possible. Your guiding rule when typing copy, therefore, should be to divide words only when it is absolutely necessary to do so in order to maintain a *reasonably* straight margin. A line of type that is five spaces shorter than the margin or three spaces longer is acceptable in business practice.

Observe the following rules about word division:

a. When dividing a word, you type the hyphen at the end of the first line, not at the beginning of the second.

b. Divide words only between syllables. A one-syllable word, therefore, may not be divided. You should not divide a two-syllable word if it has five or fewer letters. For example, do not divide words like *talked, ago, through, elate.*

c. A two-syllable word may not be divided if one of the syllables consists of only one letter. The word *consists* may be divided into *con-sists*. The word *arouse* may not be divided into *a-rouse*.

d. When a medial (middle) syllable of a word is a single vowel, that single vowel should *end* the first line and not start the second. The word *hesitate* consists of the three syllables *hes-i-tate*. It should be divided as *hesi-tate*, NOT *hes-itate*.

e. Do not divide a proper noun, a contraction, an abbreviation, or a number if at all possible.

f. If possible, do not divide a word if it is the last word of a paragraph or a page.

g. Do not end more than two successive lines with a divided word.

h. Carry over at least three or more letters.

Correct:	*Incorrect:*
shortly	short-ly
lux-ury	luxu-ry
con-sumer	consum-er

i. Divide hyphenated compound words only at a point where a hyphen naturally occurs.

sister-in-law   self-control   above-mentioned

j. As a general rule, divide words between double letters unless the word is derived from one that ends in a double letter (sma*ll*). In the latter case, the word is divided after the root word.

small-est	rub-ber
woo-ing	excel-lence
stuff-ing	win-ning

There are certain expressions that should *always* be hyphenated:

a. Compound words that begin with **self**, such as **self-conscious, self-evident, self-assurance, self-respect, self-confident.**

b. Compound words that begin with **ex, pro,** or **anti.**

For example: **ex-President, ex-Senator, pro-American, pro-United Nations, anti-Communist.**

There are other expressions that are sometimes hyphenated and sometimes not — expressions such as **up to date, high class, first rate, high grade, well informed.** As a rule of thumb, follow this procedure: Whenever any such expression comes *directly before* the noun it modifies, it should be hyphenated.

> **We have an up-to-date system.**
> **Our store caters to a high-class clientele.**
> **We deal in first-rate goods.**
> **We need a twelve-foot stepladder.**
> **He competed in the hundred-yard dash.**

When, however, the noun being modified does *not* follow directly, use *no* hyphens.

> **Our system is up to date.**
> **Our clientele is high class.**
> **Our goods are first rate.**
> **He ran in a race of one hundred yards.**

Note 1: Generally, do not use a hyphen after an adverb ending in *ly* even if it precedes the noun:

> **highly trained athlete**
> **brightly decorated hall**
> **widely heralded appearance**
> **oddly strange mixture**

Note 2: Observe this sentence: **We are short of ten- and twenty-dollar bills.**

Note the hyphen after *ten*. This sentence really says: **We are short of ten-dollar bills and twenty-dollar bills;** hence the use of the hyphen after *ten*. Here are similar examples:

> **They stock half-, three-quarter-, and seven-eighth-inch bolts.**
> **He swam in the 50-, 100-, and 220-yard free-style races.**
> **They produced 24-, 32-, 64-, and 128-page versions of the book.**

Note 3: When writing out numbers, you hyphenate compound numbers from twenty-one through ninety-nine. You do not hyphenate hundreds, thousands, or millions unless the entire number is used as an adjective directly before a noun. Observe these examples:

> **thirty-seven**
> **one hundred thirty-seven**
> **thirty-seven thousand six hundred and forty-five**
> **one hundred thirty-seven thousand six hundred and forty-five**
> BUT: **a one-hundred-thirty-seven-foot fall**
> **a six-hundred-dollar reduction**

Turn to Programed Reinforcement S87 through S102

10. PARENTHESES ( )

RULE 1.

Use parentheses to enclose expressions that are completely incidental, explanatory, or supplementary to the main thought of a sentence.

> **There is no possibility (so I am told) that this deal will be consummated.**
> **You have already learned (see Lesson 2) about nouns.**

Note 1: When a sentence ends with an expression in parentheses, place the period after the parentheses. For example:

In full consideration for our claim, we hereby agree to accept as payment the amount of Eight Hundred Dollars ($800.00).

Note 2: When a complete sentence appears in parentheses as part of another sentence, it is not started with a capital letter nor finished with a period. See the first two examples above. When a sentence in parentheses is an independent thought, it is started with a capital letter and ended with appropriate punctuation *inside* the closing parenthesis mark:

I have told the Director that you will have the goods delivered by Tuesday. (John, please don't let us down.) He will accept shipment no later than then.

Note 3: Do you place punctuation *inside* or *outside* the final mark of parenthesis? If the punctuation relates only to the material in parenthesis, place the punctuation *inside*.

His latest article ("Lost Opportunities") is certain to receive an award.

When using a telescope, never (Never!) look directly at the sun.

If the punctuation relates to the whole sentence and not specifically to the material in parentheses, place the punctuation *outside* the closing parenthesis mark.

No matter where we have traveled (in the United States and Canada at least), we have never found a better hotel. Do you see why the comma is placed *outside* the parenthesis in this sentence?

Note 4: In some instances it is proper to use either dashes or parentheses, whichever you prefer:

Right: **This offer (and it is our final offer) is too good to be refused.**

Right: **This offer — and it is our final offer — is too good to be refused.**

RULE 2.

Parentheses are used to enclose numbers or letters that itemize a list which is part of running text.

Practice serves to (a) improve your coordination, (b) increase your speed, and (c) develop your strength.

Note 1: If you had tabulated this list, you would write it as follows:

Practice serves to accomplish the following:
   a. improve your coordination
   b. increase your speed
   c. develop your strength

RULE 3.

In formal documents numbers are frequently written out both in words and figures. Parentheses are usually placed around the figures. For example:

The total fee for our service shall be Six Hundred Dollars ($600).

We acknowledge receipt of your order for six hundred (600) barrels of crude oil.

Note 1: In spelling out a dollar amount in a legal document, capitalize each word in the figure and capitalize the word *Dollar*. The figure in parentheses appears after the word *Dollar*: **Six Hundred Dollars ($600).**

Note 2: In spelling out a quantity of material, do not capitalize the numbers or the unit of measurement, and place the figures in parentheses *before* the name of the unit of measure: **six hundred (600) barrels.**

RULE 4.

Brackets [ ] are frequently used in a printed direct quotation to indicate matter that is not part of the quotation but that has been inserted by the editor.

The minister quoted the old adage: "The exception proves [tests] the rule."

11. THE DASH (—)

RULE 1.

Use the dash to indicate a major break in the continuity of thought.

The large house — and make no mistake, it was large — was completely demolished by the fire.

I know — or should I say, I feel — that you will do well.

RULE 2.

Use the dash to emphasize an explanatory phrase.

We want to tell you about our product — the Schenley car.

America — that bastion of democracy — has an obligation to all human beings.

Note 1: Properly used, the dash is an effective tool to catch the reader's eye and keep him alert. If you use the dash too often, however, you destroy its effectiveness and leave a sloppy, difficult-to-read page. The good writer uses the dash only occasionally when he wants extra *punch*. It is his *Sunday punch*, not his *left jab*.

Note 2: The dash is frequently used to set off an explanatory phrase that contains one or more commas.

The top-rated shows — Beverly Hillbillies, I Love Lucy, and Father Knows Best — have all been situation comedies.

Note 3: Don't omit the second dash. If an explanatory phrase starts with a dash, it should end with a dash too — not with a comma.

Wrong: The top rated shows — Beverly Hillbillies, I Love Lucy, and Father Knows Best, have all been situation comedies.

RULE 3.

Use the dash after an expression such as namely or that is when this expression introduces a list in tabulated form.

We are aware of three determining factors; namely —
1. **the bad weather**
2. **the rise in prices**
3. **a shortage of labor**

RULE 4.

Use a dash before the name of the author after a quotation.

Unbroken happiness is a bore; it should have ups and down. — Moliere

Note 1: In business the preferred way to make a dash on a typewriter is by striking the hyphen twice leaving no space before or after this dash.

An alternative, considered to be less formal, is to space once, strike the hyphen once, and space again.

Preferred: The officers of the company--the President, Vice-President, and Secretary-Treasurer --have approved the plans for merger.

Less Formal: The officers of the company - the President, Vice-President, and Secretary-Treasurer - have approved the plan for merger.

12. ELLIPSES (...)

Ellipses are a series of dots used in the midst of a direct quotation to indicate that part of the quotation at that point has been omitted. *Three* dots are used at the beginning of, or in the middle of, a quoted sentence. If the omitted material is at the end of sentence, a fourth dot representing the period is added. Do not use more or fewer dots than these.

If a man has freedom enough to live healthy . . . he has enough. — Goethe

According to Immanual Kant: "Freedom is that faculty which enlarges the usefulness of all other faculties. . . ."

Turn to Programed Reinforcement S103 through S112

13. CAPITALIZATION

1. Capitalize the first word of every sentence. (You should need no special examples of this.)

2. Capitalize the first word of a direct quotation that is a complete sentence.

He said, "This job must be improved upon."

"This job," he said, "must be improved upon."

Note, however, that if you are quoting an expression that is not a full sentence, you do not capitalize the first word.

He said that this job "must be improved upon."

3. Capitalize the first word of each line of poetry.

"What fairings will ye that I bring?

Said the King to his daughters three;

For I to Vanity Fair am bound,

Now say what shall they be?"

4. Capitalize each amount when spelled out in formal or legal documents, as follows:

Eighty-seven Dollars and Twenty-four Cents

Sixty-four Thousand Dollars

5. Capitalize the word *dear* in a salutation when it comes at the beginning. Do *not* capitalize *dear* when it is in the middle of the salutation.

Dear Sir:

My dear Sir:

Dear Mr. Jones:

My dear Mr. Jones:

6. Capitalize only the first word in the complimentary close of a letter.

Sincerely yours,

Yours sincerely,

Very truly yours,

7. Capitalize nouns or pronouns that refer to God or to holy books.

Please hand me the Bible on that shelf.

The Holy Scriptures tell us that God created the world in six days and that He rested on the seventh day.

8. Capitalize college degrees such as $M. D.$; radio stations such as $WQXR$; initials standing for proper names such as $F. D. R.$; abbreviations for proper nouns such as $D. C.$ for *District of Columbia.*

John Grossman, Ph. D., will address us.

He announces for WNBC.

Headlines about F. D. R. dominated the news during the New Deal.

He lives in Brattleboro, Vt.

Note the proper capitalization of Ph. D. meaning Doctor of Philosophy.

9. Capitalize the first letter of each important word in the *title* of a work of art or literature. Do not capitalize unimportant words such as *to, and,* and *the,* which occur in the *middle* of the title.

Have you read "How to Win Friends and Influence People"?

Washington's "Farewell Address" was his greatest speech.

He entitled his talk, "Russia, the Modern Dilemma."

Have you ever seen the painting, "The Blue Boy"?

10. Capitalize proper nouns. A proper noun is a noun that refers to a specific person, place, or thing. For example:

John Jones   America   Corvair

A proper noun is always written with a capital letter. Do you realize how important proper nouns are to the American system of free enterprise? Every company name, every product name, and every trade name is a proper noun. The business correspondence you will handle on the job will be filled with proper nouns. So study the *Hints* listed below. They will help you solve the capitalization problems you may face when you are in the office.

HINTS ON CAPITALIZATION OF PROPER NOUNS

HINT 1.

Always capitalize the names of *months* of the year and *days* of the week.

Classes begin on the first Monday in February.

HINT 2.

Never capitalize the names of *seasons* except in the rare instance when the season is being *personified*; that is, referred to as though it were a living being.

Our fall order was not delivered until winter.

Old Man Winter won't stop our snow tires from giving you perfect traction.

HINT 3.

Should you capitalize the name of a *direction* such as *east* or *west*?

a. When the name of a direction refers to a *specific section* of the country or of the world, it then becomes a proper noun and it should be capitalized.

The West is solid in its opposition to Communism.

The Southwest is rapidly gaining in population and industry.

The Mississippi flows through the North and the South.

b. When the name of a direction is used to refer to a point on the compass, it should NOT be capitalized.

The plane circled twice, then headed west.

Philadelphia is southwest of New York.

The Mississippi flows from north to south.

c. *Eastern, Southern, Western,* and *Northern* are capitalized when used as part of the name of a *major* world division such as a hemisphere, a continent, or a nation. They are NOT capitalized when used as part of the name of a *minor* world division such as a state, a county, or a city.

During recent years considerable economic consolidation has occurred in Western Europe.

This particular sales territory includes eastern New York, northeastern Pennsylvania, and northern New Jersey.

d. Names derived from a particular geographical locality are capitalized.

Southerner   Northerner

HINT 4.

Should you capitalize a geographic term such as *river, ocean, mountain,* or *valley?* The answer depends upon how you are using such a term. Learn these three simple rules.

a. Capitalize a geographic term such as *river* when you use it as part of the name of a *particular* river or other geographic designation:

Hudson River

Pacific Ocean

Bear Mountain

Death Valley

b. Do not capitalize a geographic term such as *river* when it is placed *before* the name of the river:

The river Jordan

The valley of the river Nile

EXCEPTION: The word *mount* is capitalized even when it precedes the name of the mountain.

Mount Everest

Mount Rainier

Mount Whitney

c. Do not capitalize a geographic term such as *river* when you use it in the plural.

Missouri and Mississippi rivers

Atlantic and Pacific oceans

Appalachian and Rocky mountains

d. Political designations such as *state, city,* or *country* are always capitalized when they are a part of the specific name of the area.

New York City

New York State

Bucks County

When a political designation such as *state, city,* or *county* is written before the *specific* name, it may or may not be capitalized, depending upon its particular meaning in the sentence.

The state of Nevada is famed for its scenic beauty.

The State of Nevada has concluded its appeal to the United States Supreme Court.

HINT 5.

Should you capitalize a word such as *hotel, highway, tunnel,* or *revolution*? The rules here are similar to those you have just studied. Generally, capitalize such a word when you are using it as *part* of a specific name.

New Yorker Hotel

Lincoln Highway

French Revolution

BUT: **French and American revolutions**

New Yorker and Pennsylvania hotels

Turn to Programed Reinforcement S113 through S123

HINT 6.

Are titles such as *president, treasurer,* or *director* capitalized? The rule preferred is this:

a. Always capitalize the title of a person when it appears *directly* before or *directly* after the name of the title-holder.

President Johnson will see you now.

Send the message to John Jones, President of Acme Steel Company.

We received the letter from James Roberts, Assistant Director of the Zenith Oil Company.

b. Generally, capitalize the title of a *high-ranking* officer even when his name does not appear in the sentence.

The Senator will return soon.

The President was not at the White House.

c. There is some disagreement about whether the title of a *less important* office holder should be capitalized when his name does not appear in a sentence. The preferred business practice is to *capitalize such titles*. After all, you express your respect for a person when you capitalize his title.

Will your Sales Manager please contact me by phone.

The letter is from the Superintendent of our Wyoming plant.

The Treasurer of our firm will be pleased to attend the dinner.

NOTE: *Vice-President* is the preferred spelling, but *Vice-president* and *Vice President* are also acceptable.

HINT 7.

Do you capitalize the name of an organization such as *company, association, commission,* or *department*?

a. These words are capitalized when they are part of the names of *specific* organizations:

243

American Steel Company
National Association of Manufacturers
Sales Department

b. These words are capitalized when they are used as *substitutes* for the complete names of specific organizations.

We in the Company take pride in our latest production record.

The Association welcomes you to its vast membership.

The Department has been awarded a trophy for outstanding employee cooperation.

BUT: **There is a company in Denver with a fine production record.**

A new association is being formed by lumber dealers across the continent.

Which department handles this problem?

HINT 8.

Capitalize the names of *specific* governmental agencies.

United States Senate   Police Department
Court of Appeals   Board of Elections
Air Force   Council of Foreign Ministers

Capitalize the names of political parties. The word *party* itself may or may not be capitalized: *Democratic Party*; *Republican party*.

HINT 9.

Certain words are derived from proper nouns but are not capitalized because they are now used as common nouns or as other parts of speech. In fact, you can make a fascinating study of former trademarks that have been deprived of their "right" to a capital letter because the courts held that the words had become part of our everyday language. Here are a few examples:

aspirin   cellophane   escalator
shredded wheat   thermos bottle

HINT 10.

Do not capitalize the name of any *school subject* or course of study except for a language or a specifically described course.

This year I am going to study shorthand and typing.

BUT: **I added Shorthand IV and Advanced Typing to my schedule.**

I am studying English, but not Spanish or mathematics.

NOTE: Capitalize the words *high school* and *college* only if the specific title of a particular school is used.

I went to Riverhead High School and then spent three years at college.

This finishes your study of the rules of punctuation and capitalization.

You have learned many rules, but they were not too difficult. Actually, almost all of these rules were merely a review for you.

You certainly knew that a period is placed at the end of a sentence that makes a statement, a question mark is placed after a question, and an exclamation point is placed after an exclamation. You know that the comma is used to separate items listed in a series, to set off introductory expressions such as *therefore,* and to set off certain explanatory expressions. You knew that quotation marks are placed before and after a direct quotation, and that the first letter of a sentence must be capitalized. You knew all this, and much more.

All in all, probably three-quarters of the rules in this lesson were completely familiar to you. You applied them automatically without a second thought. It is mastery of the other one-quarter of these rules, however, that often spells the difference between the average, run-of-the-mill office employee and the highly paid, top-notch secretary or executive.

Do you feel you have fully mastered all the rules of punctuation presented in this lesson?

Do you feel certain that every transcript you hand to your teacher and later to your employer will exhibit perfect punctuation?

Here is the turning point in your training. If you want to move up as a superior employee, make certain that you know the rules of punctuation thoroughly. Review this lesson. Then review it again if necessary. It won't take long, and it will be well worth the small effort.

Turn to Programed Reinforcement S124 through S134

	S1 A period is used at the end of a sentence that makes a statement or gives a command. Indicate whether this sentence is a statement or a command. **Put it down.** Answer: _____.
R1 command	**S2** Punctuate the following, placing a period at the end of each sentence and capitalizing initial letters of the sentences. **book sales are improving this is particularly true of paperbacks.**
R2 Book . . . improving. This . . . paperbacks.	**S3** A period is placed after an abbreviation. If a sentence ends with an abbreviation, it has (one, two) period(s). Place periods where necessary: **The shipment is being sent c o d to Global, Inc**
R3 one; . . . c.o.d. to Global, Inc.	**S4** In typing, allow _____ blank space(s) after the period at the end of a sentence; allow _____ blank space(s) after each period in an abbreviation like **c.o.d.;** allow _____ blank space(s) after each period in an abbreviation like **C. P. A.**
R4 two; no; one ● TURN TO Exercise 48	**S5** A question mark is used after a question. It is not used after the following sentence because it is really a polite _____: **Will you please come in.**
R5 command	**S6** Occasionally there may be several questions in one sentence. How would you punctuate this? **Can you think of two advertising slogans four new jingles three eye-catching phrases**
R6 Can you think of two advertising slogans? four new jingles? three eye-catching phrases?	**S7** In typing, allow _____ space(s) after a question mark at the end of a sentence; allow _____ space(s) after a question mark in the middle of a sentence.
R7 two; two	**S8** A third punctuation mark is the exclamation point. It is used after words that show feeling or strong e _ _ _ _ _ n.
R8 emotion	**S9** Use periods, question marks, and exclamation marks where needed: **What a break I got a ten-dollar raise did you**
R9 What a break! I got a ten-dollar raise. Did you? ● TURN TO Exercise 49	**S10** **He ordered pens, pencils, erasers, and paper.** This sentence illustrates the rule pertaining to the use of the comma with words listed in a s _ _ _ _ _.
R10 series	

S11
In the following sentence, do you place a comma before the word **and**? **He sent back the bills, the invoices ? and the statements.** Answer: _____.

R11
Yes

S12
☐ True ☐ False   If coordinate conjunctions (like **and**) connect all the words in a series, you place a comma before each conjunction. For example: **He polished, and waxed, and buffed the desk.**

R12
False
(Correct: **He polished and waxed and buffed the desk).**

S13
When you have a series of adjectives you (should, should not) place a comma after the last adjective. For example: **We offer fast, accurate, efficient ? service.**

R13
should not
(We offer fast, accurate, efficient service.)

S14
To decide whether to place a comma after the last item in a series, test by treating the last item as though it were alone and not part of a series. In the space below, rewrite the sentence in S13 as you would to test it. In other words, rewrite it omitting all adjectives in the series except the last.

_____

R14
We offer efficient service.

S15
When you have a series of adverbs you (should, should not) place a comma after the last adverb. Rewrite this sentence as you would to test it.
   This letter has been quickly, accurately, and efficiently ? typed.

_____

R15
should not;
This letter has been efficiently typed.

S16
You (should, should not) place a comma after the last item in a compound subject. Rewrite this sentence as you would test it:
   Filing, typing, and posting ? are my best skills.

_____

R16
should not;
Filing is my best skill.

S17
You (should, should not) place a comma after the last word in a series when it is followed by a complete sentence. Place commas where needed in this sentence:
   Filing typing and posting these are my best skills.

R17
should;
Filing, typing, and posting, these are my best skills.
● TURN TO Exercise 50

S18
☐ True ☐ False   Commas should generally be used to set off expressions that, if omitted, would not substantially change the meaning of a sentence.

R18
True

S19

☐ True ☐ False The following sentence shows that commas must set off words of direct address: **Tell me, John, are you staying late?**

R19
True

S20

Punctuate this example of direct address: **I beg you my friends to avoid squabbles.**

R20

I beg you, my friends, to avoid squabbles.

● TURN TO Exercise 51

S21

Commas are used to set off an expression that explains a preceding word. Circle the expression that should be set off by commas: **Betty the new girl is an old friend of mine.**

R21

Betty, the new girl, is . . . .

S22

A group of words that is not essential to the meaning of the sentence should be set off by commas. Are commas used correctly here? **Gasoline, that is mixed with water, is useless.**
☐ Yes ☐ No

R22
No

S23

Are commas used correctly here? **My typewriter, which is not new, works beautifully.** ☐ Yes ☐ No

R23
Yes

S24

Gasoline that is mixed with water is useless.
The word **that** is a relative pronoun. The clause **that is mixed with water** is called a ___ ___ ___ ___ ___ ___ clause. If we omit the relative clause from this sentence, what is our remainder? _____ ____ _____.
This (has, has not) changed the meaning of our sentence.

R24
relative;
Gasoline is useless;
has

S25

Since omitting **that is mixed with water** from the sentence in S24 changes its meaning, we know that this clause **restricts** our meaning to only one type of gasoline. It is therefore called a r___ ___ ___ ___ ___ ___ ___ ___ clause.

R25
restrictive

S26

A restrictive clause is a relative clause that (is, is not) essential to the meaning of a sentence.

R26
is

S27

Since a restrictive clause is essential to the meaning of a sentence, we (can, cannot) treat it as being merely explanatory. Accordingly, we (do, do not) set it off with commas because our rule says to set off explanatory expressions only.

R27
cannot; do not

S28

My typewriter, which is not new, works very well.
The clause **which is not new** is a rel ___ ___ ___ ___ clause that (is, is not) essential to the meaning of our sentence.

R28
relative; is not

S29

If we omit **which is not new** from the sentence in S28, the remainder is:

_____ _____ _____ _____ _____

This (has, has not) changed the meaning of our sentence.

R29

My typewriter works very well.;

has not

S30

Since omitting **which is not new** does not change our meaning, it is a n_____ clause. It is merely explanatory and, hence, (should, should not) be set off with commas.

R30

nonrestrictive;

should

S31

There are two types of relative clauses—restrictive and nonrestrictive. A _____ clause is merely explanatory and should be set off with commas; a _____ clause is essential to the meaning of a sentence and should not be set off with commas.

R31

nonrestrictive;

restrictive

S32

Smiling broadly, he walked in.

Smiling is the present part_____ple of the verb **to smile.**
The phrase **smiling broadly** is a p_____ial phrase.

R32

participle; participial

S33

When a participial phrase (is, is not) essential to the meaning of a sentence, it should be set off with commas.

R33

is not

S34

Insert commas where necessary in these sentences.
a) **Declaring his position the President was applauded.**
b) **The man living in sloth will never succeed.**
c) **The order being processed is the one I want.**
d) **Our representative having made his report left at once.**

R34

a) **... position, the ...**
b) **no commas**
c) **no commas**
d) **... representative, having made his report, left....**

● **TURN TO**
Exercises 52 and 53

S35

Use commas to set off words, phrases, or clauses that interrupt the natural flow of a sentence.
Punctuate this sentence: **He told me that his new firm however did not check references.**

R35

...firm, however, did not....

S36

Bad typing job, wasn't it? In this sentence a comma is used to set off a q_____that is added to a statement.

R36

question

S37

I want a winning sales campaign, not another losing one. In this sentence a comma is used to set off a
con __ __ __ __ __ __ __ __ expression added to a statement.

R37

contrasting

S38

A comma is used to set off a short direct quotation from the rest of the sentence. Punctuate this sentence and add a capital letter where necessary:
He said leave the bill of lading here.

R38

He said, "Leave the bill of lading here."

S39

The following is not a direct quotation. Change the punctuation in this sentence if necessary: **He said that the telegram came.**

R39

No change required.

S40

No comma is used before a quotation that is not a complete thought but is a necessary part of the sentence. Change the punctuation in this sentence if necessary: **Frank said he was "bushed, battered, and fatigued."**

R40

No change required.

● **TURN TO**
Exercises 54 and 55

S41

When coordinate conjunctions **(and, but, or, yet)** connect long independent clauses, you (do, do not) use a comma. For example: **The foreign car has influenced the American make, but I prefer the American type.**

R41

do

S42

Correct the punctuation in this sentence: **She is not a fast typist but, she is accurate.**

R42

. . . typist, but she . . . .

S43

To connect two independent clauses to create a compound sentence, you cannot use a comma by itself. You must either use the mark of punctuation known as a _____,
or you must use a c __ __ __ __ followed by a
c __ __ __ __ __ __ __ __ __ __
c __ __ __ __ __ __ __ __ __ __ __ such as **and, but, or, nor,**
or **yet.**

R43

semicolon;
comma;
coordinate conjunction

S44

You should not confuse a compound predicate with a compound sentence. The following is an example of a compound
_____:
We shall take the assignment and start as soon as possible.

R44

predicate

S45

The following is an example of a compound _____:
We shall take the assignment, but you may have it if you like.

R45

sentence

S46

In a very short compound sentence you may omit the comma before **and** or **or**; you must include the comma before **but** or **yet** no matter how short the sentence. Add commas where necessary in these sentences:

a) **I will go but you can't.**   b) **I will go and you can too.**
c) **I will go or you can.**   d) **I don't want to go yet I will.**

R46

a) **... go, but ...**
b) **no comma**
c) **no comma**
d) **... go, yet ...**
● **TURN TO**
  Exercises 56A and 56B

S47

A dependent clause is a group of words that contains a subject and a _____ but does _____ express a complete thought.

R47

predicate; not

S48

We will stand with you if you wish.
This is an example of a c ___ ___ ___ ___ ___ x sentence because it contains an _____ clause and a _____ clause.

R48

complex;
independent;
dependent

S49

We will stand with you if you wish.
If you wish is a _____ clause. The natural sequence of a complex sentence is for the dependent clause to come _____ the independent clause.

R49

dependent; after

S50

If you wish, we will stand with you.
In this sentence the dependent clause comes _____ the independent clause. It therefore (does, does not) follow the natural sequence.

R50

before; does not

S51

When a complex sentence is inverted so that the dependent clause comes first, you (should, should not) place a comma after the dependent clause.

R51

should

S52

When a complex sentence follows the natural sequence so that the independent clause comes first, you (should, should not) place a comma after the independent clause.

R52

should not

S53

Place a comma in each of the following sentences where necessary:

a) **In case you are opposed we'll stand with you.**
b) **They celebrated when they heard the news.**
c) **Whenever you are in town drop in.**

R53

a) **... opposed, we'll** ....
b) no comma
c) **... town, drop** ....

S54 Place a comma in each of the following sentences where necessary:

a) **On our way to town we passed the new factory.**

b) **The revised plans have been completed but we won't break ground for a month.**

c) **While you were out Mr. Smith called.**

R54
a) no comma
b) ... **completed, but** ....
c) ... **out, Mr. Smith** ....

● TURN TO Exercise 56C

S55 Use commas where necessary to avoid confusion within a sentence. Place a comma where necessary in the following sentences:

a) **Just the week before I had left for the Coast.**

b) **Ever since our orders have been increasing.**

R55
a) ... **before, I** ....
b) ... **since, our** ....

S56 Use a comma to separate words repeated in succession. Place commas where necessary in the following sentences:

a) **We have been through hard hard times together.**

b) **This will be a cold cold winter.**

R56
a) ... **hard, hard** ....
b) ... **cold, cold** ....

S57 Use a comma to indicate the omission of a word or phrase. What omitted words are indicated by the commas in these sentences:

a) **This week we made four sales; last week, three.**
Answer: _____ _____

b) **The Billing Department has twenty typewriters; the Shipping Department, twelve.**
Answer: _____

R57
a) **we made**
b) **has**

S58 Insert commas where needed in these sentences:

a) **Last year we closed in August; this year in July.**

b) **He excels in bookkeeping; she in stenography.**

R58
a) ... **year, in** ....
b) ... **she, in** ....

S59 Rewrite each of the following complimentary closes, showing proper capitalization and punctuation:

a) **yours truly**   b) **sincerely yours**   c) **very truly yours**

R59
a) **Yours truly,**
b) **Sincerely yours,**
c) **Very truly yours,**

S60 Insert commas where necessary:

a) **Since we saw you last Mr. Jackson we have built a new plant that is the largest in the East.**

b) **Naturally if you insist we will have to agree won't we?**

R60
a) **Since we saw you last, Mr. Jackson, we have built a new plant that is the largest in the East.**
b) **Naturally, if you insist, we will have to agree, won't we?**

● TURN TO Exercises 57 and Review

S61

In a business letter the mark of punctuation after the salutation is the _____.

R61

colon

S62

Before a long quotation use a _____. Before a quotation that includes one short sentence use a _____. Before a quotation that includes three short sentences use a _____.

R62

colon; comma; colon

S63

The punctuation mark you use before a formal list introduced by the words **as follows** or **the following** is the _____.

R63

colon

S64

Punctuate the following correctly: **Please ship these items to us before the 6 30 mail pickup three dozen spools two dozen balls of twine a gross of envelopes.**

R64

Please ship these items to us before the 6:30 mail pickup: three dozen spools, two dozen balls of twine, a gross of envelopes.

S65

When typing, leave _____ blank space(s) after a colon that introduces a formal list or a quotation; leave _____ blank space(s) after a colon that separates hours from minutes.

R65

two; no

● **TURN TO Exercise 58A**

S66

The semicolon is made up of two punctuation marks. It is a little stronger than a c __ __ __ a, but not quite so strong as a p __ __ __ __ d.

R66

comma; period

S67

There are four ways that the independent clauses in a compound sentence may be connected:

1. You may use a c _____ conjunction like **and** or **but** preceded by a c __ __ __ __.

2. If one of the clauses is very short, you may omit the _____ and use the c _____ c _____ by itself.

3. You may omit the conjunction and use a _____ by itself.

4. If the clauses are long and contain commas, you may use a coordinate _____ preceded by a _____ instead of a comma.

R67

1. coordinate; comma
2. comma;
   coordinate conjunction
3. semicolon
4. conjunction; semicolon

S68

Punctuate using a semicolon: **The storm affected business many firms closed completely.**

R68

...business; many....

S69

Use a semicolon in the following sentence:

There is no question but that personal contacts are sometimes valuable in business but in the long run, I think, success depends far more upon ability than upon any other factor.

R69

...in business; but in the long run....

S70

Our firm is nearly forty years old; nevertheless, it is young in spirit.

A semicolon is used here because a c_____ _____ plus a conjunction like **nevertheless** (is, is not) strong enough to "glue" the two clauses together. If the word **nevertheless** were replaced by the coordinate conjunction **but,** a comma (would, would not) be strong enough.

R70

comma; is not; would

S71

Lists introduced by expressions such as **namely, that is, for example,** and their respective abbreviations **v_____, i_____, e_____** are generally preceded by semicolons.

R71

viz.; i.e.; e.g.

S72

Punctuate this sentence:

The salesman omitted three cities namely Spokane, San Diego, and Oakland.

R72

...three cities; namely, Spokane....

S73

Dashes, not semicolons, should set off a formal list that occurs in the middle of a sentence. Punctuate the following two sentences:

a) **Only three possibilities namely stupidity carelessness or misinformation can explain this outrageous mistake.**

b) **Only three possibilities can explain this outrageous mistake namely stupidity carelessness or misinformation.**

R73

a)
...possibilities — namely, stupidity, carelessness, or misinformation — can...

b)
...mistake; namely, stupidity, carelessness, or misinformation.

S74

Punctuate the following:

Here are the receipt numbers: 6,352 4,008 and 6,927.

R74

...numbers: 6,352; 4,008; and 6,927.

S75

Review typewriter spacing. How many blank spaces do you leave after the following marks of punctuation:
a) A semicolon _____
b) A comma separating words in series _____
c) A colon introducing a formal list _____
d) A period at the end of a sentence _____

R75

a) one; b) one; c) two; d) two

● **TURN TO**
Exercises 58B and 58C

S76

Quotation marks should be placed around direct quotations. They (should, should not) be placed around indirect quotations.

R76

should not

S77

Punctuate the following, inserting capitals if necessary.
Tell me he said why I hadn't heard from you.

R77

"Tell me," he said, "why I hadn't heard from you."

S78

(Circle one.) In a direct conversation between two people: a) the entire conversation is put into one paragraph beginning and ending with quotation marks: b) a separate paragraph with beginning and ending quotation marks is used for quote of each speaker.

R78

b

S79

In a single quotation consisting of several paragraphs, quotation marks are put at the b_____ of each paragraph but at the end of only the _____ paragraph.

R79

beginning; last

S80

Titles of books are usually underlined or printed in capitals, but titles of articles and less important materials are written with _____ marks.

R80

quotation

S81

Punctuate this sentence: **The French expression nouveau-riche may be translated as the newly arrived.**

R81

The French expression "nouveau-riche" may be translated as "the newly arrived."

S82

Always place the comma and period (inside, outside) the closing quotation mark.

R82

inside

S83

Always place the colon and the _____ (inside, outside) the closing quotation mark.

R83

semicolon; outside

S84

The _____ and the _____ are always placed inside the closing quotation marks; the _____ and the _____ are always placed outside the closing quotation marks.

R84

comma; period;
colon; semicolon

S85

The question mark, exclamation mark, and dash are placed inside or outside the closing quotation marks depending upon whether they relate specifically to the material being quoted or to the entire sentence. If they relate specifically to the quoted material, you put them (inside, outside) the closing quotation marks. If they relate to the sentence as a whole, you put them _____ the closing quotation marks.

R85

inside; outside

S86

Punctuate the following sentences, adding capitals if necessary:

    a) **Why haven't I seen you before he asked**

    b) **She exclaimed this is preposterous**

    c) **Did you remember his words give me liberty or give me death**

R86

a) **"Why haven't I seen you before?" he asked.**

b) **She exclaimed, "This is preposterous!"**

c) **Did you remember his words: "Give me liberty or give me death"?**

● TURN TO Exercise 59

S87

You have studied the use of the apostrophe already. As a review insert apostrophes in the following contractions: **cant; shouldnt; wont; youll; Id**

R87

can't; shouldn't;
won't; you'll; I'd

S88

You use an apostrophe to indicate possessive (nouns, pronouns), but you do not use an apostrophe to indicate possessive (nouns, pronouns).

R88

nouns; pronouns

S89

Rewrite each of the following words as a possessive.
John our company it their

R89

**John's; ours; company's;
its; theirs**

S90

The apostrophe is used to form the plural of letters and numbers. Write these correctly: **All the t s were uncrossed in letters of the 1820s and 1830s.**

R90

t's; 1820's; 1830's

S91

A hyphen is used to divide a word at the end of a line. Do not divide a one-syllable word or a word of five or fewer letters. Circle the words in the following list that should **not** be divided.

through   thorough   rely   reliance   ability   able   straight

R91

through; rely;
able; straight

S92

Do not divide a word so that only one letter is left at the end of the first line. Circle the words in the following list that should **not** be divided:

hardness   emerge   afraid   fortunate   reserve

R92

emerge; afraid

S93

Do not carry over only one or two letters. Circle the words in the following list that should **not** be divided:

hardly emergent batted elated surely

R93
hardly; elated; surely

S94

Circle the words in the following list that should **not** be divided:

hand handed handy handily handsome

R94
hand; handed; handy

S95

When a medial syllable is composed of a single letter (like the **e** in **plan-e-tary**), that letter should be placed at the end of the first line, not at the beginning of the second line. Place a slash (/) to indicate where you should break the following words:

cal-o-rie cap-i-tal cat-a-log cel-e-brate

R95
calo/rie; capi/tal;
cata/log; cele/brate

S96

Use one or more slashes (/) to indicate where you can break the following words. If you should not break a word, put a circle around it:

a-bound ac-tion a-dopt ad-u-late af-firm-er

R96
abound; ac/tion; adopt;
adu/late; af/firmer

S97

Use one or more slashes (/) to indicate where to break the following words. If you should not break a word, put a circle around it.

a-ged a-gent a-gree-ment al-ler-gy al-ler-gic al-le-vi-ate

R97
aged; agent; agree/ment;
al/lergy; al/ler/gic;
al/le/vi/ate

S98

Words or expressions beginning with **self, ex, pro,** and **anti** are always hyphenated. Write these expressions correctly:

selfrespect antiRussian proAmerican exofficio

_____   _____

_____   _____

R98
self-respect; anti-Russian;

pro-American; ex-officio

S99

Adjective phrases such as **up to date** or **first class** are hyphenated when they come before the noun they modify; are not hyphenated when they come after the noun. Insert hyphens where proper:

a) **We use up to date methods.**
b) **This dinner was first class.**
c) **I speak from first hand experience.**
d) **They shipped low grade ore.**

R99
a) **up-to-date**
b) **none**
c) **first-hand**
d) **low-grade**

S100

An adjective phrase such as **up to the minute** (is, is not) hyphenated when it comes after the noun; it (is, is not) hyphenated when it comes before the noun.

R100
is not; is

S101

When the adjective phrase contains an adverb ending in **ly** — for example, **highly trained** — you generally do not hyphenate even when the phrase comes before the noun. Insert hyphens where proper:

    a) **He is a highly skilled workman.**
    b) **We need a well informed citizenry.**
    c) **The truth is self evident.**
    d) **We enjoyed a sincerely interested audience.**
    e) **They held a five day reunion.**

R101
    a) **none**
    b) **well-informed**
    c) **self-evident**
    d) **none**
    e) **fine-day**

S102

When writing out numbers, hyphenate compound numbers from twenty-one to ninety-nine. Do not hyphenate hundreds, thousands, or millions unless the entire number immediately precedes the noun it modifies. Insert hyphens in the following numbers:

    a) **six million four hundred eighty two thousand nine hundred fifty five**
    b) **a nine hundred fifty five dollar deficit**

R102
    a) **six million four hundred eighty-two thousand nine hundred fifty-five**
    b) **a nine-hundred-fifty-five-dollar deficit.**

    ● **TURN TO**
    Exercises 60 and 61

S103

Parentheses are used to enclose expressions that are completely incidental to the main thought of a sentence. Very often you may choose between using parentheses or d __ __ __ __ s.

R103
dashes

S104

When a sentence ends with a statement in parentheses, place the final period (inside, outside) the parentheses. For example: **Turn to Lesson 4 (page 37)**

R104
outside; **(page 37).**

S105

Foreign affairs, the cost of living (which is rising) national defense, and civil rights are major political issues.
In this sentence a comma should be placed (inside, outside) the closing parenthesis mark.

R105
outside

S106

In formal documents, a number is often written out and also expressed by a figure in parentheses. In the following two sentences, circle words that should be capitalized.

a) **The contract calls for payment of two hundred dollars ($200).**

b) **The invoice calls for two hundred (200) tons.**

R106
a) **Two Hundred Dollars;**
b) no capitals

S107

Insert parentheses in the following sentences:

a) **If I understand the truth at least insofar as it is possible to ever know the truth, Robinson has violated our trust.**

b) **Under said Agreement Licensee pays a royalty of fifteen percent 15%.**

R107
a) **the truth (at least insofar as it is possible to ever know the truth), Robinson. . . .**

b) **. . . percent (15%).**

S108

Insert dashes in the following sentences:

a) **The truth at least I think it's the truth is that Robinson has violated our trust.**

b) **We are proud of that symbol of free enterprise the New York World's Fair.**

c) **To be or not to be Shakespeare.**

R108
a) **The truth — at least I think it's the truth — is. . . .**

b) **. . . free enterprise — the New York World's Fair.**

c) **To be or not to be — Shakespeare.**

S109

The formal way to make a dash on a typewriter is to strike the _____ twice, leaving no space before or after the dash.

R109
hyphen

S110

A less formal dash is made by spacing once, striking the hyphen _____ time(s), then spacing once again.

R110
one

S111

An ellipse indicates material that has been o __ __ __ __ __ __ from a direct quotation.

R111
omitted

S112

An ellipse at the beginning or in the middle of a quotation is indicated by _____ dots; at the end, by _____ dots.

R112
three; four

● **TURN TO**
Exercises 62 and Review 12A

259

S113
Only when the name of a direction refers to a specific section of the country or the world is it capitalized. When the direction simply refers to a point on the compass, it should not be capitalized. Which of the following is correct? (Check one)
A. All directions are capitalized.
B. No directions are capitalized.
C. Directions are capitalized only when they refer to a specific section of the country or world.

R113
C

S114
Circle the direction(s) you would capitalize in this sentence: **The plant was located in the south about three miles east of Atlanta.**

R114
South

S115
Eastern, southern, western, and **northern** are capitalized only if they refer to major world divisions. They are not capitalized if they refer to a minor or local geographical divisions. Look at this sentence: **Berlin is part of Western Europe.** You capitalize **Western** because **Western Europe** is a m ___ ___ ___ world division.

R115
major

S116
He works in eastern Pennsylvania. The word **eastern** is not capitalized because **eastern Pennsylvania** is a m ___ ___ ___ world division.

R116
minor

S117
A name derived from a particular geographical locality is capitalized. **He is a Southerner, but I am a Northerner.** Circle the incorrect words in this sentence: **I am a new englander who was born in the south.**

R117
New Englander; South

S118
Geographical terms such as **river, ocean, mountain,** or **valley** are capitalized when they are used as part of a name. For example: **The Hudson River separates New York from New Jersey.**
Which of the following are correct?
A. Atlantic Ocean   B. Bear Mountain   C. Sun valley
Answer:_____

R118
A and B

S119
These same geographical terms — **river, ocean, valley** — are **not** capitalized when they precede the name. For example: **The valley of the river Jordan is wide.** Circle words that should be capitalized in this sentence: **The islands of the pacific and the valleys of the appalachians date back millions of years.**

R119
Pacific; Appalachians

260

S120
An exception is made with the word **mount** which is capitalized even when it precedes the name of the mountain. Is this correct? **He climbed Mount Everest.** Answer:_____

R120 Yes

S121
Should we capitalize geographic terms like **river** when they are used as plurals? The answer is **no.** Which is correct?
A. **The Atlantic and Pacific oceans are huge bodies of water.**
B. **The Hudson and Ohio Rivers are important to commerce.**
Answer:_____

R121 A

S122
Political designations such as **state, city,** or **country** are capitalized when they are part of the actual name of the area. Which of these are correct?
A. **New York City is the largest city in America.**
B. **Washington State borders on Canada.**
C. **Kings county is in Brooklyn.**
Answer:_____

R122 A and B

S123
Words like **hotel, highway, tunnel,** or **revolution** are capitalized when they are part of the proper name. Circle any errors in this sentence: **The Waldorf-Astoria hotel can be reached by the Lincoln tunnel.**

R123 Hotel; Tunnel

S124
Should titles such as **president, treasurer,** or **director** be capitalized? We always capitalize such titles when they appear directly before or after the name of the title holder: **President Johnson;** we capitalize high-ranking officers: **The Senator spoke.** Are these correct?: A. **I mourn President Kennedy.** B. **The Secretary of State spoke.** Answer:_____

R124 Yes

S125
As a sign of respect we also capitalize lesser titles. Which is more respectful?
A. **The Vice-President of our firm and the Superintendent of Schools met.**
B. **The vice-president of our firm and the superintendent of schools met.** Answer:_____

R125 A

S126
Names of organizations such as **company, association,** or **department** are capitalized when they are part of the name of a specific organization. Circle the word(s) you would capitalize: **The Bethlehem Steel company is a huge steel producer.**

R126 Company

S127
These same words (**company, association, department**) are capitalized when used as substitutes for the complete names of specific organizations. Which sentence is correct:
A. **The Association welcomes you as a new member.**
B. **An association of publishers may be formed.**

Answer:_____

R127 A and B (both are correct)

S128
Certain words derived from proper nouns are not capitalized: **pasteurize** from **Pasteur** or **platonic** from **Plato**. Circle the word in the following sentence that is not capitalized although it comes from a proper noun: **The best chinaware is imported from London.**

R128 chinaware

S129
School subjects are not capitalized, except for languages or specifically described courses. Circle the one subject that is capitalized incorrectly in this sentence: **He studied mathematics, English, Advanced Algebra II, and Typing in school.**

R129 typing

S130
The words **high school** and **college** are not capitalized unless they are part of a specific school name. How would you complete this sentence? **He was graduated from Jefferson ___igh ___chool, but did not go to ___ollege.**

R130 High School; college

S131
Since only important words in a book title are capitalized, circle the words you would capitalize in the title, **the cruise of the snark.**

R131 The Cruise; Snark

S132
Let's see how well you have learned to capitalize. Circle the words you should capitalize in this sentence: **My employer, carl smith, started the olympic printing company in the summer of 1964 in the southern part of new england.**

R132 Carl Smith;
Olympic Printing Company;
New England

S133
Circle the words you would capitalize in this sentence: **After moving the plant from the mohawk valley to get hudson river power, he was elected president of the printers association of america.**

R133 Mohawk Valley;
Hudson River; President;
Printers Association;
America

S134
Circle the words you would capitalize in this sentence: **Mr. smith then taught a course in english in newark college for students with high school diplomas.**

R134 Smith; English;
Newark College
● TURN TO
Exercises 63 and 64

EXERCISE 48   Using the Period

A. Cross out all incorrect punctuation in the following paragraphs and insert all necessary periods and capitals.

SCORING: DEDUCT 5 POINTS FOR EACH ERROR.

This morning we received a request to submit a bid on the equipment specifications for the new vocational school now being erected in Erie, Pa.

It is our policy, as you know, to work only through our regular dealers. We suggest, therefore, that you send a representative to follow up this opportunity for some very good business.

We can be very helpful to you in preparing your estimate on the list of hand tools, and we hope you will let us work with you. The large machine equipment, of course, is out of our line. Because of your long experience in this field, we know you will have no trouble in submitting a complete bid.

*   *   *

We appreciate the information that you gave us in your letter of October 17.

The purchasing agent for the Board of Education in Erie has given us permission to submit a bid on the equipment list for the new school. Since the bid must be submitted on or before November 19, it is necessary for us to work rapidly.

Some time ago you stated that there might be price changes after November 1. While we understand that increasing demands are being placed on the tool industry, still we must request a definite guarantee from your company that the prices in effect now will apply to the Erie school contract if it is awarded to our company.

SCORE

B_____

EXERCISE 48   The Period

B. This problem deals with the proper use of the period. Insert periods wherever necessary in the sentences below. Indicate a capital letter if a new sentence is to follow.

SCORING: DEDUCT 7 POINTS FOR EACH ERROR.

1. I will be there at eight o'clock I shall see you then
2. Step forward to volunteer that is the way to help
3. Will you open the door, please my hands are occupied
4. Work now go to lunch later
5. Mr M Franklin Smith, Jr lives in Pittsburgh, PA
6. Dr Frank R Jackson, DDS ordered these drills to be sent c o d
7. John R Boyd, Esq was officially listed as *Sup't of Arsenals* and later as *Sec'y of War*
8. He gained $245 on his first venture, but lost $15,324 later
9. Washington, DC is north of Raleigh, NC
10. The merchandise went to Cap't Johnson of Wallace Lines, Inc
11. We stayed at the YMCA in St Louis, MO
12. Mrs Johnson asked Miss Smith to visit at noon
13. Norman Wells III received his BA from Yale and his PhD from Harvard
14. Won't you please come in, Mr. Smith
15. The US 4th Army Brigade is being transferred from Ft Dix, NJ, to St. Johns, BWI, aboard the USS Enterprise

SCORE

A_____

EXERCISE 49   The Question Mark and Exclamation Point

A. At the end of each of the following sentences, place a question mark, an exclamation mark, or a period — whichever is correct.

SCORING: DEDUCT 5 POINTS FOR EACH ERROR.

1. Did you send the letter
2. Please mail it at once
3. Won't you come in, please
4. Why wasn't it filed at once
5. A fine idea
6. The director asked many questions
7. Who is there
8. I am not sure who filed the letter
9. Will you be kind enough to visit us
10. Why not take a chance

11. Why
12. Can we doubt his sincerity
13. That is the $64,000 question
14. Amazing
15. What an amazing discovery
16. Did you see the shipment
17. Have they acknowledged our order
18. Wonderful
19. Won't you please consider our offer
20. This is wonderful news, isn't it

SCORE

B_____

EXERCISE 49 — The Question Mark and Period

B. This problem deals with the correct use of the question mark. Put question marks or periods wherever you think necessary; indicate a capital if a new sentence is to follow.

SCORING: DEDUCT 10 POINTS FOR EACH ERROR.

1. Can you be there this evening ?
2. Will you please allow me to pass ,
3. Are you able to complete the exercises ?
4. Why don't you use a carbon it will help ?
5. Since our last order, have prices risen ?
6. I wonder why he was discharged .
7. Are you sure that all figures have been carefully examined and checked ?
8. He asked me where you are going tonight .
9. Can you name three generals three admirals three air chiefs ?
10. Why is he doing this I wonder .

SCORE

C_____

EXERCISE 49 — Using Punctuation

C. Insert periods, question marks, and exclamation marks wherever appropriate in the following letter.

SCORING: DEDUCT 10 POINTS FOR EACH ERROR.

Gentlemen:

Last May we ordered the new novel by George Wilson, Jr. As yet we have not received it although it is already July 15 May we ask for an explanation ?

Is the book out of print or was our order simply misplaced If it is in stock, please ship it at once, cod. If not, let us know when we can expect it .

Rush

Very truly yours ,

NAME   CLASS   DATE

EXERCISE 50 | Commas: Separating Items in a Series

This problem involves the use of commas to separate items listed in a series. Insert commas in the following sentences wherever necessary.

SCORING: DEDUCT 3 POINTS FOR EACH ERROR.

1. We will leave by car, rail, or plane on Friday.
2. The successful teacher is friendly, alert, interesting, and self-confident.
3. Our store deals in radios, TV sets, refrigerators, and similar products.
4. We have correspondence from you dated August 3, August 18, September 6, and October 15.
5. You will not be able to resist our newest model when you see its long, low, streamlined appearance.
6. Newspapers, magazines, books, and periodicals, all will be on sale this week.
7. Our rates are $8.00 for a room without bath, $10.50 for a room with bath, and $18.00 for a suite of two rooms.
8. We deal in state bonds, municipal bonds, industrial bonds, and railroad bonds.
9. We deal in state, municipal, industrial, and railroad bonds.
10. Thirty days hath September, April, June, and November.
11. We sell the finest kerosene, benzene, and alcohol lamps on the market.
12. The properties available are in Detroit, St. Louis, Cleveland, and New York.
13. For lunch we offer roast beef, salad, and bread and butter.
14. Our courses include shorthand, business English, typewriting, and bookkeeping.
15. She gave a stately, prim, correct appearance.
16. Would you be willing to spend a few dollars for a chance to break into a fast-growing, profitable, interesting, respected profession?
17. Fame, fortune, and esteem — these were his lot in life.
18. Their firm deals in the finest silks, cottons, and woolens.
19. The box is neither lightweight nor presentable.
20. I can see now the lovely green lawn, the broad gravel walk, the giant shade trees, and the perfect model of a colonial walk.
21. The new skyscrapers have been luxuriously, ornately, and decoratively designed.
22. The efficient telephone operator answers, pacifies, informs, and cajoles the caller.
23. I want you to learn to write, to compose, to correct, and to dictate letters.
24. That a modern novelist is frank, that he is imaginative, and that he is perceptive are recognized facts.
25. Ask questions politely, listen to details carefully, and follow instructions intelligently.
26. Tact, wisdom, and diplomacy — these are necessities of an enlightened, intelligent foreign policy.
27. Please try our new furniture polish.
28. To plan and design carefully, to purchase and order wisely, and to build and construct sturdily are necessary steps.
29. The firm of Webb, Prince, and Berman is well known.
30. He planned to invite workers, farmers, storekeepers, salesmen, etc.

SCORE
_____

EXERCISE 51   Commas: Set off Name of Person Addressed

This problem involves the use of commas to set off the name of a person directly addressed. In some of the following sentences commas have been omitted. Fill in all missing commas.

SCORING: DEDUCT 10 POINTS FOR EACH ERROR.

1. Thank you, Mr. Shaw, for the prompt attention given to our questionnaire.
2. We have directed Mr. James King, of our credit department, to discuss terms of payment with you.
3. They are being shown this week, Mrs. Watson.
4. Mr. Adams, we have learned that you will soon enjoy delivery of your new car.
5. I have looked further, Mr. Grover, into the Gray lumber situation.
6. Mr. Martin says that economic conditions will continue to be thoroughly sound.
7. Madam, does the approach of warm weather suggest sending your furs to storage?
8. Is it the fault of this store that your account remains inactive, Mrs. Wright?
9. Mr. White's inspection of our floor equipment was very helpful.
10. The January sales now being held throughout the store offer you exceptional values, Mrs. Hays.

SCORE
_____

EXERCISE 52   Commas: Set off Explanatory Expressions

This problem deals with the use of commas to set off explanatory expressions. Insert commas wherever proper in the following sentences.

SCORING: DEDUCT 10 POINTS FOR EACH ERROR.

1. Our representative from New Orleans, Mr. A. J. Johnson, is in town.
2. Asia, the largest of the continents, is becoming a major focus of international relations.
3. Our new location, the corner of Sixth Avenue and 42nd Street, is ideal for our type of business.
4. Our attorney, Mr. G. A. Blake, will call at your office tomorrow.
5. B. H. Brown, golf champion of the South, won the cup handily.
6. It is my pleasure to introduce H. Colin Phillips, our friend and leader.
7. Would you enjoy living in a residential park, a veritable winter wonderland of over 500 acres of high, healthy, beautifully wooded, fertile land, Mr. Smith?
8. We advise you to see either Mr. R. J. Jones, Director of the Bureau, or Mr. P. T. Smith, his assistant.
9. The speakers were H. George Brittingham, Professor of Business English, and John Rogers, Jr., Professor of American History.
10. The Mississippi, America's longest river, flows into the Gulf of Mexico.

SCORE

A_____

EXERCISE 53   Nonrestrictive Clauses

A. This problem involves the use of commas to set off explanatory expressions. Each of the following sentences involves a nonrestrictive clause — that is, a relative clause that should be set off with commas. Insert commas as necessary.

SCORING: DEDUCT 10 POINTS FOR EACH ERROR.

1. This morning we received a report from Mr. Johnson, who is our representative in New York.
2. Wellington chalk, which is the best chalk you can get, is the most economical for school use.
3. Mr. Howard Clark, who is president of the National Savings Association, sent a copy of his latest address.
4. Our customers, all of whom have been most kind to us, will be pleased to hear of our latest plans.
5. The manufacture of this equipment, which is the finest ever made, is a painstakingly exact process.
6. These lessons, which you should study every day, will provide fine background for your future work.
7. Our office furniture, all of which we bought last year, is of ultra-modern design.
8. The new secretary, who was trained at business school, is the best we've ever had.
9. The luggage, which was engraved with his initials, was presented to Mr. Phillips.
10. The park, which is noted for its old trees, was established in 1889.

SCORE

B_____

EXERCISE 53   Restrictive Clauses

B. Each of the following sentences involves an explanatory expression that should **NOT** be set off with commas because to do so would change the meaning of the sentence. Underline each such restrictive clause.

SCORING: DEDUCT 10 POINTS FOR EACH ERROR.

1. The man who does a poor job does not last long in business.
2. The advertisement that catches the eye is the one that has a certain "plus."
3. Medicine is a profession that satisfies a man's desire to serve others.
4. Water that is stagnant is putrid.
5. Anyone who works hard can succeed.
6. Only those who are geniuses gain acclaim as musicians.
7. A rumor that we heard yesterday is disturbing.
8. The ledger that is in Room 217 is the one I want.
9. The officer who leads his men bravely gains their respect.
10. We observed a downward trend that is most unsatisfactory.

NAME   CLASS   DATE

EXERCISE 53 | Commas and Explanatory Expressions

C. Each of the following sentences includes an explanatory expression. Some of these expressions should be set off with commas; some should not. Place commas around those expressions that should be set off; underline those expressions that should not.

SCORING: DEDUCT 4 POINTS FOR EACH ERROR.

1. Water that does not run rapidly becomes stagnant.

2. Your fall order which we received last week has been filled.

3. The man who runs the fastest wins the race.

4. John Doe who was tried for larceny was acquitted.

5. Deliver only those posters that you consider best as soon as you can.

6. The letter that was sent to him came back unopened.

7. This work which I feel sure you will enjoy is not very difficult.

8. The dress that I think you will like best has not yet arrived.

9. Our book is printed in type that is easy on the eye.

10. That woman who spoke to you at such great length yesterday is back.

11. This business which you have merely sampled these past months can provide ample excitement for a lifetime.

12. A red-headed woman who does not have a fiery temper is a rarity.

13. Mr. Oglethorpe is a man who knows this business inside out.

14. The order which we have been awaiting for weeks was delayed again. *either*

15. He is the man whom I would elect.

16. My teacher Frank C. Smith has been an inspiring influence. *either*

17. I myself have much to study.

18. The poet Milton wrote about heaven.

19. Our business like any other new business will benefit from experience.

20. These data all of which are interesting do not change our business prediction.

21. Knowing that sales are the lifeblood of an organization we shall hire an alert salesman.

22. The new executives that lead our top organizations have youth and vitality.

23. They shipped the merchandise in May assuming you wanted it for June 15.

24. A sales letter that paints word pictures brings maximum results.

25. His brother Albert is brighter than his brothers John and Herman.

SCORE

A_____

EXERCISE 54 — Commas and Conjuctions

A. This problem deals with the use of commas to separate words such as therefore from the body of the sentence. Insert commas wherever proper in the following sentences.

SCORING: DEDUCT 7 POINTS FOR EACH ERROR.

1. It is, however, unnecessary for you to reply at once.
2. Feel free, of course, to take as much time as you need.
3. Naturally, we were shocked to hear of the delay.
4. It is, nevertheless, imperative that your representative contact us at once.
5. We feel, on the other hand, that your client is entitled to some minor sort of relief.
6. As we understand the situation, the failure was entirely the fault of your agent.
7. To be very frank, we were satisfied with neither the lamps, the shades, nor the fixtures.
8. It is, in our opinion, impossible to predict the outcome at this moment.
9. This class, however, is the best we have had.
10. No one, naturally, can be blamed for such an innocent mistake.
11. As a rule, commas should set off nonessential information.
12. I believe, for example, that a brusque answer does much harm and little good.
13. We feel, therefore, that politeness is an exemplary quality.
14. No, they did not report on time.
15. Well, all of us make mistakes.

SCORE

B_____

EXERCISE 54 — Commas and Questions Added to Statements

B. This problem deals with the use of commas to set off questions that are added to statements and opposing ideas beginning with not. Insert commas wherever necessary in the following sentences.

SCORING: DEDUCT 10 POINTS FOR EACH ERROR.

1. You received our catalogue, didn't you?
2. We will send you east, not west.
3. It's going to be a banner month, isn't it?
4. We shall judge a man by his accomplishments, not by his looks.
5. We offered you this line last year, didn't we?
6. You can do the job, can't you?
7. Look for facts, not opinions.
8. In treating employees, one should be kind and understanding, not rude and impatient.
9. This is easy, isn't it?
10. We hold most meetings in the morning, few in the afternoon.

NAME   CLASS   DATE

EXERCISE 54 — Commas: Miscellaneous Uses

C. This problem deals with commas used in abbreviations and commas used with dates and geographical names. Insert commas and periods in the following sentences wherever necessary.

SCORING: DEDUCT 10 POINTS FOR EACH ERROR.

1. Frank Henry James is our new President.

2. We have received a letter from Morris C. Cohen Esq our attorney.

3. Frances Kearney LL.D. Ph.D. will support our fund drive.

4. Jack Kent Inc well-known publishers will give a cocktail party at the St. Regis.

5. John C. Squires Ltd our Canadian firm is quite active.

6. September 3 1912 was the date of the founding of the company.

7. July 4 1776 was a red-letter day for the U.S.

8. The affair last Wednesday August 17 was a huge success.

9. The issue for July 1964 is a particularly interesting one.

10. John James III has lived at 373 Ocean Avenue San Francisco California for five years.

EXERCISE 55 — Commas: and Direct Quotations

This problem deals with the use of the comma to set off a short direct quotation. Insert commas in the following sentences wherever necessary.

SCORING: DEDUCT 10 POINTS FOR EACH ERROR.

1. He said "This is ridiculous."

2. "We shall not stop fighting" said he "nor shall we retreat an inch."

3. "Why" I asked "doesn't he admit he was wrong?"

4. "This is the worst job I have ever seen" was what he said.

5. I told him "Either you accept our offer or we shall deal elsewhere."

6. "Send the check to my office" he wrote.

7. "Who punched the clock at 5 P.M.?" he asked.

8. "Eureka!" he shouted at the top of his lungs "I have the solution."

9. General MacArthur swore that he would return.

10. He stated "I shall return!"

NAME   CLASS   DATE

EXERCISE 56   Sentence Errors

A. This is a review problem on run-on sentences and sentence fragments. Proofread the following letter crossing out each error and writing in your correction. Review the material on run-on sentences and sentence fragments in Lesson 1.

SCORING: DEDUCT 10 POINTS FOR EACH ERROR.

My dear Miss Green:

The Drake Hotel is a comfortable and well-managed manor. Situated on a beautiful piece of land in the hills of Bell Harbor. From the heart of Baltimore it can be reached by train or automobile. In less than an hour. Although it is near the city, It is far enough removed for rest and quiet.

Majestic old trees and attractive walks add to the beauty of the grounds, the extensive lawns reach to the shore of Chesapeake Bay, fishing and boating are always in season.

If you can possibly arrange your vacation to fall in August, you will find the Drake Hotel at its most beautiful, flowers are in bloom and the shade trees are at their lushest. Of course, some of our regular guests prefer the fall when the trees are ablaze with color, And the ground is covered with a thick carpet of fallen leaves.

We extend to you and your friends, A cordial invitation to visit us.

SCORE

B

EXERCISE 56   Commas: Compound Sentences

B. This problem deals with the use of the comma in compound sentences. Insert commas wherever necessary in the following sentences.

SCORING: DEDUCT 10 POINTS FOR EACH ERROR.

1. Our letters haven't been very serious but underneath their semi-jesting tone runs the feeling that we will eventually get your business.
2. It was inspected it was tested it was tortured but it didn't fade or shrink.
3. Last year we had the pleasure of sending you one of our publications and we hope that it has proved of value.
4. Booklets and showroom demonstrations are interesting but actual performance on the job is convincing.
5. An excellent pool is available for those who like to swim and for those who like to play golf there is a beautiful 18-hole course.
6. Every lesson in the manual is easy and every principle is outlined in complete detail.
7. We tried and we succeeded.
8. Forgive our curiosity but why have we not heard from you?
9. Your offer was received and was carefully considered by the Board.
10. You have not written us for many weeks nor have you bothered to pay your bills.

SCORE

C

EXERCISE 56   Commas: Complex Sentences

C. This problem deals with the use of the comma in complex sentences. In some of the following sentences commas are missing. Insert such commas wherever necessary.

SCORING: DEDUCT 7 POINTS FOR EACH ERROR.

1. We have enjoyed full employment despite the world situation.
2. Despite the world situation we have enjoyed full employment.
3. Realizing his position John resigned.
4. John realizing his position resigned.
5. Mr. Smith despite his vast knowledge did not know the answer.
6. Despite our advice he accepted the offer.
7. Rushing to the rescue he was injured by a falling board.
8. Because of your fine past record we are keeping your account open one more week.
9. Forgetting all he had been told he stood before the audience dumbfounded.
10. While attending a convention last month I met an old friend.
11. We have accomplished much since we started.
12. As soon as the clock struck five the employees stopped working.
13. Because there were extended coffee breaks management was irritated.
14. After hearing the good news he sold his stock.
15. He will not bargain unless you do so in good faith.

SCORE
_____

EXERCISE 57 — Commas: Miscellaneous

This problem deals with the use of the comma in a variety of instances. Insert commas wherever necessary in the following sentences.

SCORING: DEDUCT 7 POINTS FOR EACH ERROR.

1. Last year our stockholders shared in profits of over $60,000,000.00.
2. On July 15, 1964, the workers in our plants numbered 6,475.
3. The contract dated August 4, 1956, is still valid.
4. He has lived at 1220 Elm Avenue, Springfield, Illinois, for eight years.
5. Despite poor January sales, our overall net profit for the past year was over $250,000.
6. We addressed the letter to Mrs. Robert Patterson, 5202 South Spruce Avenue, Madison, Wisconsin.
7. Since our last visit in December, 1963, we have reconsidered your $3,000,000 expansion plan.
8. We have reviewed your books for the month of July, 1964, and we find a $3257.50 discrepancy with our figures.
9. On December 1, 1964, we expect you to deliver 50,000 tons of No. 10 steel to our warehouse at 1614 Bruce Avenue, Pittsburgh, Pennsylvania.
10. Please change my address in your listings from Polly Jones, 616 Almond Street, New Orleans, Louisiana, to Mrs. Robert Mayer, 327 Elm Avenue, Miami Beach, Florida.
11. Ever since, we have avoided telephoning.
12. Only three hours before, we saw him alive.
13. It has been a long, long, process of waiting.
14. Whoever spoke, spoke in vain.
15. Our arms budget exceeds $48,000,000,000.

SCORE
_____

REVIEW EXERCISE 11 — The Period, Question Mark, Comma

This is an overall problem dealing with the use of all the marks of punctuation you have already studied. Insert commas, periods, or question marks wherever necessary in the following letter.

SCORING: DEDUCT 5 POINTS FOR EACH ERROR.

Gentlemen:

Your letter, and the booklet, "Live Records," reach, us at a time when our bookkeeping system is a matter of great concern. This booklet, therefore, has received our careful attention.

Since, our office force was reduced last year, the

(continued)

marked development of business during the past year has increased the urgency of our bookkeeping problem Though we have been considering the use of bookkeeping machines for a long time we are not yet convinced however that such a large outlay of money would result in a satisfactory return Nevertheless something must be done to relieve the pressure which is becoming great of our work

Will you have your representative Mr. Roberts call on Monday May 10 at ten o'clock to discuss arrangements

It is our intention to have Mr. Roberts examine our ordering billing and shipping procedures. Above all we want him to meet our bookkeepers and clerks and after he forms an impression of them we would like him to submit a written report of his recommendations with respect to personnel This would seem to be a reasonable approach wouldn't it

Are you aware of the many many new products that are being offered by our firm to customers throughout North America Central America and South America Since January 1963 we have been involved in a $3000000 expansion of our product line that has succeeded despite great odds Today we stand first in volume of sales in this field and we intend to maintain this position

Our problem is to handle the bookkeeping load and that I believe is exactly what your firm can help us achieve We look forward therefore to Mr. Roberts' visit

Sincerely

SCORE

A_____

EXERCISE 58   The Colon

A. This problem involves the use of the colon. Insert a colon in each of the following sentences wherever proper. Add other punctuation where necessary.

SCORING: DEDUCT 10 POINTS FOR EACH ERROR.

1. We have recorded your order as follows one wooden cabinet one chair three metal files one desk

2. He is quoted as saying "My only regret is that I have but one life to give for my country."

3. At precisely 456 P. M. our plane departs.

4. The following is stock on hand 3000 #10 envelopes, 2500 #13, and 1500 #17.

5. This is what he said "No amount of money could ever repay you for the fine unselfish job you did on behalf of your nation."

6. The letter began "Dear Sir I wish to thank you for your help."

7. The President stated "My fellow Americans I speak to you today on a matter of grave importance."

8. The problems we must face are these avoiding nuclear war upholding liberty developing free societies.

9. We listed three stock prices $5.52, $5.59, $6.01.

10. The following furniture was ordered three tables four chairs and four sofas.

SCORE

B_____

EXERCISE 58   The Semicolon

B. This problem involves the use of the semicolon. Insert a semicolon in each of the following sentences wherever proper. Add other punctuation where necessary.

SCORING: DEDUCT 10 POINTS FOR EACH ERROR.

1. We have not received your exam as yet consequently we have delayed sending your next lesson.

2. This is a fine surprise we were just thinking of you.

3. We have done our best the rest is up to you.

4. There are two reasons for our decision namely your determination and your doggedness.

5. To be perfectly frank I am sorry to see him go but I know that try as you might you had no alternative but to fire him.

6. The market went up for some stocks others, however, declined in value.

7. All of us were concerned about the employment picture for the year as presented by the government but following your advice we felt it our duty to remain calm.

8. Our Society includes James Brown the eminent painter Jack Jules the famous caricaturist and Cynthia Prince the well-known columnist.

9. He had one principle namely to do unto others before they did unto him.

10. The manager spoke to the staff about staying late however it was to no avail.

EXERCISE 58　　Punctuation Review

C. This problem involves the use of the colon, semicolon, comma, and period. Insert these marks wherever proper in the following sentences.

SCORING: DEDUCT 10 POINTS FOR EACH ERROR.

1. We offer a choice of three models the stately Classical the functional Colonial or the streamlined Modern.
2. Once again we are extending the time however in the future there will be no further extension
3. Standing up in the Assembly Patrick Henry shouted "Give me liberty or give me death"
4. Mrs. Housewife just mail the enclosed card postage is prepaid
5. The traits that I most admire in a man are these honesty wisdom and perseverance
6. During the past few months which have been especially hectic I inspected the following divisions the Tennessee factory the Missouri offices and the Louisiana warehouse
7. Therefore we are pleased to be able to extend this invitation but bear in mind that much as we would prefer that it be otherwise this must be our last offer
8. You Mr Smith have already received our final offer henceforth we shall not bother you again
9. To err is human to forgive divine.
10. Since our last report we have restudied the figures you submitted but despite our attempts to reconcile them the surplus figures do not coincide.

EXERCISE 59　　Quotation Marks and Other Punctuation

A. This problem deals with the use of quotation marks and other marks of punctuation. Insert all necessary punctuation in each of the following sentences. Capitalize where necessary.

SCORING: DEDUCT 5 POINTS FOR EACH ERROR.

1. He told his secretary Marie give your full attention to this purchase order.
2. do you manufacture these they asked
3. He spoke with authority saying you may be certain that our firm adheres only to the highest standards of business ethics
4. Your article southeast asia has created a stir.
5. did you receive any compensation for writing the coming battle of congress
6. He asked the question how can we justify our own failure to help them
7. Of all the men I know he said none compares with mr Jones
8. try our new air conditioner the ad stated it will bring comfort to your home or office
9. The enclosed booklet make your own weather will show you how to maintain your volume of business during summer months
10. How are sales for your book make your own weather

(continued)

11. In your letter you write that the price of shipment will soon go up

12. Shakespeare wrote the evil that men do lives after them the good is oft interred with their bones.

13. Nathan Hale shouted my only regret is that I have but one life to give for my country

14. don't give up the ship the commander bellowed.

15. let us know by return mail he wrote whether you will accept the offer.

16. he accused his competitor of being a blind pig-headed mule.

17. rush help or — were the last words we heard

18. Great was all he could shout.

19. Did you read the article can you diet

20. tomorrow and tomorrow and tomorrow — Shakespeare

SCORE

B

EXERCISE 59	Using Quotation Marks

B. Properly punctuate the following passage.

SCORING: DEDUCT 5 POINTS FOR EACH ERROR.

Memorandum to J. P. Roberts

We received a letter from Modern Offices Inc that reads as follows

Gentlemen We have your letter of June 15 in which you enclosed the specifications for the safe equipment to be installed in the new offices of the Martin Manufacturing Company

We shall be glad to send you pictures and details of Western safes that meet these requirements

It would be more convincing however to have you and your customer visit us in Cleveland May we therefore extend an invitation to you and your customer to come to Cleveland at our expense

Please let us know when it will be most convenient for you and we shall make the necessary hotel reservations.

Cordially yours

In view of the invitation extended to us in this letter I think we should very seriously consider sending a representative to inspect the Western safes in Cleveland

NAME   CLASS   DATE

EXERCISE 60   The Apostrophe

A. This problem deals with the proper use of the apostrophe. Choose the correct word.

SCORING: DEDUCT 10 POINTS FOR EACH ERROR.

1. (It's, Its) a wonderful opportunity for you.   1. _It's_
2. Can this be (yours, your's)?   2. _yours_
3. (Your, You're) offer is most interesting.   3. _Your_
4. The (women's, womens') coats are in here.   4. _women's_
5. (There, They're) are three reasons for this decision.   5. _There_
6. Give them (their, they're) due.   6. _their_
7. (They're, Their) fed up with this type of bickering.   7. _They're_
8. Send us a gross of (No. 10s, No. 10's) and a hundred (No. 17s, No. 17's).   8. _10's_ _17's_
9. A (mans, man's) success is measured in terms other than money.   9. _man's_
10. The company sent (its, it's) form letter.   10. _its_

EXERCISE 60   Possessives and Contractions

B. This problem deals with the use of the apostrophe in forming possessives and contractions. In the following letter insert apostrophes and other punctuation wherever necessary.

SCORING: DEDUCT 5 POINTS FOR EACH ERROR.

Dear Miss Roberts:

We can't understand the failure of your firm's representative to visit any of our shops during his two-week visit to our city. It's apparent to us that your sales staff misunderstands our company's position in this city. We're not a small chain of widely separated stores. Ours is a

(continued)

large organization with no two stores more than ten blocks apart, and none of them more than a few minutes' walk from the center of town.

Our figures for the past half year's sales reflect this concentration in our city's prime market area. These sales figures show that ours is a very profitable operation. One's personal tastes shouldn't influence his decisions in business matters. Hard facts and figures should be the businessman's only criteria.

We'll be very much pleased to open our books and records to your firm at your representative's convenience. Wouldn't you be foolish to let this opportunity go by unnoticed? It's not too late to change your mind.

Each of our shops has its own individual management and its own individual personality. All of them are famous for their consistently fine goods -- the best in men's women's and children's clothing.

We're justly proud of the reputation we've established among our town's most respected people. Won't you please accept this invitation to send one of your representatives to inspect our stores and our books. We're looking forward to your reply within a few days' time.

Sincerely,

SCORE

A_____

EXERCISE 61   The Hyphen

A. This problem involves the use of the hyphen to divide words at the end of a line. Assume that each of the following words comes at the end of a line. In the spaces provided, write the two parts into which the word should be divided. Consult your dictionary if necessary.

SCORING: DEDUCT 10 POINTS FOR EACH ERROR.

1. problem   *prob*   *lem*
2. narrate   *nar*   *rate*
3. amount   _____   _____
4. hopeful   *hope*   *ful*
5. message   *mess*   *sage*
6. natural   *natu*   *ral*
7. question   *quest*   *tion*
8. inert   _____   _____
9. innate   *in*   *nate*
10. legible   *lege*   *ble*

SCORE

B_____

EXERCISE 61   Compound Words

B. This problem deals with compound words. Some compound words are written as one word. Others are hyphenated. Still others are written as two separate words. Below is a list of compound words written separately. In the space provided, write them properly.

SCORING: DEDUCT 5 POINTS FOR EACH ERROR.

1. self evident   1. *self - evident*
2. letter head   2. *letterhead*
3. ex President   3. *ex - President*
4. self control   4. *self - control*
5. vice chairman   5. *vice - chairman*
6. father in law   6. *father - in - law*
7. all right   7. *all right*
8. can not   8. *cannot*
9. not withstanding   9. *notwithstanding*
10. real estate   10. *real estate*

(continued)

11.	ex governor	11.	_ex - governor_
12.	type written	12.	_typewritten_
13.	editors in chief	13.	_editors - in - chief_
always 1 word 14.	over due	14.	_over due_
15.	post card	15.	_postcard_
16.	self conscious	16.	_self - conscious_
cut it? 17.	any body	17.	_anybody._
18.	vice president	18.	_vice - president_
19.	no one	19.	_no one_
20.	some thing	20.	_something_

SCORE

_____

EXERCISE 62	Parenthesis, Dash, and Hyphen

This problem involves the use of the parenthesis, the dash, and the hyphen. Insert all necessary punctuation in the following sentences.

SCORING: DEDUCT 10 POINTS FOR EACH ERROR.

1. It is self-evident—at least it should be so—to a reasonable man that our economic outlook is brightening.

2. Please look at our advertisement (you can find one in this month's issue of the New Era) to see what we mean by vibrant layout.

3. You should be able to collect the facts (and we mean all the facts) with little trouble if you are willing to apply yourself.

4. And the Licensee hereby agrees to pay Licensor on the first day of each month commencing on January the first, Nineteen hundred and sixty-five the sum of (one hundred dollars ($100.00).

5. As you have already learned (see Lesson XIV) a pronoun should agree in person and number with its antecedent.

6. We are interested—I might say extremely interested—in the report of those men who attended your factory demonstration.

7. As a result of our long experience (never forget we have been in business for over a hundred years) we feel it our duty to urge you to reconsider your decision.

8. Our representative, Mr. Fred Perry (didn't you meet him at our last convention) will be glad to assist you in any way possible.

9. This chance (and it's your very last chance) is a fine opportunity.

10. Practice to (a) listen carefully (b) speak clearly (c) make your point.

EXERCISE 63   Proper Nouns

A. This problem involves capitalization of proper nouns. Some words that should be capitalized are not capitalized. Other words that should not be capitalized are capitalized. Cross out all incorrect letters and write the correct form above each.

SCORING: DEDUCT 7 POINTS FOR EACH ERROR.

1. The Medlock Tool Co. appreciates the Information it received from you on October 17.

2. Our Local board of education requests bids on the new School .

3. The Boardman Vocational Institute has a new superintendent, Samuel Jones.

4. Allen and White, Inc., received your Order for the Fall line early in September.

5. Mr. Robert C. Phillips, chairman of the Firm of Phillips and Sons, intends to open up the West as its newest market.

6. The Carlsbad Hotel is located South of Main Street.

7. The Advertising Agency of Bemis, Baumer, and Beard offers exceptional coverage throughout the northwest.

8. We have inquired of our Attorney, Mr. John L. Dowings, to ascertain our Rights against the Omega Insurance Co.

9. The Assistant Director of The Lakeland Hotel is John Doe, Jr.

10. The president left the White House by Limousine at Noon and rushed to the airport.

11. The Bookkeeper passed his C. P. A. Examination.

12. Our Vice-president went south for the Winter.

13. The U. S. S. President Pierce is in its Berth in Liverpool, England, ready for a difficult crossing of the Atlantic Ocean.

14. The american society for the prevention of cruelty to animals is known as the A. S. P. C. A. .

15. According to Mr. James A. Downing, Secretary of the American Association of Manufacturers, the northwest is a fertile field for expansion; however, Secretary Downing warns against too great reliance upon the federal government. He feels that congress will not make any substantial Appropriations during its Spring session.

EXERCISE 63 — Capitalization of Proper Nouns

B. This problem involves capitalization of proper nouns. In the sentences below, some words that should be capitalized are not capitalized. Other words that should not be capitalized are capitalized. Cross out all incorrect letters and write the correct form above each.

SCORING: DEDUCT 7 POINTS FOR EACH ERROR.

1. The chevrolet is a popular car in the south.
2. The first monday of each Month is a good time for a Meeting.
3. Our fall styles are put into production in the Spring.
4. The Southern part of texas is hottest in the Summer.
5. The ohio river flows from East to West.
6. Every person of Spanish descent should know some latin.
7. Our Employer had a British accent.
8. The united nations building is near the east river.
9. The River Nile is longer than the Hudson river.
10. The united states supreme court is our highest tribunal.
11. The meeting was addressed by Frank James, president of Neon, Inc.
12. The american medical association claims to speak for most Doctors.
13. The department Supervisor of stern's department store spoke yesterday.
14. It is sometimes wise to italicize words like platonic or pasteurize.
15. He was graduated from High School and went to Yale university.

SCORE

A_____

EXERCISE 64 — Capitalization

A. The following paragraph is written without any capital letters. Cross out each small letter that should be capitalized. Write the capital letter above it.

SCORING: DEDUCT 10 POINTS FOR EACH ERROR.

on wednesday, january 17, president James Jackson delivered his winter message to stockholders of the apex screen co. in a speech entitled, "meeting the mosquito menace," he explained the firm's expansion into the northwest as part of man's never-ending struggle against the insect kingdom. calling for "a screen on every window," he demanded greater efforts in southern parts of the united states, where the mosquito problem was most biting.

EXERCISE 64 — Capitalization Review

B. The following letter is written without any capital letters. Cross out each small letter that should be capitalized. Write the capital letter above it.

SCORING: DEDUCT 5 POINTS FOR EACH ERROR.

Mr. John Murphy
17 Lexington Avenue
New York, New York

My dear Mr. Murphy:

Are you one of the many New York city businessmen who would like to spend a few days or a few weeks in the country, but whose business interests demand that you not venture far from Manhattan? The Hotel Gramatan in the hills of Westchester county, midway between the scenic Hudson River and Long Island sound, offers you a most inviting home 28 minutes from Grand Central Terminal, the heart of the shopping and theater district.

The hotel is of moorish design, and the wide spanish balconies encircling it are literally "among the tree tops."

Accommodations are on the american plan, and the rates are considerably less than the cost of equivalent accommodations in town: single room and board, $50 per week and upward; large room and private bath with board for two people, $90 per week and upward.

an excellent golf course, eight of the best tennis courts in westchester county, a string of fine saddle horses, good roads for motoring and driving are offered.

walter e. gibson, drama critic of the <u>new york times</u>, visited the hotel gramatan in july of last year. upon his return to new york, he wrote the following in his column, <u>going on in new york</u>: "the hotel gramatan is one of the finest hotels i have ever visited. its european cooking is tops."

why don't you take a drive up the scenic hutchinson river parkway and visit the gramatan some time this fall?

very respectfully yours,

CLASS   DATE   NAME

REVIEW EXERCISE 12A   Punctuation

This problem deals with capitalization and punctuation. The following letter is written with no punctuation marks and no capital letters. Insert all punctuation marks. Where a letter should be capitalized, cross out that letter and write the capital letter above it.

SCORING: DEDUCT 5 POINTS FOR EACH ERROR.

Randall and Peck Inc.
35 Draper Avenue
Rochester 10 New York

Gentlemen:

The enclosed booklet "Make Your Own Weather" will show you how to maintain your volume of business through the hot summer months. Read about our new Scott portable cooler that will bring summer comfort to homes, offices, hospitals, and hotels in your city. It is an air conditioning unit that is both quiet and beautiful. It is almost as easy to install as a radio, and it can be moved from room to room, and from building to building. You cannot afford to overlook this opportunity.

One large industrial user of the Scott portable cooler wrote us as follows:

"Our plant is located in the south where we face tremendous heat problems during most of the year. We had considered installing other air conditioning units, but all of them were too expensive. Then we learned about the Scott cooler last spring. We ordered one of the Scott air conditioners for our executive office, and were so satisfied with its superb performance that our purchasing manager was instructed to order Scott coolers for the entire plant. I can't recommend the Scott cooler too highly."

Take the advice of this successful businessman and the thousands like him; try the Scott cooler.

To help our dealers we have arranged a demonstration at the factory on April 8 and 9. We invite your sales and service managers to attend this meeting at our expense.

Very truly yours,

SCORE

B_____

REVIEW EXERCISE 12B   Punctuation

This is a review problem on punctuation. Insert all omitted punctuation marks in the following passage.

SCORING: DEDUCT 5 POINTS FOR EACH ERROR.

HOW BANKS OPERATE

The ordinary idea of a bank is of an institution where one deposits money for safekeeping and withdraws it as it is needed. There are many people who think of a bank in no other terms, who give no thought to the manner in which a bank profits by these operations.

The two fundamental concerns of a bank are borrowing and lending money. When you deposit money in a bank, whether it is in a checking or a saving account, you are lending it money. The bank in turn lends this money, or a part of it, to others at a rate of interest that is higher than that which you receive. The difference is the profit made by the bank. Such an institution must keep a surplus on hand with which to accommodate your withdrawals, or the checks that you issue.

As a general rule, a checking account balance draws no interest. The depositor receives service for the use of his money. A savings account, however, draws a small rate of interest, and the bank profits by lending your money at a higher rate than it pays.

Another commonly used service of a bank is provision of storage facilities for money, securities, important papers, jewels, and other valuables. These are guarded in what is known as a safe deposit vault, a place that is rented for a certain sum per year for this purpose.

Banks sell service. They hire, borrow money, and they rent, lend money. When one hires money he has to pay the rent, which is interest. He also has to provide collateral or security, which may be sold in case the money is not repaid.

In addition the banks offer many other services to their clients or customers. They collect drafts, checks, and coupons from bonds; they pay checks issued by depositors; they extend credit; and they act as trustees, administrators, executors, and guardians. They advise clients with regard to the investment of money in securities, land, or business of any kind. They are usually able to advise and assist in all kinds of financial transactions.

Thurs. test.
Conjunctions
Common errors.
✓   Chapter 9 - 10.

INDEX

293

Bobby's hat
thanksgiving turkeys
a workmans' lunch
businessmen's lunch
stenographer's pad
secretaries' typewriters
for pete's sake
  arms' length
a birds eye view
women's dresses

never use womans'